# MOBILE LEARNING

*Mobile Learning: The Next Generation* documents the most innovative projects in context-aware mobile learning in order to develop a richer theoretical understanding of learning in modern mobile-connected societies. Context-aware mobile learning takes advantage of cell phone, mobile and pervasive personal technologies to design learning experiences that exploit the richness of both indoor and outdoor environments. These technologies detect a learner's presence in a particular place, the learner's history in that place or in relation to other people and objects nearby and adapt learning experiences accordingly, enabling and encouraging learners to use personal and social technologies to capture aspects of the environment as learning resources and to share their reactions to them.

**John Traxler** was Professor of Mobile Learning (the world's first) and is now Professor of Digital Learning in the Institute of Education at the University of Wolverhampton, UK. He is a founding director and current Vice President of the International Association for Mobile Learning, Associate Editor of the *International Journal of Mobile and Blended Learning* and *Interactive Learning Environments*.

**Agnes Kukulska-Hulme** is Past-President of the International Association for Mobile Learning, Professor of Learning Technology and Communication in the Institute of Educational Technology at the Open University, UK and Programme Manager for the Next Generation Distance Learning research programme in the institute.

# MOBILE LEARNING

## The Next Generation

*Edited by John Traxler and
Agnes Kukulska-Hulme*

Routledge
Taylor & Francis Group

NEW YORK AND LONDON

First published 2016
by Routledge
711 Third Avenue, New York, NY 10017

and by Routledge
2 Park Square, Milton Park, Abingdon, Oxon OX14 4RN

*Routledge is an imprint of the Taylor & Francis Group, an informa business*

© 2016 Taylor & Francis

The right of John Traxler and Agnes Kukulska-Hulme to be identified as authors of the editorial material, and of the authors for their individual chapters, has been asserted by them in accordance with sections 77 and 78 of the Copyright, Designs and Patents Act 1988.

*Library of Congress Cataloging-in-Publication Data*
A catalog record for this book has been requested.

ISBN: 978-0-415-65835-5 (hbk)
ISBN: 978-0-415-65836-2 (pbk)
ISBN: 978-0-203-07609-5 (ebk)

Typeset in Bembo
by Apex CoVantage, LLC

Printed and bound in Great Britain by
TJ International Ltd, Padstow, Cornwall

# CONTENTS

# FIGURES AND TABLES

## Figures

## Tables

# CONTRIBUTORS

**Marco Arrigo** works at the National Research Council of Italy, Institute of Educational Technologies of Palermo. He is a coordinator and scientist responsible for several national and international projects on educational technologies and mobile learning. His research interests are new technologies in distance education, cooperative learning systems and intelligent agents. Currently he works on application of ICTs to the educational field. In particular, he is working both on mobile learning applications (technologies and methodologies), and on speech applications to allow blind people to access online learning environments.

**Brenda Bannan** is associate professor at the College of Education and Human Development, George Mason University, USA. Her research interests primarily revolve around the articulation of integrated design and research processes in learning technology design and development. She is the author of numerous articles and book chapters on the emerging method of design research in education related to areas such as mobile learning, augmented reality, enquiry-based instruction, language learning and cognition, motivation and special education.

**Teresa Cerratto-Pargman** is an associate professor of human-computer interaction (HCI) and a member of the board at the Department of Computer and Systems Sciences at Stockholm University, Sweden. Her research interests are in the areas of technology-enhanced learning (TEL), interaction design and HCI. In particular, in the field of TEL, she has studied collaborative writing, the introduction of language technologies into second-language learning, computer-mediated communication and mobile learning. A central theme in Teresa's work is the study of the relationship between writing and technology from sociocultural perspectives on literacy and tools. She uses qualitative methods for describing and explaining developmental aspects of sociotechnical practices observed in everyday writing and learning experiences.

**Gill Clough** is a research associate with the Institute of Educational Technology at the Open University. Her PhD focused on analysing the informal learning opportunities afforded by context-aware mobile technologies, looking at the activities of the worldwide community of geocachers.

**Giovanni Fulantelli** has been a researcher at the National Research Council of Italy, Institute for Educational Technology since 1991. He is a member of the scientific board of the institute. His research activities focus on innovative and effective e-learning processes, both from technological and methodological perspectives. He is a coordinator and scientist responsible for several national and international projects on educational technologies. He has been a contract professor at the University of Palermo.

**Manuel Gentile** is a researcher at the Institute of Educational Technologies of the National Research Council in Palermo. His main research interests include the definition of methodologies and environments to support learning with particular attention to entrepreneurship education. He has been involved in several research projects at the national and international level, within which he uses his expertise in the design and implementation of mobile learning platforms, serious games and systems for the collaborative production, sharing and organization of learning resources.

**Christian Glahn** is the director of the Blended Learning Center at the HTW Chur, Switzerland. He studied and researched the fields of computer and educational sciences in Germany, Austria, the Netherlands and Switzerland and has been active in the area of technology-enhanced learning for more than 15 years. He holds a MSc in media education and a PhD in information systems. He is experienced in bridging innovative context-aware technologies and formal training, non-formal learning and performance support in universities, services and industries. His research focuses on integrating smart technologies into existing technology-enhanced learning environments in higher education as well as security and defense organisations.

**Angela Hamilton** is program lead at the Institute for Simulation and Training (Mixed Emerging Technology Integration Lab), University of Central Florida, USA. She provides program-level management for METIL's R&D projects and functional teams (games, instructional, 3D and technical). In addition to helping shape the METIL research agenda, she focuses on partnership and opportunity development in the healthcare, corporate, academic, military, government and non-profit domains.

**Jieun Kim** is assistant professor at Hanyang University. Her research focuses on the investigation of design cognition and emotion in diverse commercial and industrial contexts. These include developing a gesture-based serious game for rehabilitating stroke patients and designing cognitive appliances for those with memory loss.

**Agnes Kukulska-Hulme** is professor of learning technology and communication in the Institute of Educational Technology at the Open University and past president of the International Association for Mobile Learning. She has been researching mobile learning since 2001, most recently as part of the European MOTILL project on mobile lifelong learning, the MASELTOV project on smart and personalised technologies for social inclusion, the British Council project on Mobile Pedagogy for English Language Teaching and the SALSA project on immigrant language learning in the next generation of smart cities. Her discipline background is in language learning and communication.

**Teemu H. Laine** holds a PhD in computer science from the University of Eastern Finland. His current research as assistant professor at Ajou University focuses on context-aware games for education and wellbeing. His other research interests include educational technology, context-aware middleware, context modeling and reasoning, extensible software architectures and ICT for development.

**Ahreum Lee** is a PhD student at Research Institute of Serious Entertainment, Hanyang University, South Korea. Her research interests are life-logging service design, mobile learning and human-computer interaction.

**David Metcalf** is senior researcher and director of the Institute for Simulation and Training (Mixed Emerging Technology Integration Lab), University of Central Florida, USA. Combining an academic grounding and continued university involvement with a strong history of industry-centered training and simulation, his work at METIL bridges the gap between corporate learning and simulation techniques and non-profit and social entrepreneurship.

**Marcelo Milrad** is a full professor in media technology at Linnaeus University, Sweden. His current research focuses on the design and development of mobile and wireless applications to support collaborative learning. He has published over 170 papers in international journals, refereed conferences, books and technical reports. He has also presented and given lectures about his work in more than 40 countries worldwide. During the last few years, he has been serving as a program committee member in a number of international scientific conferences such as CSCL, ICALT, WMUTE, ICCE and mLearn.

**Eeva Nygren** is a PhD candidate at the University of Eastern Finland. Nygren received a post-graduate degree (Licentiate of Philosophy) in mathematics in 2005 from the University of Joensuu. Since then she has worked as a mathematics teacher and vice principle at the Evangelical Folk High School of Kitee. Her main research interests are integrating educational technology into teaching, especially games and motivation.

**Hokyoung Ryu** is associate professor at the Research Institute of Serious Entertainment at Hanyang University. His research interest includes practitioner's HCI and designing issues, cognitive information design, learning technology and game-based learning (serious games).

**Mike Sharples** is professor of educational technology at The Open University. His research involves human-centred design of new technologies and environments for learning. He inaugurated the mLearn conference series and was founding president of the International Association for Mobile Learning. He is the associate editor in chief of *IEEE Transactions on Learning Technologies*.

**Juliet Sprake** is a senior lecturer in the Design Department at Goldsmiths, University of London. Juliet is interested in mobile learning, participatory sensing and designing alternative methods for navigating the urban landscape. An important aspect of her work is using technologies to sense and record change in the material fabric of our built environment so that buildings can be described as 'learning-enabled'. She has written about some of this in her book, *Learning-through-Touring*, and enjoys working with digital artist Peter Rogers to make interactive apps, tours and games for finding ways into, up and around the city.

**Davide Taibi** is a researcher at the Institute for Educational Technologies at the National Research Council of Italy. His research activities are mainly focused on the application of innovative technologies in the e-learning field, with particular emphasis on mobile learning, semantic web and linked data for e-learning, standards for educational processes design, open educational resources and learning analytics. He has participated in several European funded projects in the mobile learning and open educational resources areas. He has been a contract professor at the University of Palermo.

**John Traxler** was professor of mobile learning (the world's first) and is now professor of digital learning in the Institute of Education at the University of Wolverhampton, UK. He is a founding director and current vice president of the International Association for Mobile Learning and executive committee member of the USAID mEducation Alliance. He was conference chair of mLearn 2008, the world's biggest and oldest mobile learning research conference, one of the first to recognise the growing significance of context. He has co-written a guide to mobile learning in developing countries for the Commonwealth of Learning and is co-editor of the definitive book *Mobile Learning: A Handbook for Educators and Trainers* with Agnes Kukulska-Hulme.

# 1

# INTRODUCTION TO THE NEXT GENERATION OF MOBILE LEARNING

*John Traxler and Agnes Kukulska-Hulme*

## Introduction

Over the past two decades, mobile learning has evolved and matured to the extent that arguably we can now think of it as "just learning" (Kukulska-Hulme, 2010). In many places, use of mobile technology is increasingly taken for granted and may appear to be fading into the background, with teachers and learners adopting mobile phones and tablets as just another tool. Yet our aim in this book is to show that specific recent technological developments, as well as ways in which education is being reconceived, are still remarkable and that many new challenges need to be discussed and explored. We believe it is particularly important to pay attention to the fact that the next generation of mobile learning is becoming 'context-aware'. Context-aware mobile learning takes advantage of mobile phones, and other mobile, connected and pervasive personal technologies, in the design of learning experiences that exploit the richness and uniqueness of the learner's indoor or outdoor environment. These technologies detect a learner's presence in a particular place, their history in that place and perhaps their presence in relation to other people and objects nearby, and adapt the learning experiences accordingly. They also enable and encourage learners to capture aspects of the environment, approaching the environment as a learning resource, and to capture and share their reactions to it.

We have put this book together to document the most innovative projects in context-aware mobile learning and use these to develop a broader and richer theoretical understanding of learning in modern mobile connected societies. We are also keen to contribute to a critical engagement with the growing popular, non-educational, non-formal, uses of context-aware technologies and devices at the moment when the availability, diversity and capability of retail context-aware *apps* is reaching saturation. In addition, the book has contributions that place context-aware mobile learning in the wider context and history of mobile learning and, as appropriate, educational technology and e-learning. Issues of scale, ethics, evaluation and sustainability are also addressed within the wider social context. The book consolidates progress in the field, and so it will be a valuable reference for teachers and students using educational technology in schools, colleges and universities in the developed world, as well as for researchers, developers and directors working in education and in the heritage, museum, culture, tourism, environment and landscape sectors. A brief review of books that typically populate the mobile learning space illustrates the continued production of general texts, some of undoubted quality, alongside slowly increasing numbers of more specialist texts that show the gradual maturity of the market. National programs in various countries and sectors continue to publish substantial booklets and books in order to highlight their own funded projects and programs. This book marks an era of more depth and specialisation. The realisation that context-awareness in mobile learning was to be significant for many of us dates back to mLearn 2008, the annual research conference of the International Association for Mobile Learning. That year's conference was entitled 'The Bridge from Text to Context', punning on its Ironbridge venue in the UK. A considerable proportion of contributions showed contextual mobile learning reaching a critical mass. The history of contextual mobile learning has, however, been by no means straightforward, and our contributors tackle the preliminary definitions and early developments from a variety of different perspectives.

## The Activities and Achievements of Mobile Learning

The diverse mobile learning community of researchers, developers, promoters, practitioners and policy makers has persuasively demonstrated that mobile devices can deliver learning to people, communities and countries where other educational interventions have been too expensive, difficult, dangerous or demanding. The community has demonstrated that mobile devices can extend, enhance, enrich, challenge and disrupt existing ideas and assumptions about learning. The community has also challenged and changed existing conceptualisations and theories of learning and has shown that mobiles can raise motivation for learning, most especially amongst disenfranchised and disengaged learners.

The community has, however, worked largely within institutional contexts, often positioned at the vanguard of e-learning, buying into the rhetoric of innovation and working top-down. There have been many small-scale, fixed-term subsidised projects staffed by enthusiasts, growing largely out of the conceptions, foundations, aspirations and limitations of e-learning. These developments took place when technology was scarce, fragile, difficult and expensive; now technology is ubiquitous, easy, cheap and reliable. The context for mobile learning has changed from the legacy of learning with computers to the ubiquity of the social use of mobiles.

If we look back at the last 15 to 20 years, we see several overlapping generations, or paradigms, representing some kind of historical progression. We suggest
that these might be:

- Techno-centric learning, where the defining feature was merely that the
  learning took place on a mobile digital device. Various dedicated graph-
  ing calculators fell into this paradigm and perhaps the experiments with
  the connected classroom, where the mobile technology worked with other
  components such as an interactive whiteboard to form a managed learning
  environment. Little contextual mobile learning was represented in this phase
  or paradigm because of its inherent conservatism, though the scope for personalisation of learning might now be recognised as part of "user-generated
  contexts" (Cook, Pachler, & Bachmair, 2013).
- Industrialised learning, where technology is used for its capacity to ensure
  quality whilst producing efficiency gains and increased throughput in large-
  scale formal education. This is a continuation of learning with computers,
  perhaps taking it from batch processed production line learning to flexible
  manufacturing systems learning, from mass production to mass customisation. Little contextual mobile learning has been represented in this paradigm
  to date, probably because of high editorial investment needed to create usable
  content and interactions for large-scale systems.
- Enriched learning, still a legacy from learning with computers, where the
  extra affordances of mobile technology, for example location-awareness,
  image-capture or augmented reality, combined with existing affordances of
  computers, enable the curriculum to become more flexible, vivid, personalised, situated and authentic. This was where contextual mobile learning was
  often to be found in its early days.
- Extended learning, another legacy from learning with computers, this time
  taking learning to people, communities and regions where traditional educational interventions were too expensive, dangerous or difficult, to dropped-
  out kids or rural communities for example. Sadly to date few examples of
  contextual mobile learning are found in this phase or paradigm, probably
  because the deployment depends on learners' own mobiles, which must be
  presumed to have adequate and uniform capability.
- Encouraging learning, yet another legacy of learning with computers, exploiting the apparent capacity of mobile technologies to enthuse and encourage
  learners, especially disengaged and disenfranchised learners. The relationship
  between mobiles, encouragement and achievement was, however, always a
  difficult one for evaluation to capture and quantify.
- User-generated learning, marking a distinct shift away from the existing institutions, curricula and professions of education as understood and expressed
  in the earlier phases, and instead characterised by contributions from across
  cyberspace, phonespace and the Twittersphere. This is apparent also in the vast
  number of apps and podcasts. The financial return on either is so minimal

that clearly there are other institutional, corporate or personal motivations involved. The institutional one is usually an educational mission, the corporate one is usually about branding, presence and image, but that still leaves a large number of individuals and groups contributing for diverse and diffuse reasons.

• Learning for mobile and connected societies, where the technologies of mobility have transformed the balance of what can or must be known and learnt because they have or they are transforming the societies themselves. The transformations include the assets, artefacts, transactions, commodities, corporations and resources that constitute the economic life of those societies and how they are organised; a continuation of the epistemological revolution that started with computers, gathered momentum with networks and accelerates with mobiles. These technologies have become pervasive, embodied and prosthetic, around us, on our bodies and maybe soon within us. One of our contributors tackles exactly these issues, but several others allude to the changing nature of learning and knowing.

The reason behind this exploration of the generations, paradigms and implicit definitions of mobile learning is to provide contrasting lenses with which to analyse the contributions in the current volume. It does not necessarily imply that these generations have been mutually exclusive, sequential, global or even well populated with examples. We see the current book as indicative of a transition or generational change in writing about mobile learning, a transition from the generic to the specific, acknowledging the increasing familiarity amongst readers with the general ideas, principles and history of mobile learning and perhaps an increasing familiarity amongst the wider world with the technologies and applications available.

'Generation' is also a term used to characterise the wider population, specifically the division or transition from 'immigrants' to 'natives' (Prensky, 2001), or from 'visitors' to 'residents' (White & le Cornu, 2011). Whatever the rigour or relevance of these concepts, they can be loosely correlated to earlier remarks about a change in the culture and context of mobile learning, as mobile technologies change from being scarce and difficult (with progress taking place amongst relatively small research communities) to being ubiquitous and pervasive (with progress being driven by commercial and social activities and pressures). In these various senses, we see contextual mobile learning as the next generation.

## Contents, Structure and Overview

This introductory chapter ensures that readers from any part of the mobile learning community and any part of the e-learning community globally have the necessary background to appreciate and understand the subsequent more specialised contributions. Having introduced the activities and achievements of the mobile learning community, we provide an explanation for the distribution and nature of the book's case studies and explain the structure of the book. The chapters merge case study with reflection, recommendation and discussion. In order to facilitate cross-referencing, comparison and analysis, we encouraged contributors to use a template that highlighted the following elements:

- Background (e.g., heritage, landscape, school, museum, zoo, city)
- Sector (e.g., children, adults, informal learning, work-based learning, community)
- Country or region
- Theoretical/pedagogic perspective
- Technology
- Deployment (e.g. funding, scale, timescale, maturity, evaluation)
- Originality, interest or impact

In subsequently organising the chapters of this book, we have been forced to address the issue of the classification and categorisation of contextual mobile learning in order to provide us with a structure and a sequence. The classification of mobile learning in general and contextual mobile learning in particular is a fascinating and thought-provoking exercise (as can be seen in, for example, Frohberg, Göth and Schwabe, 2009; Sharples, 2006; Winters, 2007; Traxler, 2007; Park, 2011). It is, however, ultimately futile as the technologies, the pedagogies and their appropriation progress rapidly and relentlessly, and case studies never populate the sample space regularly, even if it were possible to actually define the axes of that space. We have therefore opted for a progressive, albeit imperfect, sequence of chapters, moving from accessible ones requiring least prior knowledge to, later, more demanding ones. This is not straightforward since any chapter is a mixture of technology, pedagogy and context. We highlight this developmental progression as we preview the book's contributions.

Our first contributors, Metcalf and Hamilton, provide a very positive overview of the technologies of contextual mobile learning and their applications from a US perspective, with numerous examples from academia, industry, commerce and the military. These graphically illustrate the power and diversity of the apps and peripherals now routinely available in the commercial market place and the potential for further pedagogic and academic exploitation. Arrigo, Fulantelli, Gentile and Taibi are by contrast firmly rooted in Italian educational contexts and report on the impact of mobile technologies in a range of projects based on a common methodological background and on a common mobile platform. The system is significant for encouraging learners to write onto the context as well as read from it; their mobile devices can tag the physical places that they visit with textual notes, photos, audio recordings and social tagging in authentic environments. The practical focus is on three projects across three different educational sectors or levels, each one showing context crossing between formal and informal settings and across hardware platforms. The technology platform facilitates a close relationship between physical objects and the digital objects created during the learning activity and motivates collaboration amongst learners to build shared knowledge. The theoretical framework is the hypothesis that, in a mobile environment, knowledge building can be analysed on the basis of three spaces: social, information and geographical—the social being the social interactions between students, the information being the cultural artefacts and the public statements produced by students and the geographical being the physical places.

Clough also discusses the synergy between mobile and social technologies in a study showing how the development of context-aware mobile technology alongside Web 2.0 social spaces facilitated location-based informal learning. The study demonstrates how these technologies transform the ways in which learners engage with their physical environments and with each other. Clough's theoretical framework is a constructivist one, used for assessing meaningful learning with technology and providing an understanding of how context-awareness has influenced informal learning activities.

Sprake's contribution looks at informal learning in urban spaces and another that explores the value and nature of learner contributions, this time in recording motion and emotion and creating stories and tours for subsequent visitors. She introduces some fascinating and valuable concepts and metaphors, such as 'stumbling upon' and 'turning a corner', that draw together space, geography and learning. Laine and Nygren use contextual resources, such as nearby objects, and specifically investigate the role of technology integration in context-aware learning spaces to identify disturbance factors that may disrupt the learning experience, some coming from the physical context. They present results of technology integration evaluation of their mathematics game that combines a virtual story and physical fraction rods and discuss its deployment across widely different countries. The theoretical framework for Lee, Kim and Ryu is situated learning theory (Lave & Wenger, 1991) for the analytic phase and activity theory (Engeström, 1999) for design activities. This too focuses on informal learning, this time in healthcare, working with stroke patients.

Bannan introduces methods for analysing the learning context drawn from mobile design research, specifically addressing the design of two mobile applications implementing contextually-aware features. A design research framework is presented for the systematic implementation of applied methodologies conducted through cycles of data collection and analysis to improve the design of the location-aware mobile applications. Fundamental to the process of mobile design research is an understanding of the context of learning that is more than merely the learning environment and tools. This chapter supports the position that this type of analysis is important when attempting to design for context-aware applications and takes a broader view of context, embracing interactions amongst persons, content, learning context and functionality, in fact much of what other authors term the 'user-generated context' (Cook, Pachler, & Bachmair, 2013).

Pushing context beyond physical environment and technological environment is a theme as we move through subsequent chapters. Sharples sees context as a central construct for designing and understanding mobile learning and proposes three different conceptions of context to guide research, learning through context, learning in context and learning about context, based in specific examples. In learning through context, a learner experiences context as a means to satisfy learning goals. For learning in context, the learner is situated within an environment that is configured to enable effective learning. When learning about context, the natural surroundings become the object of learning. Like Bannan, Sharples explicitly addresses the design of contextual mobile learning and, in passing, questions whether contextual mobile learning design can be moved beyond specific contexts to something more generic or abstract. This leads to questioning the cultural relativism of contextual mobile learning.

Cerratto-Pargman and Milrad, working in a Swedish context, articulate the problem of fostering sustainable learning innovations and focus on three examples of research projects in order to provide a critical analysis of the barriers and constraints experienced by researchers and teachers. They discuss factors, stakeholders and lines of action identified when attempting to introduce mobile technologies and sustain innovative educational practises. These are valuable insights given the often small-scale, fixed-term nature of projects and the inputs of advocates and subsidy that sometimes characterise the work of the mobile learning community. Glahn tackles similar issues in looking at contextual learning in large formal organisations, specifically those in the security and defense sectors. He argues that the organisational factors have not received sufficient attention by research and development and explores the core challenges, identifying four, namely 'technological availability', 'organisational framing', 'educational approaches' and 'authoring of learning resources'.

In the last contribution, Traxler discusses the significance of context and learning in the context of the dynamics between widespread mobile technology and societal change, specifically in the nature of epistemology, arguing that the apparently stable dichotomy between the learner and his or her context is increasingly fluid and fragmented. The final chapter draws together the themes of the earlier individual contributions and explores the credibility of contextual learning as the next generation of mobile learning. This necessitates looking at evolving factors and trends in the wider educational and social environment. There are technical, demographic and business trends. There are trends around education such as industrialisation, globalisation, competition and consumerisation and there are trends within education such as MOOCs, OER and BYOD. There are also ongoing challenges such as scale, theory, sustainability, ethics, evaluation and design. This is the environment of contextual learning and the environment of the next generation of mobile learning.

## References

Cook, J., Pachler, N., & Bachmair, B. (2013). Using social networked sites and mobile technology for bridging social capital. In G. Trentin & M. Repetto (Eds.), *Using network and mobile technology to bridge formal and informal learning* (pp. 31–56). London: Chandos.

Engeström, Y. (1999). Activity theory and individual and social transformation. In Y. Engeström, R. Miettinen & R. Punamaki (Eds.), *Perspectives on theory* (pp. 19–38). Cambridge: Cambridge University Press.

Frohberg, D., Göth, C., & Schwabe, G. (2009). Mobile learning projects: A critical analysis of the state of the art. *Journal of Computer Assisted Learning, 25*(4), 307–331.

Kukulska-Hulme, A. (2010). Mobile learning as a catalyst for change. *Open Learning: The Journal of Open and Distance Learning, 25*(3), 181–185.

Lave, J., & Wenger, E. (1991). *Situated learning: Legitimate peripheral participation.* Cambridge: Cambridge University Press.

Park, Y. (2011). A pedagogical framework for mobile learning: Categorizing educational applications of mobile technologies into four types. *The International Review of Research in Open and Distance Learning, 12*(2), 78–102.

Prensky, M. (2001). Digital natives, digital immigrants. *On the Horizon, 9*(5), 1–6.

Sharples, M. (Ed.). (2006). *Big issues in mobile learning.* Nottingham: University of Nottingham.

Traxler, J. (2007). Defining, discussing and evaluating mobile learning. *The International Review of Research in Open and Distance Learning, 8*(2), 1–12.

White, D., & le Cornu, A. (2011). Visitors and residents: A new typology for online engagement. *First Monday, 16*(9). Retrieved from http://firstmonday.org/ojs/index.php/fm/article/view/3171/3049

Winters, N. (2006). What is mobile learning? In M. Sharples (Ed.), *Big issues in mobile learning* (pp. 7–11). Nottingham: University of Nottingham.

### Books and Resources

There are an increasing number of general introductions and overviews of mobile learning, and these may help readers with the wide context of mobile learning, including the following:

ADL. (n.d.). *ADL mobile learning handbook.* Retrieved from https://sites.google.com/a/adlnet.gov/mobile-learning-guide/home

Ally, M. (Ed.). (2009). *Mobile learning: Transforming the delivery of education and training.* Retrieved from http://www.aupress.ca/index.php/books/120155

Ally, M., & Tsinakos, A. (Eds.). (2013). *Global mobile learning implementations and trends.* Beijing: China Central Radio & TV University Press. Retrieved from http://en.crtvu.edu.cn/images/stories/globalmobilelearning.pdf

Ally, M., & Tsinakos, A. (Eds.). (2014). *Increasing access through mobile learning.* Commonwealth of Learning. Retrieved from http://www.col.org/PublicationDocuments/pub_Mobile%20Learning_web.pdf

Berge, Z., & Muilenburg, L. Y. (Eds.). (2013). *Handbook of mobile learning.* New York, NY: Routledge.

Brown, E. (Ed.). (2010). *Education in the wild: Contextual and location-based mobile learning in action.* Nottingham: Learning Sciences Research Institute, University of Nottingham. Retrieved from http://www.lsri.nottingham.ac.uk/ejb/preprints/ARV_Education_in_the_wild.pdf

Crompton, H., & Traxler, J. (Eds.). (2015). *Mobilizing mathematics: Case studies of mobile learning being used in mathematics education.* New York, NY: Routledge

Danaher, P., Moriarty, B., & Danaher, G. (2009). *Mobile learning communities: Creating new educational futures.* London: Routledge.

Herrington, J., Herrington, A., Mantei, J., Olney, I., & Ferry, B. (Eds.). (2009). *New technologies, new pedagogies: Mobile learning in higher education.* University of Wollongong. Retrieved from http://ro.uow.edu.au/newtech/

Huang, R., Kinshuk, & Spector, M. (Eds.). (2013). *Reshaping learning: Frontiers of learning technology in a global context.* Berlin: Springer.

JISC. (2005). *Innovative practice with e-learning guide.* Retrieved from http://www.jisc.ac.uk/media/documents/publications/innovativepe.pdf

JISC. (2009). *Emerging practice in a digital age.* Retrieved from http://jisc.ac.uk/media/documents/programmes/elearning/digiemerge/Emergingpracticeaccessible.pdf

JISC. (2013). *Mobile Learning.* Retrieved from http://www.jiscinfonet.ac.uk/infokits/mobile-learning/

Keegan, D. (n.d.). *Mobile learning: A practical guide.* Ericsson. Retrieved from http://www.ericsson.com/res/thecompany/docs/programs/incorporating_mobile_learning_into_mainstream_education/book.pdf

Kukulska-Hulme, A., & Traxler, J. (Eds.). (2005). *Mobile learning: A handbook for educators and trainers.* London: Routledge

Marshall, S., & Kinuthia, W. (Eds.). (2013). *On the move: Mobile learning for development.* Hershey, PA: IGI Global.

McConatha, D., Penny, C., Shugar, J., & Bolton, D. (2013). *Mobile pedagogy and perspectives on teaching and learning.* Hershey, PA: IGI Global.

Metcalf, D., & De Marco, J.M. (2006). *mLearning: Mobile learning and performance in the palm of your hand.* Amherst, MA: HRD Press.

Miller, C., & Doering, A. (2015). *The new landscape of mobile learning.* New York, NY: Routledge.

Naismith, L., Lonsdale, P., Vavoula, G., & Sharples, M. (2005). Literature review in mobile technologies and learning. *Report 11.* Bristol: NESTA Futurelab. Retrieved from http://www2.futurelab.org.uk/resources/documents/lit_reviews/Mobile_Review.pdf

Needham, G., & Ally, M. (Eds.). (2008). *M-libraries: Libraries on the move to provide virtual access.* London: Facet Books.

Pachler, N., Cook, J., & Traxler, J. (2015). *Key issues in mobile learning: Research and practice.* London: Continuum.

Pachler, N., Pimmer, C., & Seipold, J. (2011). *Work-based mobile learning: Concepts and cases.* Bern: Peter Lang.

Parsons, D. (Ed.). (2011). *Combining e-learning and m-learning: New applications of blended educational resources.* Hershey, PA: IGI Global.

Parsons, D. (Ed.). (2012). *Refining current practices in mobile and blended learning: New applications.* Hershey, PA: IGI Global.

Parsons, D. (Ed.). (2013). *Innovations in mobile educational technologies and applications.* Hershey, PA: IGI Global.

Pegrum, M. (2014). *Mobile learning: Languages, literacies and cultures.* New York, NY: Palgrave Macmillan.

Quinn, C. (2012). *The mobile academy: mLearning for higher education.* San Francisco, CA: Jossey-Bass.

Retta, G. (Ed.). (2009). *The evolution of mobile teaching and learning.* Santa Rosa, CA: Informing Science Press.

Retta, G. (Ed.). (2010). *Mobile learning: Pilot projects and initiative.* Santa Rosa, CA: Informing Science Press.

Ryu, H., & Parsons, D. (Eds.). (2009). *Innovative mobile learning: Techniques and technologies.* Hershey, PA: IGI Global.

Traxler, J., & Wishart, J. (2011). *Making mobile learning work: Case studies of practice.* Bristol: ESCAlate. Retrieved from http://dera.ioe.ac.uk/14768/1/8250.pdf

Vavoula, G., Pachler, N., & Kukulska-Hulme, A. (2009). *Researching mobile learning: Frameworks, methods and research designs.* Oxford: Peter Lang.

Wexler, S., Brown, J., Metcalf, D., Rogers, D., & Wagner, E. (2008). *Mobile learning: What is it, why it matters, and how to incorporate it into your learning strategy.* Retrieved from http://www.elearningguild.com/research/archives/index.cfm?id=132&action=viewonly

# 2

# TECHNOLOGIES AND APPLICATIONS FOR CONTEXT-AWARE MOBILE LEARNING

*David Metcalf and Angela Hamilton*

## Introduction

"If content is king, then context is queen." Wayne Hodgins frequently made this pronouncement whilst he was at Autodesk and serving as the committee chair for IEEE LOM (Learning Object Metadata) for Standard 1484 (quoted in Duval, 2010). Context denotes information about ourselves and the world around us and is especially important in mobile settings, where the individual, activity and environment each introduce a host of variables. Fortunately, much of this context can be captured and acted upon.

Data such as user location, proximity to other people and devices, and time of day have been commonly used to enhance context in mobile learning applications, and recent technical and instructional innovations have led to increased capabilities to gather a range of contextual information—including kinesthetic, environmental, cognitive, physiological and social factors—and then adapt and support learning accordingly.

In 2006, we predicted, "location-aware learning, augmented reality, mobile collaboration, mobile gaming and simulation, and expert location await us" (Metcalf, 2006, p. 131). The early potential and promises of technologies such as these have been further enhanced with advanced content and real-time data—whether images taken from a camera, Global Positioning System (GPS) coordinates, or even biometric information. These inputs can give information about our identity or perhaps our health or state of being. All of these can influence the settings, affordances, availability and readiness for learning.

In this chapter, we will survey a range of supporting technologies, such as GPS, image recognition, augmented reality, peripheral devices and social media, and provide case examples of practical applications of those technologies for learning.

We will also identify future trends and innovations that will expand both the capabilities and use of context-aware mobile technologies and applications.

## GPS and Accelerometers

Location can be an important contextual factor for learning. With GPS now a standard feature on smartphone and tablet devices and the availability of application programming interfaces (APIs) that allow developers to integrate with Google Maps and other navigation tools, instructors have an important toolkit for delivering tailored learning content.

Ride & Drive (Allogy Interactive, 2014) is an example of a learning platform that uses both location-based and activity-based context to guide users on mobile tours with smartphones and tablets (Figure 2.1). Course creators use the authoring tool component to associate video, audio and other media with GPS coordinates. When users reach the designated waypoints on the map, the mobile app automatically launches relevant content. For example, in a course created for auto dealerships, the app guides a group of salespeople on a test drive of the latest model of a popular brand of car to educate them on the types of information they would need to communicate to potential buyers. Whilst the driver navigates the car along the defined path, passengers listen to audio narration and view a series

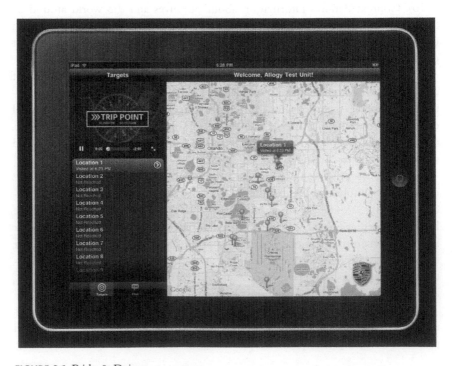

**FIGURE 2.1** Ride & Drive

of videos about various features and benefits. The course also leverages the device's accelerometer (which measures tilt and motion) to trigger related content, such as when a hairpin turn along the route triggers a module on traction control.

## Image Recognition

Whilst mobile device cameras have long been used to capture images from our surroundings, image recognition technology is broadening the scope of use beyond merely storing or sharing static images. We now have access to mobile apps that process the visual information from the images and then search for or automatically trigger links to related content.

Learning applications that leverage image recognition technology can support either guided lessons (in which instructors embed objects in the environment and link to specific content) or experiences where learners explore their surroundings and seek out on-demand content for reference and enrichment. Whether engaging in objectivist or constructivist experiences, mobile users are typically goal-oriented and require "instantaneous search and retrieval" to meet their information needs (Weiss, 2002, p. 66).

QR (Quick Response) codes are now ubiquitous in the commercial sector for marketing and product information, amongst other uses, and have also become common tools for mobile learning. Objects can even be geotagged to provide additional context on location. Our colleagues at the Center for Learning and Knowledge Technologies (CeLeKT) in Sweden have several projects that use QR codes for embedding learning scenarios in authentic settings. For example, the AMULETS project—designed to engage elementary students in collaborative problem solving—used QR codes to launch instructions for activities and challenges that were spread over time and across various indoor and outdoor locations. QR codes were also used as a form of multiple-choice assessment in which students had to scan the correct code to proceed to the next mission (Kurti, Milrad, & Spikol, 2007).

The CeLeKT research team also served within a consortium of partners in a European Union-funded project for Open Science Resources (OSR) to aggregate digital science education content from various European science centres and museums, seeking to overcome challenges in interoperability and language through robust context-sensitive metadata structures. To enhance access and context and support formal and informal science learning in or out of the museum setting, the consortium's technical partners (including the University of Central Florida) envisioned OSR supporting a combination of several image recognition technologies on mobile devices, from QR codes to advanced visual search, drawing from the rich set of metadata in the OSR repository to launch additional information, related content, or physical and virtual pathways through learning. The results of this effort included an open repository of STEM assets (http://www.osrportal. eu/en/repository) that can be cross-utilised in museums, classrooms and virtual environments using mobile devices, static displays and computers.

Recent developments in visual search capabilities are helping overcome limitations of text-based searches. Visual search has an important advantage in identifying unknown objects within the user's environment. For example, when travellers encounter an unfamiliar landmark or product logo, without prior knowledge they may not have any idea of what search terms to enter into a text-based search engine. Visual search tools like Google Goggles enable them to simply point their mobile device camera at the object and wait for the results.

Augmented reality takes image recognition a step further by enhancing the camera view of the environment with an information overlay. Layar, SnapTell, Junaio and Aurasma are examples of popular augmented reality browsers that use the device capabilities such as GPS, compass, accelerometer and the camera to identify and link to information on points of interest in the user's vicinity. They use image recognition to launch interactive multimedia content such as web URLs, images, videos, audio or 3D models from defined trigger images.

Within our Mixed Emerging Technology Integration Lab (METIL) at the University of Central Florida's (UCF) Institute for Simulation and Training, we have used augmented reality triggers to launch a diverse range of learning content, from 2D posters with anatomical images that launch interactive 3D versions of the same content to instructive videos for combat trauma care. Developed for the US Army medical component, the paper-based cards use two-dimensional images and text to describe the sequential steps of various lifesaving medical procedures for disaster situations as well as combat. The cards can be used independently or with an augmented reality browser to launch videos or 3D assets that provide higher-fidelity demonstrations of the steps and procedures (Figure 2.2).

**FIGURE 2.2** Cards triggering learning content on combat trauma care

## Peripheral Devices

One interesting aspect of context awareness is the ability to leverage streams of data from peripheral devices that connect to mobile devices and into the overall mLearning ecosystem of available online resources to which the mobile device acts as a gateway.

What do we mean by peripherals? Anything from digital pens that record audio and notes to biometric fingerprint scanners on a mobile device, near-field communication (NFC) sensors, barcode readers, visual search software, or sensors for healthcare, like blood pulse oximeters, blood glucose meters, EKGs or EEGs, that are mobile-enabled to deliver real-time or near real-time streams of data to the mobile device through ANT+ or Bluetooth. These are just a few examples of the many ways we can infer context and know the right pathway for delivering learning or performance interventions to help someone more readily learn or complete their tasks.

With the rapid expansion of the mHealth market in recent years, health is yet another contextual factor that we can leverage to deliver personalised and adaptive educational content and support. Physiometric devices include basic fitness trackers and specialised devices for monitoring chronic conditions.

One example is a suite of physiometric devices that can connect to electronic health records, medical informatics knowledgebases, other health and wellness courses, and online communities through mobile devices. The picture below shows one example of a test bed with a variety of health and fitness devices that can send either real-time or near real-time data (Figure 2.3). With this mobile crash cart filled with peripherals, sensors and devices, students, faculty and staff at the UCF College of Medicine effectively have a suite of sensors for gathering real-time clinical data and also informing medical education teams about the condition of an individual in order to better assess learning readiness and well-being as part of learner context. Stress and arousal levels and performance readiness for kinesthetic tasks can all be assessed. This is just one example of the suite of sensors that can further enable the next generation of contextual learning using advanced mobile technologies and the peripherals that support them in an overall mLearning ecosystem.

Another example of peripherals supporting education can be found in the Intelligent Home, a collaborative initiative between the Lake Nona Institute, Dais Technologies, University of Central Florida, Florida Blue and others. Intelligent homes are state-of-the-art residences designed with multiple cooperative and connected interfaces that encourage individuals to make healthful choices. Within the home environment, integrated mHealth devices and interfaces enable ambient education and coaching, monitoring and telemedicine to promote health and well-being. Physiometric data provide the necessary contextual information on fitness, risk factors, disease states and other factors to enable the delivery of customised education, coaching or healthcare.

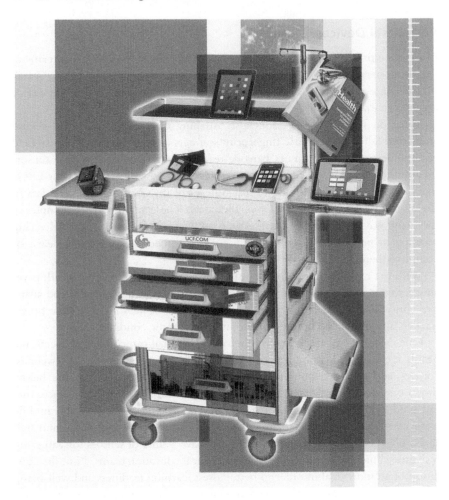

**FIGURE 2.3** Mobile crash cart

## Social Media

Social media tools can connect learners through collaboration and competition, especially within the social context of group events or cohort learning. Socially-aware mobile applications may pull data from users' social profiles or may situate learning and encourage engagement within the shared context of groups (Duval, 2010).

Within UCF METIL, we have supported live events at conferences such as *Training Magazine*'s Learning 3.0 event in Chicago and Training 2011 in San Diego. We developed a social game called Tower Challenge for the Chicago event to encourage attendees to learn about the city, the conference topics and social media platforms. Built within the Moving Knowledge Engine, the game challenged players to engage with their environment and fellow attendees by answering Chicago- and conference-themed trivia and challenges. To meet the challenges and interact with the game and each other, they used the same technologies they were learning about such as GPS, QR Codes, augmented reality, camera images and social media feeds. Scores were posted to online leaderboards and Twitter accounts to drive motivation and engagement within the social context of the peer group.

We have also employed leaderboards in other social contexts, such as a leadership training program for Google team members who were identified as future leaders within the organisation. We leveraged the Moving Knowledge Engine as a multimodal mobile communication platform to use e-mail messages to link participants to a diverse range of existing free or paid resources in the cloud (e.g., videos, articles, e-learning content) to create a flexible yet seamless curriculum and provide scaffolding to drive the 'Learning Story'. The engine's ability to track learners' 'interaction footprints'—both individual and social—was vital for the delivery of adaptive content as well as learner reflection (Glahn, 2009).

To take advantage of the social context of the program and its participants—highly driven emerging leaders at Google—we introduced game-like elements to drive competition. Moving Knowledge served as a game engine to track scores on learning activities and award points for participation in synchronous debrief and collaboration sessions via web conferences and forums, quizzes and other interactions. Results were posted to an online leaderboard, where participants could see how they rated amongst their peers. Before 2009, Google had previously run pilots for leadership training using off-the-shelf e-learning programs from well-respected sources, which achieved a 30% start rate, but completion rates that were far lower. Whilst the new leadership program remained voluntary, the new cloud-based resource structure and competition incentives drove completion rates above 90% (Clow & Metcalf, in press).

## Reflections

Understanding the implications of context-aware learning from government, industry and educational settings shows commonality and transferability across multiple sectors of society. The potential to cross-utilise mobile technology in transmedia activities can provide meaningful outcomes for learning and performance (Raybourn, 2014). Combining mobile technology with augmented reality, health sensors, e-learning elements, and simulation and game techniques can enable rich narrative and experiential learning. Examples that show student and employee outcomes prove that contextual characteristics of mobile learning solutions are additional enablers that can be combined with other learning interventions. Further studies should be conducted to determine the optimal blend of contextual and mobile learning assets with other learning interventions in transmedia solutions. There may be distinct differences and potential negative implications to overuse of media, movement between modalities and heuristics that can help determine the proper design.

## Future Trends and Innovation

As expressed in many of the examples throughout this chapter, the use of context will continue to drive innovation. A particular interest to this research team is the notion of adding physiometrics and cognitive context to the already robust suite of location-based and activity-based sensing possible with GPS chips and accelerometers. Through our work in *mHealth* (Krohn & Metcalf, 2012), we are seeing rapid adoption of physiometric, medical and cognitive sensors that could inform the context for both learning and health-related activities. Having insight into someone's state of attention, engagement and level of arousal could determine changes in the approach that one takes to delivery methods, length of learning interventions and learning modality (e.g., didactic versus experiential). There is an existing research base for this activity in places like pilot training with the US military—leveraging biometric sensors to determine the most appropriate cognitive cue (visual, aural, kinesthetic, etc.), populating a heads-up display, whispering or shouting information into an earpiece or vibrating the stick in a cockpit (Reinerman-Jones, Barber, & Jackson, 2012).

Some of this research is already being leveraged by groups like the UCF ACTIVE Lab at the Institute for Simulation and Training, where a suite of cognitive sensors is being used for evaluation of learning outcomes within virtual environments, and also for more advanced capabilities like sending data from a wireless suite of sensors including functional near infrared imaging that can send information from the neocortex into the wireless network. Currently, concentration on simple yes or no answers to questions can send a distinct signature that allows you to project basic thought patterns over the internet. The implications for this line of research are substantial.

Biometric sensors are becoming less intrusive and being put into new practical applications for wellness tracking; for instance, Band-Aid-sized sensors like the eye ribbon can replace much of the tracking that is done by bulky Holter monitors requiring a full chest harness. The ability to understand cognitive workload as well as physical stress level has significant implications for future study and uses, particularly when linked to the method of delivery and amount of content delivered over mobile phones or requested from participants in learning, human performance or simulation exercises. This level of real-world data will also allow simulations, whether delivered over computer, mobile device or live (or some combination thereof), to be more realistic and in tune with the real context of the learner. This will be particularly true in high-stress job situations such as pilot training, surgical training, military exercises and other mission critical tasks.

We look forward to the world that context awareness in our learning and other areas of life will produce and hope to continue to advance the state-of-the-art in this important area alongside many of you who are reshaping the way we learn and the world around us.

## References

Allogy Interactive. (2014). Retrieved from http://allogy.com/products/ride-along

Clow, J., & Metcalf, D. (in press). Developing leaders @ Google: The new era of leadership development in the cloud. Harvard Business Review Digital.

Duval, E. (2010). From scarcity to abundance (and from mass production to hyper-personalisation): The snowflake effect. Presented at *Knowledge Integration in an Organizational Network*, Venlo. Retrieved from http://www.slideshare.net/erik.duval/from-scarcity-to-abundance-and-from-mass-production-to-hyperpersonalization-the-snowflake-effect-3588866

Glahn, C. (2009). *Contextual support of social engagement and reflection on the web* (Doctoral dissertation). Open University of the Netherlands, Heerlen.

Krohn, R., & Metcalf, D. S. (2012). *mHealth: From smartphones to smart systems*. Chicago, IL: HIMSS.

Kurti, A., Milrad, M., & Spikol, D. (2007). Designing innovative learning activities using ubiquitous computing. Proceedings from *7th IEEE International Conference on Advanced Learning Technologies* (pp. 386–390).

Metcalf, D. S. (2006). *mLearning: Mobile learning and performance in the palm of your hand*. Amherst, MA: HRD Press.

Raybourn, E. (2014). A new paradigm for serious games: Transmedia learning for more effective training and education. *Journal of Computational Science, 5*(3), 471–481.

Reinerman-Jones, L. E., Barber, D., & Jackson, M. (2012). Real-time physiological measures. Presented at the Department of Defense Human Factors and Ergonomics Technical Advisory Group, Dayton, OH.

Weiss, S. (2002). *Handheld Usability*. Chichester: John Wiley & Sons.

# 3

# INTEGRATING MOBILE TECHNOLOGIES IN THE ITALIAN EDUCATIONAL CONTEXT

*Marco Arrigo, Giovanni Fulantelli, Manuel Gentile and Davide Taibi*

## Introduction

This chapter focuses on a research activity aimed at investigating the impact of mobile technologies on Italian educational contexts. In particular, the authors report on three mobile learning projects they have carried out over the past four years at the Institute for Educational Technologies (ITD) of the National Research Council (CNR) of Italy.

The three projects are based on a common methodological background and on a common mobile platform; however, they have been aimed at different target groups: secondary school students, university students and adults. Each project has uncovered specific issues concerning the use of mobile technologies for learning, and the chapter presents the benefits of m-learning in three levels of education.

The projects have been carried out using the MoULe (Mobile and Ubiquitous Learning) system (Arrigo et al., 2007), an online environment for collaborative learning, the design of which has been inspired by recent Web 2.0 technologies (Figure 3.1). By means of smartphones, MoULe enables educational activities based on the exploration of a geographical place. The MoULe system is built on the Moodle learning management system. It is accessible both through computers used by students in the classroom or at home, and through mobile devices during on-site learning activities (for example, school trips or guided visits).

The system includes specific functionalities to search and access information spaces, to communicate and to annotate places according to their geographical coordinates. Data stored in the system (including data uploaded into it by users) are enriched with information concerning geographical localisation (via the GPS technology integrated into the devices) so that the system provides users with information specific to the place they are visiting and, at the same time, automatically associates the students' activities to their geographical location. Accessing the

**FIGURE 3.1** The MoULe

online environment through the mobile devices offers the same functionalities as accessing it through desktop computers. Administrators can use MoULe to design educational paths; they can monitor users' activities in real-time and evaluate the quantity and quality of interactions amongst users. The MoULe system won the GOLD Award at mLearn 2009 in Orlando, Florida, in recognition of mobile learning excellence for the education category.

The three projects described in this chapter share a common model for the mobile knowledge building process (mKBP) (Gentile et al., 2007), fostering social learning interactions, formal and informal learning (Eshach, 2007; Arrigo, 2011) and environmental tagging (Taibi et al., 2007; Vinu et al., 2011). The collaborative knowledge building process is supported by the MoULe system using the wiki as a tool to foster collaboration between participants. Students in the classroom and on site use the wiki to share and create new knowledge. In this type of educational activity that draws from the social constructivism paradigm, knowledge is not transferred from teacher to student, but is the result of collaborative activities oriented towards the development of conceptual artefacts and collective understanding through social negotiation. In a similar way, the project FABULA (Rossitto, Canova Calori, & Divitini, 2011) aims to support collaboration between participants in learning experiences that take place in city contexts. In this project, particular attention is given to the creation and sharing of knowledge and experiences between participants.

The social dimension of learning has played a key role in the design of the learning activities carried out in the three projects. The tools of the MoULe system have been designed following a Web 2.0 approach. Social activities have played a key role in mobile learning experiences in the last few years; amongst others, the project Tweetalyser (Montebello, Camilleri, & Refalo, 2011) has followed a similar approach to the MoULe experience, making use of Web 2.0 tools such as Twitter and other social networks to create systems that support the social dimension of learning.

With respect to formal and informal settings, the system developed in the MoULe experience is accessible both through desktop computers used by students in the classroom or at home, and through mobile devices during on-site learning activities. In the three projects described in this chapter, participants experienced classroom and on-site activities alternately, thus playing different roles. This approach allows participants to perform both formal activities in the classroom and informal activities on site. A positive evaluation of the combination of classroom learning activities and mobile learning activities has been presented by Silander, Sutinen, and Tarhio (2004), where an SMS-based application for collaborative concept map building was developed and tested.

Concerning environmental tagging, in the MoULe system participants can use mobile devices to tag the physical places that they visit with textual notes, photos and audio recordings, thus experiencing social tagging in authentic environments. They build a representation of on-site learning activities and position themselves both in the physical space and in the community. Two important features have been developed in the methodology proposed by MoULe in the three projects: the close relationship between physical objects and the digital objects created during the learning activity, and the collaboration amongst students to build knowledge in a shared and motivating way. The Toponimo geosocial game (Sweeney, Sharples, & Pemberton, 2011) is concerned with similar issues; GPS data have been used to link physical locations to words, images and sound files related to a particular location. In Dingli and Seychell (2011) a virtual mobile city guide is presented, and learning aspects are merged with the experience of exploring a new city. The camera is used to take photos and to share them with friends.

The projects described in this chapter address three key levels of education: secondary schools, university and adult education. These three educational contexts have specific characteristics, and the issues regarding the implementation of mobile learning experiences for each context are considered separately. Bradley and Holley (2010), Grund (2011) and Hartnell-Young and Heym (2008) describe applications of mobile devices to support learning at secondary schools, whilst Maruyama (2012) and Isabwe, Oysaed, and Reichert (2011) analyse the use of mobile technologies in university settings. Lifelong learning supported by mobile devices has been widely discussed in Jancke, Götter, Vogt, and Zawacki-Ritchter (2012), Sharples (2000) and Arrigo et al. (2007).

### The Mobile Knowledge Building Process Model

The mKBP model (Figure 3.2) is an extended version of the model proposed by Stahl (2000). In particular, the mKBP focuses on mobile learning scenarios

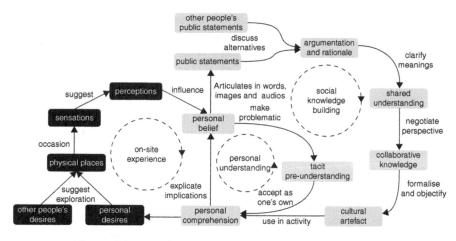

**FIGURE 3.2** The mobile Knowledge Building Process model

investigating how the on-site experience can modify a student's beliefs and thus his or her cognitive state. Stahl splits the collaborative knowledge building process into a set of phases centred around two cycles regarding personal understanding and social knowledge building. In addition to Stahl's model, the mKBP takes into account how the use of mobile devices can support students in positioning themselves both in the physical space and in the community space.

On the basis of mKBP, the authors studied the evolution of a mobile collaborative learning experience through its interactions with the social, the information and the geographical spaces. Moreover, according to the socio-constructivism paradigms, knowledge is not transferred from teachers to students, but is the result of participative and collaborative activities. When these activities take place in a mobile environment, it is extremely important to consider how temporal and spatial factors can influence the learning process.

Basically, in adopting the mKBP we hypothesise that, in a mobile environment, the knowledge building process can be analysed on the basis of three spaces: social, information and geographical. The social space represents the social interactions between students that occur in the knowledge building process. Next, the information space concerns the cultural artefacts and the public statements produced by students as a result of their learning experience. Finally, the geographical space represents the physical places.

## Three Mobile Learning Experiences in Italy

In order to summarise the key concepts for each of the projects presented in this chapter and provide readers with an easier way of comparing them, the authors have used the evaluation grid tool designed and developed within the MOTILL project (Arrigo, Kukulska-Hulme, Arnedillo-Sánchez, & Kismihok, 2013). Using this tool the authors attempt to provide a systematic analysis for practises in four areas: management, pedagogy, policymaking and ethics. A synthesis of policy and ethical issues is reported since they are less central to the aim of this chapter than other issues.

The first project was carried out over two years from 2007–2008 at the Institute for Educational Technologies of the National Research Council of Italy, involving six secondary schools in Palermo. It was the first application of the MoULe system, so the pedagogical and technical testing of the efficacy of the system was central to the project. The testing methodology was designed in two cycles, each lasting for a four-month period. Moreover, each testing cycle was designed in two phases: the MoULe system prototype was first tested with the teachers, and then the MoULe system and pedagogical model was tested with both students and teachers. In the first phase, after being introduced to the methodologies and technologies of mobile learning, the teachers were encouraged to design the learning activities for their students to carry out during the next phase.

Whilst the first phase with the teachers followed a more theoretical approach to mobile learning, the second phase was more practical: the students started learning about the main functionalities of the MoULe system and getting used to the mobile devices. Then the teachers explained the outside learning activity they had designed in the first phase, which varied according to the type of school. Finally, the students carried out the learning task in the classroom and on site. At the end of the testing phase, the students worked collaboratively to produce a hypermedia artefact about the sites they had visited.

The second project was carried out in 2010 at the University of Milano-Bicocca in the course on sociology of business innovation as part of the master's degree in human resource training and development in the Department of Education. In this experience the 10 students involved were divided into three groups, each with a different theme. Each group was assigned the task of creating collaborative hypermedia about their group topic using the wiki tool by collecting media footage—such as images, texts or audio interviews—on site using mobile devices equipped with satellite tracking systems. Unlike the previous experience, students involved in this project were provided with a smartphone supplied with GPS for 24 hours a day, not only during the testing phases.

Finally, the third project was carried out in 2011 with adults excluded from the educational cycle. In this experience the authors investigated the use of mobile technologies for lifelong learning in order to boost the number of people involved in training programs and, consequently, to help people to find a job. A course for 40 adult students currently excluded from the educational cycle and living in a disadvantaged area of Palermo (the Zen suburb) was organised using mobile devices. The course focused on the use of mobile technologies to design innovative mobile tourist guides; these guides aggregated not only information about the town's places, but also about the crafts from the past that are disappearing from Palermo. In this third project, an updated version of the MoULe system for iOS

TABLE 3.1 Synoptic table of the three projects

| | Objectives | Target | Technology | Funds | Period |
|---|---|---|---|---|---|
| **Mobile technologies in secondary school curricula** | Producing hypermedia artefacts about the physical places they visited | 114 secondary school students | HP 6915 and I-MATE K-JAM Windows Mobile GPRS/EDGE network | Sicilian government within the CORFAD project | 2007–2008 |
| **A MoULe experience at the university of Milano–Bicocca** | Investigating implicit and explicit readiness of Italian university students towards m-learning | 10 university students | HP 6915 and I-MATE K-JAM Windows Mobile GPRS/EDGE network | University of Milano–Bicocca | 2010 |
| **Mobile lifelong learning for adults excluded from the educational cycle: the Zen project** | Building a tourist guide to the city of Palermo | 40 unemployed young people and adults | iPhone iOS v. 4 UMTS network | Assessorato Regionale dell'Istruzione e Formazione Professionale della Regione Sicilia | 2011 |

devices was used. This new version was designed to overcome the connection issues observed in previous projects and provided a more usable interface than the previous version. Students used the iPhone 4 and iPad 2 with iOS 4.x.

In Table 3.1, key facts are highlighted to provide an overview of the projects. In the following sections, the three projects are described in depth.

## Mobile Technologies in Secondary School Curricula

### *Management*

#### *Rationale*

This study aimed to support students using context-sensitive handheld devices in collaborative knowledge construction. The specific goal was to track students during the whole collaborative knowledge building process and reconstruct the physical exploration of their learning space. In this way the student activities created an augmented space consisting of physical objects, as well as the didactic objects and items they produced.

#### *Technologies and Media Utilised*

Students accessed the MoULe platform with mobile devices, as well as desktop PCs, to collaborate and create shared knowledge about topics proposed by their teachers. In this way they used a single system in which on-site learning activities could be alternated with classroom learning activities so that the knowledge building process was supported in both learning environments. In particular, students used two types of mobile devices: HP 6915 and I-MATE K-JAM running the Windows Mobile operating system and connected to the GPRS/EDGE mobile network.

#### *Stakeholders and Agency*

The project involved teachers and students from six different secondary schools in Italy and the researchers at the CNR. In particular, 29 teachers of different subjects (science, arts, languages, etc.) and 114 students in the fourth year of secondary school took part.

Researchers supported teachers in planning educational activities based on the MoULe system. Initially, the researchers exercised control over activities; later, teachers worked in groups to define and design the learning experience.

During the testing of the system with students, teachers defined some practises principally aimed at developing collaborative work between students on site and those in the classroom. Nevertheless, each student was free to define his or her own practises of use for both the mobile environment and the e-learning platform.

## Organisational Support

This research was developed within the framework of the CORFAD project, a Sicilian government initiative that aimed to develop a centre of knowledge for distance learning. Six researchers from the CNR were involved in the whole project.

The MoULe activities in this experience required at least one smartphone for each pair of students. Apparatus and connections (WIFI or GPRS/EDGE/UMTS) were provided by the CNR, these being the principal costs for implementing a similar didactic experience. Both teachers and head teachers identified costs as the main obstacle to the diffusion of mobile learning for scholastic activities.

## Risk Assessment

Schools generally consider outside activities difficult to manage. The running of the project involved procedures of careful planning and control of the activities. Some of the factors that differentiate this experience from others involving mobile learning include:

- Mobile learning activities are often planned to take place in indoor sites (museums) or in circumscribed areas (university campuses, other defined places). Instead this study did not impose any restrictions of this kind; the teachers were left free to choose both the places and the types of activities to carry out whilst exploring locations. At least, the places were chosen as a result of discussions and were definitely not predefined.
- Many mobile learning activities take place in a setting that is already equipped with, for example, Wi-Fi, labelled items or radio frequency IDs (RFID), etc. This experience, on the other hand, involved a 'natural' setting where there were confusion, complexity and a wealth of stimuli.
- The researchers were involved throughout the entire project, as it is not easy for teachers to become autonomous in the use of these devices. Moreover, the technology is constantly being updated and mobile applications rapidly become obsolete. Other problems can be related to the wireless connections, which are often not sufficiently broad to support multimedia communications, and to the GPS that is unable to communicate positions during indoor activities.

## Supporting Transitions

The transition between formal and informal learning was promoted by the design of experimental activities based on alternating on-site and classroom learning, and by the learning environment created, which was accessible through the use of both mobile devices and desktop computers.

During these learning experiences, the students discovered different sources of information and different ways of extracting, elaborating, constructing and storing knowledge. This transition from non-structured knowledge to situated learning is probably one of the most important transformations needed for managing one's own lifetime learning.

## Achievement of Economic Goals

The studies only indirectly addressed economic issues. The students involved were not at work, but in educational institutions. However, the way the activities were organised has some features in common with the work organisation of some innovative firms. The students used new technologies and new modalities to interact and collaborate. With the help of these devices, they discovered the value of their cultural heritage as preserved in certain places and by certain people, and they integrated these sources to create valuable web sites, full of very useful information.

## Quality Assurance

The research studies resulting from this project have been reported in various national and international scientific articles, many of which analyse the quality and quantity of the experimental activities. The research shows the impact mobile technology had on the evolution of social relationships within the group of students involved. The analytical methods used also show a correlation between the activities carried out in the physical location, the social interactions and the conceptual space in which the process of knowledge construction took place. This model of analysis of mobile learning activities is the most innovative aspect of the project.

## Pedagogy

### Impact on Subjects Being Learnt

Mobile technology modified and enriched the didactic activities carried out during the project. During the on-site visits, the mobile devices allowed the students to move around in an augmented physical space, with information available from a variety of different sources. Moreover, the students, both on site and in the computer lab, were able to make further additions to the information space. Furthermore, the use of mobile devices opened up a communication channel between the two groups of students, promoting a collaborative process of knowledge construction.

### Learning Behaviours, Activities and Processes

The learning activities took place both in the classroom and on site. Generally a class of students was divided into two groups. The group that went out of the school was given handheld devices (usually one device for each pair of students), whilst the members of the other group who went to the computer lab each had a PC. All the students were thus able to access the MoULe environment to carry out the learning tasks.

Learners made use of mobile devices principally to create artefacts, rarely to seek information or communicate by means of synchronous and asynchronous tools. From desktops, they shared images and texts, created wiki pages and collaborated with students outside. Teachers occasionally intervened to help students, usually only to set the wiki pages, to establish the priority of topics or to decide the relevance of information.

## Development of Competences

The students acquired competences in using online educational tools, particularly applications that promote processes of collaborative knowledge construction and improve their abilities to work in a group. They worked using social network tools, such as the wiki editor, forums and chat.

## Achievement of Educational Goals

This study promotes collaborative learning processes during on-site learning activities. The on-site activities, which may be guided visits, school trips, etc., give students the opportunity to widen their cultural and social horizons. Moreover, this experience provides teachers and schools with tools that enable them to exploit the educational potential of these activities. From an educational point of view, the system was oriented to addressing some scholastic organisational issues.

## Support for Learning across Contexts

This study takes place partly in the classroom and partly in a location outside the school. The transition between the various contexts is facilitated by the use of mobile technology that opens up a communication channel with the classroom environment.

The learning activities were carried out in different physical contexts, in the classroom, outdoors and across different cultural environments, applying a collaborative approach. One of the aims of the system was to introduce the constructivist paradigm into everyday life situations: students learnt that the objects around them could be transformed into learning objects.

## Policy

From a political prospective we can observe how the learning tasks connected to this project enabled the students to extend their knowledge of the local area and to discover social, cultural and economic aspects of their city. Consequently, the experience extends the meaning of learning into new contexts and raises some questions about the possibility of recognising similar experiences as part of institutional curricula. The recognition of mobile learning programs is a national problem.

Moreover, the diversity of the learning tasks carried out by the schools shows that the educational model used in this study can be transferred to different educational contexts, and the technologies to wider areas. Two practical examples of the transferability of the research are the two other projects described in this chapter. Furthermore, considering that the use of mobile learning represents a new experience in Italian schools, policymakers should evaluate the opportunity of extending this practise to wider contexts, creating networks between different schools and integrating learning activities with other social and cultural initiatives.

Finally, the results of this experience have highlighted some important issues related to lifelong learning. Amongst others, the need to train teachers in m-learning to fully exploit its educational potential and the use of mobile devices integrated into a scholastic context to sustain student motivation and scholastic performance.

### Ethical Considerations

During the learning experience, a wiki platform was activated with access restricted to students participating in the project. At the end of the project, most of the schools involved decided to publish the contents produced during the learning experience on the web (only for viewing, not editing). Problems related to copyright and fair use were discussed with teachers and students during the experience. The system has a specific interface that also permits cognitively impaired students to use the mobile application.

The researchers explained the privacy issues regarding the use of personal images and of movies in which students appear. Students and parents were informed about the implications of the research and about the use of the various materials produced by the students in scientific publications. Personal data were stored in private archives that are not possible to consult from outside.

## A MoULe Experience at the University of Milano-Bicocca

### Management

#### Rationale

This project was carried out at the University of Milano-Bicocca (Pieri & Diamantini, 2011; La Guardia, Arrigo, & Todaro, 2012) in collaboration with the CNR. The main aim was to investigate the implicit and explicit readiness of Italian university students to use m-learning.

## Technologies and Media Utilised

Like in the previous experience, the MoULe platform was used. For three months, each student was provided with a smartphone supplied with GPS.

## Stakeholders and Agency

This study involved two professors and 10 students following a course in the sociology of business innovation as part of the master's degree in human resource training and development at the Department of Education, University of Milano-Bicocca. It further involved a researcher and a technician at the same university and five researchers from the Italian National Research Council, Institute for Educational Technology of Palermo.

Researchers from the CNR trained university teachers to use the MoULe platform. Teachers, supported by the CNR researchers, designed a learning path for students defining the points of interest (POIs), the learning objectives and the functionalities that students could use during their learning activities. Teachers also trained students to use the system. The management of these activities was carried out by university teachers, CNR researchers and a technician who coordinated and supported learners when needed.

## Organisational Support

The experience began in March 2010 and ended in June 2010. During the whole three-month period, a mobile device was provided to each student by the CNR, whilst maintenance costs to carry out this project were sustained by the University of Milano-Bicocca. For instance, it was necessary to pay for a national telephone provider with GPRS technology to provide mobile internet connectivity.

The CNR managed the MoULe platform on its server, which was specially adapted for these activities, and also trained teachers and students at the University of Milano-Bicocca to use the system. Moreover, the CNR supported university teachers in learning path design and POI identification. The university teachers designed the learning path for their students and supported them when needed. Since students used mobile devices independently 24 hours a day, no costs for on-site tutors were sustained. Staff costs to carry out this experience were sustained both by CNR and University of Milano-Bicocca.

## Risk Assessment

A loss of motivation was one of the main challenges to address in this project. During the design stage it was decided not to provide any tutors for on-site activities. As a consequence of this, and as the students worked alone all the time and mainly outside the university, a loss of motivation was observed. In fact, to resolve any issues the students had to contact tutors and technicians online and wait for solutions and clarifications. This factor, as an example, was demotivating for students who had problems with the technology. To tackle this problem and minimise the risk of it happening, a forum and chat service were used to support students during their mobile learning activities. Moreover, with regard to techno-logical risk, as reported by a student involved in this project:

> M-learning is too much a *victim* of the technological evolution. It is still in its infancy. For example, at the beginning Internet was for a few, then every-thing became 'automatic' so Internet was used by everybody. Put mobile technology in the hands of everyone and it can make m-learning univer-sally possible.

Students have also reported difficulties in using MoULe because it is some-times slow due to the GPRS network and out-dated devices used. Moreover, their expectations were related to their experiences of social networks like Facebook, where they can do everything without knowing anything about the technology.

## Supporting Transitions

As reported above, this experience was introduced into the curricula activities of the sociology of business innovation course of the master's degree in human resource training and development at the Department of Education, University of Milano-Bicocca. Students involved experienced a new way of producing an artefact, and this was included in the evaluation for passing the subject. In par-ticular, students experienced the transition between formal and informal learning, carrying out activities based on alternating on-site and classroom learning using an LMS as well as a mobile device at any time and anywhere for three months without any constraints.

During these three months, students used mobile devices independently and discovered how to use these devices for learning on the go for their univer-sity subject, but also for their hobbies. For instance, a student reported after the MoULe experience, "I really like m-learning, I like cooking, and on the train I would like to take cooking classes via m-learning."

## Achievement of Economic Goals

The introduction of mobile learning in a university setting allowed students to learn anywhere and at any time during the day. M-learning seems to offer solu-tions and to resolve issues related to attending lessons at university. Students can study at home and even carry out a designed learning activity related to the sub-ject on the go. This opportunity was much appreciated.

## Quality Assurance

One of the innovatory values of this research is the introduction of the potentiality of mobile devices in a university setting. In fact, in Italy m-learning is not very common yet. Almost all universities have experimented with e-learning, and it is now integrated into the teaching of many subjects, but only a very few universities have introduced m-learning systematically.

However, this innovation has not been fully evaluated since it has considered only students' readiness to use mobile learning. Results of this research have been presented at some international conferences in the field of m-learning (Pieri & Diamantini, 2011; La Guardia et al., 2012).

## Pedagogy

### Impact on Subjects Being Learnt

Using the MoULe system, students were able to learn on site about the subject of study. Moreover, they reported that the use of m-learning in a university setting had great potential.

### Learning Behaviours, Activities and Processes

Basically the activities as well as the procedure were the same as those carried out in the other experiences reported in this chapter. However, the main difference between this study and the others reported is that in this case students used mobile devices that were available 24 hours a day and no on-site tutor was provided. Thus, they carried out their mobile activities without any interference or help, and they managed their own studies.

### Development of Competences

Students acquired competences in using a mobile learning platform, and some of them appreciated the fact that the MoULe experience introduced them to m-learning opportunities. In particular, some students who commute found m-learning to be very useful on the tram and train.

### Achievement of Educational Goals

This study promotes awareness of the potentiality of mobile devices for learning. It has also introduced students to collaborative learning processes during on-site learning activities. Moreover, students have acquired competences in using the LMS and mobile LMS.

On the other hand, this experience provides teachers and universities with tools that enable them to exploit the educational potential of mobile learning in a university setting, though this research has highlighted that the introduction of mobile learning into universities needs to deal with and overcome some technological and pedagogical issues. These are problems that need tackling at a national level.

### Support for Learning across Contexts

Throughout their experience with the MoULe platform, students collaborated in learning activities both inside and outside the classroom and for the whole day. In particular, students in the same theme group worked together outside formal educational settings, using the system to communicate and exchange information at any time. They used mobile devices to interact with each other anytime and anywhere, sharing information correlated to their position.

### Policy

This study does not specifically address policy and social issues. However, it is easily transferable to other subjects and universities in local, national and international contexts. In fact, the experience can be replicated in other contexts at very little cost if students use their own mobile devices. On the other hand, from a policymaker's point of view, the importance of this study is strictly correlated to its aim and further integration of mobile learning into university settings in both formal and informal contexts. Thus, this research could support other universities in adopting mobile learning.

### Ethical Considerations

In this experience students used MoULe on mobile devices in all their everyday activities (e.g., at university, at home, travelling, walking around, etc.). Consequently, every action they performed was traced by the system. This might be an ethical concern if it is not well managed. In fact, students' habits should be mapped and analysed for educational scope only (e.g., to study their learning path).

## Mobile Lifelong Learning for Adults Excluded from the Educational Cycle: The Zen Project

### Management

#### Rationale

The main objective of the project was the training of unemployed young people and adults in innovative activities involving tourism. More precisely, the project aimed at using mobile devices integrated with more traditional ICT tools to build a tourist guide for the city of Palermo by using mobile devices and providing tourists with the mobile city guide. A second important objective of the project was to improve—and in some cases to introduce—ICT as one of the key competences for the information society.

## Technologies and Media Used

In this study, a modified version of the MoULe platform was used. It was a simplified version with no access to wikis or to the specialised search engine via mobile phones. Furthermore, the interface of the mobile application was simplified. No major change to the desktop side of the platform was made.

During the on-site activities, each student was provided with an iPhone with iOS v.4. The GPS integrated in the device was used for the geolocalisation functionalities, and devices were connected to the UMTS mobile network.

## Stakeholders and Agency

The target group of the project was unemployed young people and adults from a disadvantaged area of the city of Palermo. Different stakeholders were involved in the project: head teachers, teachers and administrative staff from a state middle school in the selected area, researchers at the CNR, and a private tourist agency.

Researchers designed and managed the whole study by instructing other stakeholders in the general aims and the specific activities of the project and by scheduling the calendar for the activities. The work in the classroom was managed by the researchers in strict collaboration with the schoolteachers. Sightseeing tours were conducted by personnel from the tourism company, even though the researchers managed the specific m-learning tasks. Finally, students were autonomous in the management of the information gathering tasks.

## Organisational Support

The project was funded by the Assessorato Regionale dell'Istruzione e Formazione Professionale della Regione Sicilia. The financial management of the project was entrusted to the school, which also played a key role in the organisation of the practical activities.

The research activities were coordinated and managed by the National Research Council, supported in the definition of itineraries to be followed by students by personnel from the tourism organisation and the provision of information sheets concerning the sites to be visited. Schoolteachers also played a central role regarding the implementation of activities.

## Risk Assessment

Amongst the main challenges of the project, we can list first the risk of a high dropout rate of participants, which could even have affected the funding of the project. The risk is extremely high in initiatives like the one reported here since the participants are mainly adults who are unemployed, have pressing family commitments and are busy looking for a job.

Another risk derives from the diversity of actors involved in the project and the difficulties associated with developing a unique approach to the teaching model: the priority for the school was the participation of people in the course, regardless of whether they were in the classroom or on the city excursion. The staff from the tourism organisation behaved like real tourist guides, providing many details about the sights visited by the participants, thus reducing the students' learning autonomy. This particularly was in contrast with the goal of researchers at the National Research Council, whose primary interest was that students should have a high degree of autonomy during the trial and play an active role in the construction of knowledge. Although this was a risk at the level of project management, its effects on the pedagogical aspects could be particularly serious. In order to face these challenges, we worked on continuous motivation for students on the one hand, and on the other we made great efforts to coordinate the partners in order to develop a common view of the project.

## Supporting Transitions

The initial approach to the project was based on formal learning since the project included, especially at the beginning, a course for students consisting of upfront activities in the classroom, with a teacher who illustrated the topics to the class in a traditional model and guided them in practical exercises in a computer lab. However, as soon as the class started to use the mobile devices during the city tours, they began to acquire a greater degree of autonomy in the management of their learning and became the authors of the knowledge to be developed. Through the use of mobile devices, the relationship between students and teachers changed radically, as they became a single group committed to revising the information acquired in class with the learning experience in the field. We therefore observed a meaningful shift from formal to informal learning.

## Achievement of Economic Goals

The project addresses one of the greatest issues facing southern Italy: youth unemployment. Youth unemployment climbs as high as 40% in some parts of Sicily, which compounds the huge social burden of older adults who have lost their jobs, as their reintegration into the workforce is extremely complex and their skills are often no longer required by the labour market.

Another important aspect concerns the level of education of the people involved, as we tried to involve people with a low level of education and literacy, who are therefore even more impaired in the work market. The choice of the Zen suburb was not accidental, as it is one of the most disadvantaged areas in Palermo.

## Quality Assurance

The main innovation lies in the fact that we have introduced mobile devices in the context of requalification of unemployed people, using a new instrument like the iPhone to promote a project for the recovery of crafts from the past. The dimension of this innovation is particularly significant if we consider the disadvantaged suburb where we introduced the practice.

The impact in terms of knowledge and skills acquired by the students is a significant indicator of the success of the project. In addition, the dropout rate was very low, especially if compared to other experiences of adult education. Finally, the researchers applied an ethnographic approach to collecting field observations, and noted a significant correlation between socio-relational links and their impact on the collaborative learning processes. The results achieved during the study were presented to a national conference organised at the end of the project.

## Pedagogy

### Impact on Subjects Being Learnt

The introduction of mobile technologies has not caused any change to the subjects to be learnt. What has changed is the way in which students learn the subjects.

### Learning Behaviours, Activities and Processes

The learning activities were based on the same approach as reported for the other experiences. Specifically in relation to the learning behaviour, we have observed that with the progress of the trial, as students became more familiar with the technological tools, there was an increased autonomy in the management of learning.

We do not have data to say whether this is actually due to the improvement of technical skills or if the reason is to be sought in the socio-educational aspects. In fact, the collaboration between students favoured a reduction of distances in the class group, not only amongst students but also between students and tutors. In addition, students were able to better understand the aims of the project and its philosophy, thus reducing their fears around not only the technology, but the course as well.

### Development of Competences

The project has provided students with several competencies in different sectors. First, the project has improved the ICT competencies that are considered one of the key competencies for the information society. Some students had no basic competence in the use of computers, so for them the project was an invaluable opportunity to reduce the digital divide.

A second sector of competencies concerns the mobile devices and the technological features and user potentials of smartphones, in particular iPhones. Finally, specific competencies on the planning and organisation of tourist guides were developed throughout the project.

## Achievement of Educational Goals

One of the most important challenges for the information society is to promote lifelong learning mechanisms. This project is directly aimed at promoting educational paths for adults, which is a central topic at the international level. In addition, the project aims to reduce the digital exclusion of adults from the society, which is a second extremely important topic in the international lifelong learning agenda.

## Support for Learning across Contexts

One of the strengths of the project is that it was planned with the tacit aim to facilitate transitions between different learning contexts: in the classroom and in the field, formal and informal, and so on. The way in which students can make these transitions is inherent in the methodological approach of the project, which includes activities such as gathering materials in the field that are then sent to the classroom. Since students alternate between groups in the classroom and in the field, all students experience the transition.

## Policy

The political and social impact of the project is huge because of the selected target group. By requalifying adult persons who are unemployed, the project aims at improving their employability and, consequently, at supporting social mobility and inclusion.

The results of this study can be easily replicated in different contexts and regions, both at national and international levels. Because of the high social value of the initiative, policymakers should sustain it extensively, especially by supporting the creation of start-ups at the end of the project.

## Ethical Considerations

Copyright issues and fair use were a central topic of the training course. Actually, people usually ignore copyright infringement on the web, especially when they are novices and have no experience browsing. Privacy issues, like the use of personal data (including images and movies acquired in the field), were also discussed with students.

## Comparative Analysis and Discussion

In this section the distinguishing features of the three projects are summed up and an attempt is made to find the commonalties and differences amongst the three experiences and derive some conclusions based on them. The three projects were carried out in three different contexts (school, university and adult education) with different objectives: the integration of mobile technology into a school's teaching curriculum, the assessment of the implicit and explicit readiness of university students to use m-learning, and the requalification of unemployed adults in the tourism sector.

The projects covered a period of about five years, and during this time mobile technologies made great advances. An analysis of the changes in mobile technologies that have become available on the market includes:

- a dramatic improvement in terms of the quality of mobile devices;
- an equally significant improvement in the mobile network in terms of coverage and bandwidth;
- an increase in the diffusion and use of smartphone devices.

These changes resulted in specific requirements for an update of the MoULe system, whilst they reduced some of the more evident problems reported as limitations of the system during the first experience and during the experience at the University of Milano-Bicocca (Pieri & Diamantini, 2011).

In the activities carried out in the schools and in the Zen project, the teachers and the research staff were physically present to provide didactic and technological support to the learners, especially during the on-site activities. In contrast to this, the students at the university in Milan used the MoUle platform without the physical presence of teachers and researchers.

The three initiatives faced different types of risk: in the secondary school project the difficulty of managing and integrating the m-learning activities with the curricular activities represented the main risk, whilst in the university trial the greatest risk was loss of motivation. Finally, a high dropout rate was the main risk during the Zen project training course.

From a technological point of view, the risks present in the first two projects (in terms of connection problems and slowness of the devices), decreased during the Zen project for the reasons described above.

Whilst financial savings were not significant in the context of the school, the other two initiatives have highlighted the potential of mobile technologies to reduce the costs of education and lifelong learning.

In the activities carried out at the school as well as in the Zen project, students were provided with educational materials and fact sheets designed by the teachers and/or tutors as a guide for the visiting experience. In the project carried out at the university, the students had to organise the activities by themselves.

As described in the evaluation grids, during the projects at school as well as at the Zen project:

- the learning activities took place both in the classroom and onsite;
- the students made use of mobile devices principally to create artefacts;
- the students shared images and texts, created wiki pages and collaborated with students outside the classroom.

From this point of view, the experience at the university was quite different. In fact, the students could use mobile devices 24 hours a day and no tutor support was provided for the activities on site.

Analysing the projects from the point of view of the relationship between humans and technology, it becomes evident that the first two projects were based on the assumption that technology was a core element for scaffolding an experience of mobile learning. However, an analysis of the results of the first experiments soon demonstrated (Seta et al., 2008) that the active participation of teachers, both in designing and monitoring activities, was a crucial element for success. The techno-centric approach gradually declined over time, leading to the creation of studies in which the role of the teacher or tutor became central.

Similarities are more evident by observing other aspects: all three projects combined formal and informal learning. The transition between the two was promoted by the design of a learning path alternating on-site and classroom activities, and by tools available in the MoULe platform.

Regarding the pedagogical aspects, the projects shared the same didactic approach based on the collaborative construction of artefacts as the original synthesis of a learning path that is also a physical path and that becomes a tangible artefact. Furthermore, the projects were based on socio-constructivism paradigms. In fact, a knowledge building process for mobile learning experiences (Gentile et al., 2007) was defined. Through this model, the evolution of the learning experience through its interactions with the social, information and geographical spaces was analysed.

All the projects developed skills along several dimensions: technological expertise related to the use of both mobile devices and more generally of ICT tools for training, expertise on specific topics defined within the single experiment and transversal competences such as collaborative work.

To sum up, the three projects share a common underlying structure but differ widely from the point of view of the educational challenges faced. In particular, whilst during the school project the activities were designed to address scholastic and organisational issues, the study at the university aimed to promote awareness of the potentiality of mobile devices for learning. The challenge for the Zen project was to be able to conduct an effective learning activity with unemployed people with no experience with ICT.

Despite their differences in targets and specific objectives, the projects share a common aim: encouraging the growth of awareness of the effectiveness of mobile learning. Finally, not only does the analysis of the projects demonstrate the portability and flexibility of the learning activities based on a unique platform (the MoULe system), but also it shows how mobile learning represents a flexible methodology that can be adapted to different contexts.

## References

Arrigo, M. (2011). Mobile formal and informal learning on the iOS platform. Proceedings from *EDULEARN11* (pp. 6715–6722).

Arrigo, M., Di Giuseppe, O., Fulantelli, G., Gentile, M., Novara, G., Seta, L., & Taibi, D. (2007). A collaborative m-learning environment. Proceedings from *mLearn 2007: 6th International Conference on Mobile Learning* (pp. 13–21).

Arrigo, M., Kukulska-Hulme, A., Arnedillo-Sánchez, I., & Kismihok, G. (2013). Meta-analyses from a collaborative project in mobile lifelong learning. *British Educational Research Journal, 39*(2), 222–247. doi:10.1080/01411926.2011.652068

Bradley, C., & Holley, D. (2010). How students in higher education use their mobile phones for learning. In M. Montebello, V. Camilleri & A. Dingli (Eds.), Proceedings from *mLearn Conference* (pp. 232–239). 20–22 October, Malta.

Dingli, A., & Seychell, D. (2011). Mobile edutainment in the city. Proceedings from *IADIS International Conference on Mobile Learning 2011*. 10–12 March, Avila.

Eshach, H. (2007). Bridging in-school and out-of-school learning: Formal, nonformal, and informal education. *Journal of Science Education and Technology, 16*(2), 171–190.

Gentile, M., Taibi, D., Seta, L., Arrigo, M., Fulantelli, G., Di Giuseppe, O., & Novara, G. (2007). Social knowledge building in a mobile learning environment. In R. Meersman, Z. Tari & P. Herrero (Eds.), *Lecture notes in computer science* (Vol. 480, pp. 337–346). Berlin: Springer.

Grund, B.F. (2011). High school teachers face the challenge of integrating the mobile phone in the classroom. Proceedings from *IADIS International Conference on Mobile Learning 2011*. 10–12 March, Avila.

Guhr, J.D., & Gair, A.G. (2012). Mobile device trends and their implications for mobile learning at higher education institutions. Proceedings from *IADIS International Conference on Mobile Learning 2012*. 11–13 March, Berlin.

Hartnell-Young, E., & Heym, N. (2008). *How mobile telephones help learning in secondary schools*. Coventry: BECTA.

Isabwe G.M.N., Oysaed H., & Reichert, F. (2011). Future concepts for university teaching and learning. Proceedings from *IADIS International Conference on Mobile Learning 2011* (pp. 307–309). 10–12 March, Avila.

Jancke, A., Götter, R., Vogt, S., & Zawacki-Richter, O. (2012). Iacademy: An innovative mLearning approach for lifelong learning. Proceedings from *IADIS International Conference on Mobile Learning 2012*. 11–13 March, Berlin.

La Guardia, D., Arrigo, M., Todaro, G., & Allegra M. (2012). Mobile vocational learning for all. In M. Allegra, M. Arrigo, V. Dal Grande, P. Denaro, D. La Guardia, S. Ottaviano &

G. Todaro (Eds.), *Mobile learning for visually impaired people* (pp. 41–51). Rome: Italian National Research Council—Institute for Educational Technology.

Maruyama, Y. (2012). An investigation into university students' experiences and perceptions of using mobile phones. Proceedings from *IADIS International Conference on Mobile Learning 2012*. 11–13 March, Berlin.

Montebello, M., Camilleri, V., & Refalo, M. (2011). Tweetalyser: A Twitter based data mining system with recommendation capabilities. Proceedings from *10th International Conference on Contextual and Mobile Learning*. mLearn.

Pieri, M., & Diamantini, D. (2011). A MoULe experience at the University of Milano-Bicocca in Italy. Proceedings from *IADIS International Conference on Mobile Learning 2011* (pp. 77–84). 20–26 July, Rome.

Rossitto, C., Canova Calori, I., & Divitini, M. (2011). Exploring a city: Understanding situated learning experiences. Proceedings from *IADIS International Conference on Mobile Learning 2011*. IADIS Press.

Seta, L., Taibi, D., Gentile, M., Fulantelli, G., Arrigo, M., & Di Giuseppe, O. (2008). Design e valutazione di una esperienza di mobile learning. *TD-Tecnologie Didattiche, 44*(2), 44–56.

Sharples, M. (2000). The design of personal mobile technologies for lifelong learning. *Computers and Education, 34*, 177–193.

Silander, P., Sutinen, E., & Tarhio, J. (2004). Mobile collaborative concept mapping: Combining classroom activity with simultaneous field exploration. Proceedings from *2nd IEEE International Workshop on Wireless and Mobile Technologies in Education*.

Stahl, G. (2000). A model of collaborative knowledge-building. In B. Fishman & S. O'Connor-Divelbiss (Eds.), Proceedings from *Fourth International Conference of the Learning Sciences* (pp. 70–77). Mahwah, NJ: Erlbaum.

Sweeney, T., Sharples, M., & Pemberton, R. (2011). Toponimo: A geosocial pervasive game for English second language learning. Proceedings from *10th World Conference on Mobile and Contextual Learning*. 18–21 October, Beijing.

Taibi, D., Gentile, M., Arrigo, M., Seta, L., Di Giuseppe, O., Novara, G., & Fulantelli, G. (2007). Social tagging in a mobile learning environment. Proceedings from *9th IEEE International Symposium* (pp. 447–452).

Vinu, P. V., Sherimon, P. C., & Krishnan, R. (2011). Towards pervasive mobile learning: The vision of 21st century. *Social and Behavioral Sciences, 15*, 3067–3073.

# 4

# MOBILE INFORMAL LEARNING THROUGH GEOCACHING

*Gill Clough*

## Introduction

There has been considerable research into how context-aware mobile and social technologies can be used to support learning in formal and semi-formal contexts. However, less is known about the informal learning opportunities presented by context-aware technologies and how these opportunities manifest themselves in practice.

This chapter describes a study to identify how context-aware mobile technology has influenced informal learning and to classify the informal learning opportunities using a constructivist framework for assessing meaningful learning with technology (Jonassen, Howland, Moor, & Marra, 2003) that was devised originally for use in formal learning settings. This deeper understanding of how context-awareness drives informal learning activities may offer insights that can inform the ways we deploy context-aware technology in formal learning.

Informal learning was identified as a widespread phenomenon as early as the 1970s (Tough, 1979; Livingston, 1999; Burbules, 2006); however, little is known about the impact that context-aware mobile technologies and widespread social networks have had on the ways people go about informal learning. Over the years, the combination of features packed into each mobile device has increased rapidly, and new ways that these devices might support informal learning have emerged. In particular, the powerful connectivity (voice, e-mail, internet) combined with additional features (camera, video, GPS) have had a transformative effect on the ways that people engage with each other and with their physical environments. These technological developments have influenced informal learning activities that people undertake, creating learning opportunities where previously there were none and changing the nature of those that already existed.

This study focused on the technologically-mediated activities of the Geocaching community, a geographically dispersed group who use mobile and Web 2.0 technologies to link the virtual social spaces of the internet with the physical spaces in the surrounding landscape. It explored how Geocachers use the location-awareness provided by Global Positioning System (GPS) mobile devices combined with Web 2.0 technology to sustain their dynamic online community, and revealed the different ways that these activities translated into informal learning for the members of the community.

Geocachers form a worldwide community who create location-based challenges for each other, coordinating their activities through a website and web forum. In its most basic form, Geocaching is a sort of GPS-guided treasure hunt in which participants hide caches somewhere in the landscape and share the GPS coordinates of the hide location with other community members via the web. Other Geocachers then read the description of the cache on its webpage (hosted on the Geocaching community website), load the location coordinates onto their own GPS device and travel to the location to search for the cache, guided by the GPS signal. Having found a cache, a Geocacher signs the paper logbook in the cache and logs the find on the website along with a short description of the experience and any images they want to upload.

There are different types of Geocache, and each is represented by a different icon on the Geocaching website. Some of the most common are listed below:

- Traditional Geocache—a container of some sort containing a logbook and pencil and, if large enough, additional trinkets or tokens.
- Multicache (offset cache)—two or more locations. The physical cache container is at the final location, although each location may also have a cache. You need to locate each cache in order as each one contains a clue to find the next one.
- Earthcache—a virtual cache that teaches you something about the processes that formed the earth. The description contains information about the location and, in order to log it, you need to complete some task to demonstrate that you've been there such as taking photos at the location, making observations or measuring water temperature gradients.
- Puzzle cache—a cache where you need to solve some sort of puzzle in order to find the cache. This could be a puzzle that you do at home in order to work out the GPS coordinates, or it might require you to visit one or more locations and solve clues to get to the final cache.

## Methodology and Methods

The Geocaching website provides an online interactional space for community members, acting as a repository for community knowledge and retaining a persistent record of interactions between members. In it they can engage in constructive conversations via the Groundspeak Geocaching web forums, learn from the community resources and build up an online experiential narrative of place through the Geocache descriptions and find logs.

The journey from novice to experienced community member involves learning (Lave & Wenger, 1991; Wenger, 1998; Jonassen et al., 2003). This learning journey may consist of practical skills, problem-solving skills, cultural practices and conceptual knowledge at different stages, in different physical locations and using a range of technologies. To gather data on all aspects of community activities, this study used the Geocaching website both as a data source and as a means of locating and recruiting participants from the worldwide Geocaching community. The community website was viewed as "a form of social space" (Hine, 2005), and data were drawn from the collected narratives and traces created there by its inhabitants. The study used three methods of data collection:

- Web survey—an online questionnaire providing self-reported data on the target research areas of mobile and Web 2.0 technology use and informal learning.
- Geocaching community resources and outputs from the Geocaching website and forums—providing evidence to support the findings.
- Case study interviews of participants selected from the web survey respondents—conducted by telephone or e-mail to provide real-world examples to illustrate the findings.

The website Geocaching.com is the focal point for Geocaching activities, and its web forum Groundspeak offers a vehicle for community discussions. In November 2007, when this research was conducted, there were 40,284 account holders registered with the main Geocaching.com website and 489,646 active caches worldwide. By 10 December 2013, the number of Geocachers worldwide had grown to over six million, and the number of active Geocaches to 2,278,550.

The web survey was online for three weeks between 8 and 28 June 2007. It generated 659 responses, providing both quantitative and qualitative data. The qualitative data that participants provided through their free-text responses was comprehensive, totalling over 107,000 words and providing a rich data set. The survey attracted a broad spread of Geocachers. Of the 659 who completed the survey, 70% were male and 30% female. Over 60% of participants were aged between 30 and 50. From the survey respondents, five participants were selected and interviewed for case studies, four by telephone and one by e-mail, and their responses used to supplement the free-text responses from the survey.

## Framework for Analysis

Geocaching is an activity that uses both mobile and fixed technologies to link the collaborative virtual spaces of the internet with the physical spaces in the landscape in order to support the main community activity of hunting for Geo-caches using GPS devices. This interweaving of the virtual and the physical distinguishes the Geocaching community from other online communities, and offers novel ways of creating and maintaining cohesive social networks together with new opportunities for learning.

These opportunities for learning include both those with a clear skills focus, such as learning to use a GPS device, learning to read and interpret geographical coordinates and learning the ability to spot a well-hidden Geocache, as well as incidental learning opportunities that are inbuilt in the activity of Geocaching (for example, learning more about the history of an area or learning about the geographical and other processes that have formed the landscape). The informal learning opportunities occur at different points during the stages of community participation and involve mobile and Web 2.0 technologies to varying extents. However, it can be difficult to assess informal learning, as there is no official curriculum or assessment criteria. To address this challenge, the study used a constructivist framework originally created to assess meaningful learning with technology in a formal school setting (Jonassen et al., 2003).

Jonassen et al. proposed a shift in the way educators conceive of technology use in education, suggesting that they "begin to think about technologies as learning tools that students learn with not from" (Jonassen et al., 2003, p. 11), and this perspective matches the ways in which technology is likely to be deployed by informal learners who are unconstrained by imposed formal learning structures. Jonassen et al. applied a constructivist perspective to the use of technology in schools to create technology-based activities that would support meaningful learning. They defined meaningful learning as occurring when students were actively engaged in making meaning, and broke down this definition of meaningful learning into five "interrelated, interactive, and interdependent" attributes (Jonassen et al., 2003, p. 9), with the most meaningful learning activities supporting combinations of these attributes. These five attributes are:

**Active** (Manipulative/Observant)

Learners develop knowledge and skills in response to their environment, manipulating objects and observing and learning from the results.

**Constructive** (Articulative/Reflective)

Learners reflect on activity and observations and articulate what they have learnt. Thus when new experiences appear contradictory, they can engage in a meaning-making process to develop their mental models and make sense of their observations.

**Intentional** (Reflective/Regulatory)

People think and learn more when they are motivated to do so in order to achieve a cognitive goal. Technologies should engage learners in articulating what they are doing, making decisions, choosing strategies and findings answers, thereby enabling them to use their constructed knowledge in new situations.

**Authentic** (Complex/Contextualised)

Learning is more effective when situated in a meaningful context rather than being oversimplified and presented in isolation.

**Cooperative** (Collaborative/Conversational)

Collaboration is a natural human activity, with most collaboration taking place through conversations. Collaborative learning relies on socially negotiated understandings that help learners build on and learn from their own and each other's knowledge to construct new knowledge.

Jonassen et al.'s five attributes were sub-defined into rubrics that could be used to assess the extent to which both technologically mediated learning activities and the environment in which they took place promoted meaningful learning in a formal setting. Their criteria included references to environments both *inside and outside school*, and to *students, educators and interested adults*. For this study, these references were adapted to suit the informal setting of the Geocaching community environment, and concepts that were derived from a formal school situation, such as *learning expectations, responsibilities* and *outcomes*, were removed as they did not apply to informal learning. Nevertheless, the fundamental assessment criteria were retained in order to see whether rubrics for assessing formal learning mediated by technology could provide a productive framework for analysis of informal technology-mediated learning such as that arising from Geocaching.

## Informal Learning when Seeking a Geocache

When web survey participants were asked, "Did you feel that you or a member of your caching group ever learned something as a result of searching for a cache?", 89% (n=659) selected "Yes". When asked for details, participants reported learning on a wide range of topics. For example, one participant wrote: "Certainly, we have learned about history, geology, celestial navigation, and nature" (Survey response 248). Participants were invited to provide some textual detail about what they felt they had learnt through looking for Geocaches. These responses, together with data from the case studies, are used below to illustrate the informal learning opportunities described in this chapter.

## *Intentional Learning Opportunities when Seeking a Geocache*

The most obvious intentional learning opportunity arising out of joining the Geocaching community is that of learning more about Geocaching, or how to go about it. Becoming a member can act as a trigger for informal learning, for example:

> I have read two books specific to GPS technology and Geocaching since I have started. (Survey response 538)

Certain types of Geocache involve a deliberate learning goal created by the person who set the cache. For example, the aim of Earthcaches is to teach people something about the geological and geographical forces that shape the landscape. The success of this aim is reflected in the web survey responses, in which 74% (n=336) felt they had learnt as a result of seeking an Earthcache (n=336 reflects the fact that only 336 of the web survey respondents, about half, had searched for an Earthcache):

> We went to an Earthcache that involved dinosaur tracks and we have several small children and they learned from that experience. (Survey response 374)
> Earthcaches are quite often very interesting and it's definitely a way to improve knowledge and also it makes learning fun. You definitely remember things that you have learnt about, i.e. rocks and glacial formations when you have visited a site and seen an example. (Survey response 382)

These learning opportunities may extend beyond the experience of seeking the Earthcache, resulting in intentional informal learning opportunities that take the form of research both before and after the event:

> In Colorado Springs, caches led us to Garden of the Gods, which we then explored more fully, including the museum. (Survey response 52)
> Garden of the Gods Earthcache is a good example. I did a little bit more reading both before and after about the area and the geology. (Survey Response 109)

Solving the challenges devised by the creators of puzzle caches may also result in learning opportunities:

> We think that puzzle caches which require you to search the internet are often excellent for expanding your knowledge. We have often gone beyond the answer required to find out more just for our own interest. (Survey response 211)
> Some "hightech" caches have required to learn something new in mathematics and information technology. Thanks to pair of caches, I came to know birds and genetics. (Survey response 490)

However, even the traditional cache consisting of a box or container hidden somewhere in the landscape also presents learning opportunities linked to the location. Geocache creators can put considerable efforts into creating caches that give an interesting and educational experience to the Geocachers who seek them.

The first part of this experience involves reading the Geocache description. This may present a learning opportunity in itself. Geocaching can also trigger deliberate informal learning activities that complement the Geocaching activity:

> Not only have we picked up interesting bits of history, but we have actually gone out of our way to develop skills for Geocaching. My wife and I have taken classes to learn to rappel for Geocaching, we have also learned how to kayak, studied plants and animals and trailcraft, we have taken classes on field first-aid in order to help out other people we hike with. Geocaching has really been a great inspiration to learn for us. (Survey response 71)

Finding the Geocache and experiencing the location also inspire follow-up research. 73% (n=659) responded "yes" when asked if they'd been inspired to follow up in some way as a result of Geocaching, for example when finding a cache placed in a historical site or an area of great natural beauty:

> We have also bought a book about wild flowers and reptiles so that we can identify plants reptiles that we see on the trail. (Survey response 108)
>
> Many times we have come back and 1) looked up initials on a gravestone; 2) researched a specific park area for more information regarding its background; or 3) researched a specific event referenced in a cache site. Mostly it is Internet research; however several books have been purchased in the efforts. (Survey response 612)
>
> A virtual named We Three Kings inspired me to read the War of the Copper Kings and learn more history about Montana. We also enjoyed a Gandhi inspired cache in a peace garden which inspired my husband to pick up Gandhi's autobiography. Another cache, a virtual in New Orleans whose name I cannot remember, inspired me to read the book A Confederacy of Dunces by Toole. (Survey Response 49)
>
> Many caches have sent me to Google a subject, read a book, or watch a documentary. For example I've done research on SC's role in the American Revolution after visiting several sites while caching. A cache in Washington DC involved free Blacks in the district, their church, and the underground railroad, and another in Germany was an old Roman encampment protecting trade routes. Each had me doing much reading before and after. (Survey response 245)

Table 4.1 illustrates how the learning opportunities encountered when Geocaching map onto Jonassen et al.'s rubric for assessing intentional learning with technology.

**TABLE 4.1** Intentional learning opportunities when Geocaching

| *Rubric for Assessing Intentional Learning* | | |
| --- | --- | --- |
| Goal-directedness | Choosing a cache type that involves explicit learning opportunities or engaging in advance or follow-up research about a particular Geocache are both goal-directed activities. | ✓ |
| Setting own goals | Demonstrated by selecting a Geocache to seek that involves research or learning (e.g., puzzle caches or Earthcaches), or when engaging in research before or after finding a Geocache to enhance understanding. | ✓ |
| Regulating own learning | Geocaching is an optional activity as are the learning opportunities encountered as a result, therefore Geocachers set and regulate their own goals both with regard to Geocaching and any resulting learning opportunities they engage with. | ✓ |
| Learning environment promotes articulation of learning strategies with others | Logging a Geocache find involves writing some sort of textual note about the experience. There is opportunity to recount experiences with hints for others based on what has been discovered about the location, or to add hyperlinks and stories about related locations. | ✓ |
| Articulation of goals as focus of activity | Researching in advance of a Geocache represents the enactment of a specific learning goal. | ✓ |
| Technology use in support of learning goals | Both GPS devices and Web 2.0 are integral to the activity of Geocaching. | ✓ |

However, many learning opportunities that occur when Geocaching are unintentional learning opportunities. That is to say, the Geocacher did not set out with the intention to learn, but was presented with an unexpected learning opportunity as part of the experience:

> One cache my family and I found on vacation had a magnificent birds nest within sight of the cache. After snapping several photos, we researched bird-watching sites to identify the type of bird it was. We thought it might have been an eagle but after about an hour we decided it was an Osprey ... we would have NEVER done anything like that without caching. (Survey response 455)
>
> Some Geocaches have taken me to beautiful places I didn't know existed. Such as neat nature preserves, historical sites, etc. . . . Return visits allowed me to further explore the area. (Survey response 473)

The rubric for assessing intentional learning opportunities works when applied to informal learning opportunities that require intent on the part of the learner, for example engaging in research about a location before seeking a Geocache or looking up more information after having found the Geocache. However, many informal learning opportunities are unintentional. This suggests that informal learning with technology may exhibit characteristics that are not captured through Jonassen et al.'s five attributes of meaningful learning with technology.

## *Active Learning Opportunities when Seeking a Geocache*

Geocaching is an activity that involves using information provided by others to get outdoors and hunt for Geocaches in the landscape. This requires a variety of tools. Technological tools include the Geocaching website, through which the cache is selected and from which the information is downloaded, mobile devices, including some form of GPS device with which to navigate across the landscape to locate the cache, and maps, either electronic or paper. Combining these artefacts in the real-world context of a Geocache hunt offers many informal learning opportunities, primarily amongst them being how to effectively use the tools. This was reflected in the free-text survey responses to the request for details about what people learnt when Geocaching:

> Learning how to use a GPS and map and compass skills. (Survey response 121)
> Better familiarity with land navigation techniques without the use of a gps. (Survey response 325)
> It helps brush up your map reading skills. (Survey response 157)
> How to navigate better and use of maps. (Survey response 202)

By logging the find and posting up any photos, a Geocacher reflects and reports on the experience. However, Geocaching as part of a family or friendship group offers additional opportunities for discussion and reflection during the activity:

> I know my children have learned a great deal. While out in nature, I have a great venue in which to teach my children about animal and plant life, history, geology, history, technology, and even mathematics and cryptology. (Survey response 106)
> We use Geocaching in general as a way to teach our son about the outdoors. And caching often makes us find out interesting little snippets of local history / geology. (Survey response 278)
> I think that most caches teach our children something about the world about us, whether geology, history, nature, etc. There is also the aspect of learning about conservation and caring for the things about us; and about how to be safe when out and about; and of course navigation, distance,

bearings and reading maps correctly. Probably the best thing is that we interact with our kids whilst out caching and share the experience as a family. (Survey response 229)

Table 4.2 maps the learning opportunities encountered when Geocaching onto the rubric for assessing active learning with technology.

The informal learning opportunities available when Geocaching map coherently to the rubric for assessing active learning in a formal setting. The activity of Geocaching has many characteristics in common with other successful semi-formal, technology-mediated mobile learning activities undertaken with students. For example, it involves cooperation in the creation and sharing of content, similar to the Deptford Mudlarking and the Victoria and Albert Museum studies (Futurelab, 2006; Sprake & Thomas, 2007), and offers individuals the opportunity to use technologies to map information to location and share this with others.

### Constructive Learning Opportunities when Seeking a Geocache

Geocaching is a leisure activity with no external force driving individuals to join in. Any informal learning opportunities that they take up result from intrinsic interest, rather than extrinsic compulsion. This constructive approach was reported both for adult Geocachers and their younger family members:

I have a 7-year-old who is getting very good with a gps and starting to understand compass and map work. (Survey response 555)

**TABLE 4.2** Active learning opportunities when Geocaching

| *Rubric for Assessing Active Learning* | | |
| --- | --- | --- |
| Learner interaction with real-world objects | Geocachers use a variety of artefacts in the context of a real-world goal of navigating through the landscape to reach a particular point. | ✓ |
| Observation and reflection | Logging a find represents post-activity observations and reflections; however, group Geocaching offers many opportunities for face-to-face interactions. | ✓ |
| Learner interactions—manipulating controls in environment | Navigating across the landscape using a map, GPS unit and/or a compass places control of all the variables in the environment in the hands of the Geocacher. | ✓ |
| Effective tool use | Successfully finding Geocaches implies effective use of all the technological and other tools available. | ✓ |

My family has learned to use GPS. (Survey response 361)

My daughter says she learned not to give up. My kids learned that the GPS equipment is only so accurate and reliable and that you cannot rely on this measuring device to pinpoint a cache. You must eventually open your eyes and search for logical places. (Survey response 243)

Table 4.3 maps the learning opportunities encountered when Geocaching onto the rubric for assessing constructive learning with technology.

Geocaching is fundamentally an activity built around sharing experiences of location and real-world problem solving. Both through learning how to use GPS to successfully find a cache and by solving the challenges explicitly built into certain cache-types, Geocachers engage in meaning-making activities to create their own understandings. These activities are informed by the details provided by other Geocachers as well as by the characteristics of the locations they visit and map readily onto the rubric for assessing constructive learning with technology.

## Authentic Learning Opportunities when Seeking a Geocache

Geocaching presents real-world challenges. These vary according to the cache, but they often involve learning opportunities in a range of subjects. For example:

Puzzle caches in particular have given me the opportunity to learn about different languages, encryption methods and historical information. For example, a cache in my area is related to the methods of encryption used in WWII and the method that British soldiers were able to break the Lorenz cipher. I have not solved this puzzle yet, but I have learned a lot about history which I had either never learned, or forgotten. I also solved a puzzle which required learning the Babylonian number system. (Survey response 53)

**TABLE 4.3** Constructive learning opportunities when Geocaching

| *Rubric for Assessing Constructive Learning* | | |
| --- | --- | --- |
| Resolving dissonance between observed and what is known | Learning opportunities arising out of solving the challenge that is finding the Geocache. Learning opportunities that are triggered by the Geocaching experience, researching out of interest rather than compulsion. | ✓ |
| Constructing mental models and meaning making | Navigating using a GPS device, mapping the virtual representation on the device onto the physical features of the landscape, using maps. | ✓ |

Yes—a magnet based cache in particular stands out. I only did science to GCSE level, but I don't ever remember being taught that magnetic power was accumulative. I did a cache where there was a +3 magnetic power holding a cache in place, and you could only swap the polarity on two of the magnets. Where could you find something else to remove the magnetic power out here in a wheat field? We did it! (Survey response 136)

Table 4.4 maps the learning opportunities encountered when Geocaching onto the rubric for assessing authentic learning with technology.

Because Geocaching is set in the real-world context of seeking out hidden locations in the landscape, the problems and challenges encountered are authentic. In addition, when setting the Geocache, community members use the features of the landscape in order to increase the challenge and adventure, thereby ensuring that the experience is enjoyable. This maps well onto the characteristics of the rubric for assessing authentic learning.

### Cooperative Learning Opportunities when Seeking a Geocache

When Geocachers join the online community, they engage in informal learning as they try to understand and participate in the community activities. The opportunities for cooperative informal learning intensify as they seek their first Geocache and return to log it on the website. For example:

When hunting caches with groups it requires lots of teamwork. Whether we find it together or don't find it all, the team enjoys the success and not one individual. (Survey response 567)

**TABLE 4.4** Authentic learning opportunities when Geocaching

| *Rubric for Assessing Authentic Learning* | | |
|---|---|---|
| Complex challenges in real-world context | Geocaching is a real-world activity involving complex and varied challenges. | ✓ |
| Learners exercise higher-order thinking | Navigating to a traditional Geocache and solving the challenges of multicaches, puzzle caches or Earthcaches involves higher-order problem solving skills. | ✓ |
| Learners identify and define problems inherent in challenges | Geocachers often face ill-structured sequences of challenges that they need to overcome in order to find and log the cache. | ✓ |
| Problems involve complex solutions rather than "right answers" | The overarching "problem" is to find the Geocache. This may involve learning opportunities in a range of real-world subjects. | ✓ |

At times caching partners are very knowledgeable in geology, biology, botany and other things, even just the history of the area. As we hike each person imparts his/her knowledge of the area or surroundings. (Survey response 266)

Our family learned to work as a team . . . and to use each others unique talents effectively. (Daughter has quite a knack for sniffing out elusive micros, husband has a knack for being "right on top" of a cache but not finding it, so we just watch wherever he starts going around in circles.) We have also learned to be patient. Sometimes you just need to stop and think before you find a cache. (Survey response 31)

These quotations demonstrate how groups of Geocachers interact with others in activities where cooperation results in success, engage in negotiation in which all members' ideas are valued and distribute roles and responsibilities throughout the team. However, even in these examples of cooperative Geocaching, it is difficult to pinpoint any "interaction with experts". In fact, this interaction with experts takes place in virtual space rather than in physical space, through use and assimilation of the cache description (written by the 'expert' who set the cache) and by viewing the logs and images of Geocachers who have gone before. There may also be direct e-mail communication with the cache owner, for example solving some form of challenge related to the cache location and e-mailing the response to the cache owner in order to log the find. These virtual forms of expert interactions are not reflected in the rubric for assessing cooperative learning with technology.

Also, unlike in a formal setting where the teacher is the expert, the role of expert may shift according to what activity a Geocacher takes part in. When setting a Geocache and researching and writing the cache description, a Geocacher takes on the role of expert. However, that same Geocacher may take on the role of learner when seeking a Geocache hidden by another. Table 4.5 maps the learning opportunities encountered when Geocaching onto the rubric for assessing cooperative learning with technology.

As well as failing to allow for implicit collaboration, the rubric for assessing cooperative learning does not allow for the cooperative learning opportunities encountered by Geocachers who cache solo. They are not obviously interacting with others such that interaction results in success in the same way as groups of Geocachers. However, the information they are using to inform their experience of location was created cooperatively by other members of the Geocaching community. When they log their find and upload photos, they are contributing to that narrative, contributing to enrich the "persistent digital narrative of location" (Clough, 2010, p. 33) for other Geocachers. The phrase "persistent digital narrative of location" describes the online resources linked to physical location that are created collaboratively over time, consisting of the accumulated contributions of community members. This contribution may even

**TABLE 4.5** Cooperative learning opportunities when Geocaching

| *Rubric for Assessing Cooperative Learning* | | |
| --- | --- | --- |
| Interaction with others in activities where collaboration results in success | Geocaching as a team where each member of the team contributes to the finding of the cache. | ✓ |
| Interaction with experts | Emphasis in the rubric is on explicit collaboration with experts, whereas Geocaching collaboration is more implicit, through reading and reasearching. Also, the role of Geocacher encompasses both being an expert (when creating a cache) and a learner (when seeking a cache set by another). | X |
| Social negotiation in which ideas of all members are valued | All members of the Geocaching group can help, contributing through their specialised knowledge to solving the problem of finding the Geocache. | ✓ |
| Acceptance and distribution of roles and responsibilities | Roles and responsibilities shift easily within a Geocaching group. | ✓ |

evolve into changes to the cache description and learning opportunities for the person who hid the cache:

> Visiting a cache early in the morning in winter I was joined by an elderly gent who was at the same spot to do Tai Chi. We chatted I told him what I was up to and he explained some of the historical significance of the site. The cache setter had not known of the significance of the place. It was both [an] ancient route out of the city and had featured in a book by R L Stevenson. I posted this in my log and the setter subsequently amended the cache page. (Survey response 217)

The role of the Geocache hider moves from that of consumer of information about the location to contributor. This is not so much an "acceptance and distribution of roles and responsibilities" as an *inherent* distribution of roles and responsibilities enabled by the way in which the Geocaching community make use of Web 2.0 technologies.

Table 4.5 illustrated how the learning opportunities encountered by Geocaching *groups* mapped onto the rubric for assessing cooperative learning with technology. However, the learning opportunities created through innovative community use of Web 2.0 technologies are not accounted for by this rubric.

Learning opportunities when finding a Geocache begin with the consumption of information from within the Geocaching community, reading the cache description and downloading the coordinates. Further learning opportunities emerge as the Geocacher moves through the landscape, using the GPS to navigate, using maps, and referring to the cache description and logs. Connected mobile and Web 2.0 technologies provide Geocachers with a medium through which to access and contribute relevant information, and the GPS-mobile devices act as tools to guide them through the landscape. These technologies are not used in isolation, but are deployed in combinations according to the preferences of the individual Geocachers. This suggests a temporal element to the learning opportunities that may vary according to the technology choice of the individual Geocacher.

Seeking, finding and logging Geocaches represents a regular contribution to the community. When a Geocacher finds a Geocache, their experience of the cache location is guided by the description given by the Geocacher who hid the cache and informed by the accumulated narratives of other Geocachers who have previously found it. This connection is instantiated when the find is logged on the website. Thus, by simply going Geocaching, a Geocacher is contributing to the community by adding to the narrative created by another Geocache. However a stronger commitment is required when a Geocacher makes the effort to create and hide one or more Geocaches for others to find.

## Informal Learning when Creating a Geocache

In order to create a Geocache, the Geocacher needs to collect together information about the location, double-check the coordinates to be sure that they provide an accurate guide and finally upload all this information using a webform to create the Geocache description. Placing a Geocache in a location is an invitation to other members of the Geocaching community to visit that spot. Often, caches are placed in places of outstanding natural beauty or historical significance, but they may also be placed in quiet 'hidden corners' that might easily be overlooked. When asked "Do you hope that Geocachers seeking and finding your Geocache(s) would learn something in any way?", 71% (n=659) of web survey participants responded "yes". When asked what they hoped people finding their caches would learn, participants described introducing people to the history of an area, local geography and nature. In their responses to the web survey, Geocachers described how they would research information to place on the cache page:

> [I learn] bits and bobs about areas and nature—I learn more setting my own caches as I research them to add info to the cache page. (Survey response 213)
>
> Doing a little research led me to learn more about and appreciate the area myself. (Survey response 372)

Participants' descriptions of how they went about creating Geocaches would often describe research efforts to provide more detail about the Geocache.

## Intentional Learning Opportunities when Creating a Geocache

Any research undertaken in order to create a cache depends on the location and type of Geocache. For example, Earthcaches need geological or geographical knowledge:

> I did a lot of research about the areas which gave me a greater understanding of why the geology was like it was. (Survey response 157)
>
> I researched Sites of natural National importance, SAMs and SSSIs and selected two major locations: Severn Bore (natural large wave on Severn Estuary under specific conditions) and Glaciers in Southern England. (The Wombles)
>
> I had to do research to find out why these areas existed so I could craft my pages to educate the visitors. I knew nothing going in, so everything I learned about karst geology and piedmonts is a direct result of these caches. (Survey response 71)

Setting traditional Geocaches or multicaches may require some research into the history of an area:

> I have begun researching ghost towns in Texas after visiting a cache located at one and as a result have placed caches in 20 ghost towns in my area to bring others to visit them. Am working on more currently. (Survey response 460)

Table 4.6 maps the learning opportunities when creating a Geocache onto the rubric for assessing intentional learning with technology.

When creating a Geocache, external resources, such as links to related websites or additional information obtained through research, are brought into the community by the Geocacher hiding the cache. This results not only in the creation of new learning opportunities for other community members as they seek the cache, but also in an altruistically motivated form of learning opportunity for the Geocache creator with the aim of creating learning opportunities for others. The cache descriptions may contain links to other websites or other evidence of learning on the part of the creator, but this does not represent a clear articulation of learning strategies with others.

## Active Learning Opportunities when Creating a Geocache

Creating a Geocache involves collecting together information about a particular location and creating a Geocache description webpage. Earthcaches involve creating webpages that describe some form of learning challenge for Geocachers

**TABLE 4.6** Intentional learning opportunities when creating a Geocache

*Rubric for Assessing Intentional Learning*

| | | |
|---|---|---|
| Goal-directedness | Deliberate research in order to learn more about a location in order to create an engaging Geocache. | ✓ |
| Setting own goals | Geocacher chooses location to place the cache and upon which to focus the research. | ✓ |
| Regulating own learning | Hiding Geocaches is an optional activity, therefore Geocachers set and regulate their own goals. | ✓ |
| Learning environment promotes articulation of learning strategies with others | Cache descriptions seldom contain details of the research the creator has undertaken, therefore this characteristic is not explicitly represented in this setting. | X |
| Articulation of goals as focus of activity | Researching in advance of creating a Geocache represents the enactment of a goal. | ✓ |
| Technology use in support of learning goals | Web 2.0 resources may be used in conjunction with other resources in order to supplement the information on the cache page. | ✓ |

to complete once at the Earthcache location in order to log the find. Creating a Geocache or an Earthcache incorporating a learning challenge for others often requires research into the area and several visits with a GPS unit to select the cache site and take accurate coordinate readings.

> I'm putting an Earthcache together, covering a group of copper mines, I've read a couple of books on the topic and been out several times to identify remaining structures on the ground. Finding suitable learning activities is proving the hard bit to do. But I'm getting close. (Survey response 281)
>
> This is something that I am in the process of. I am trying to create one for Hunters Creek, which is a glacial-formed ravine. Do a water-hike down far enough, and you are looking up at steep shale cliffs on both sides. I am in hopes of getting this published this summer. In the meantime, it's a lot of research. (Survey response 307)

Table 4.7 maps the learning opportunities encountered when creating a Geocache onto the rubric for assessing active learning with technology.

## Constructive Learning Opportunities when Creating a Geocache

According to Jonassen et al.'s assessment rubric, constructive learning involves routinely wrestling with new experiences, becoming experts at identifying and solving problems and striving to resolve any dissonance between what is observed

**TABLE 4.7** Active learning when creating a Geocache

*Rubric for Assessing Active Learning*

| | | |
|---|---|---|
| Learner interaction with real-world objects | Geocachers use various artefacts including GPS devices or GPS apps on smartphones, webpages for the cache description and digital or smartphone cameras to provide images for the description. They need to connect them together to transfer data (text, images and coordinates) between them. They also need to visit the cache location on more than one occasion. | ✓ |
| Observation and reflection | Researching in order to write a richer description of the location is evidence of both observation and reflection. | ✓ |
| Learner interactions—manipulating controls in environment | Navigating across the landscape using physical map and compass, GPS unit and/or smartphone GPS apps as well as creating the cache webpage places control of all the variables in the environment in the hands of the Geocacher. | ✓ |
| Effective tool use | Successfully setting up a Geocache for others to find implies effective use of the tools available. | ✓ |

**TABLE 4.8** Constructive learning opportunities when creating a Geocache

*Rubric for Assessing Constructive Learning*

| | | |
|---|---|---|
| Resolving dissonance between observed and what is known | Learning in order to construct a learning experience for others provides intrinsic motivation for engaging with learning opportunities and involves ensuring enough information on the cache page to guide others there but not so much as to remove all challenge and learning opportunities. | ✓ |
| Constructing mental models and meaning making | Navigating using a GPS device, mapping the virtual representation from the device onto the website and constructing a meaningful description of the Geocache or Earthcache that will stimulate others to think and learn. | ✓ |

and what is known, operating on a sincere desire to know (Jonassen et al., 2003). Table 4.8 illustrates the constructive learning opportunities that occur when Geocachers research additional information and combine this with their pre-existing knowledge to create a rewarding Geocache for others to seek and find.

## Authentic Learning Opportunities when Creating a Geocache

Creating a Geocache involves similar real-world problem solving skills to seeking and finding a cache. Both require skills in using a GPS to identify location. However, hiding a cache involves creativity and an element of cunning. Traditional caches need to be hidden in sensible places that will not be discovered by casual passers by. Multicaches need the cache creator to use information from one location and translate it into the coordinates for the next location. Creating challenges and puzzles involves learning opportunities for both the cache creator and the cache hider, and selecting and describing interesting locations is an activity that involves interacting with real-world objects and places:

> I always try to hide caches that have some meaning, something to learn or something to see. My best cache is hidden in a local cemetery where a B-25 bomber crashed during WWII on a training run to Florida. Its truly amazing how many locals are totally unaware that this event ever occurred in our little town. I get lots of positive feedback from the finders of this cache. (Survey response 260)

Table 4.9 shows how the learning opportunities when creating a Geocache map onto the rubric for assessing authentic learning.

## Cooperative Learning Opportunities when Creating a Geocache

Researching in order to place a Geocache seems at first glance like an individual learning activity. Participants mentioned using the internet as a research tool:

> Did research on creating the geological history of the area. Lots of research from government websites. (Survey response 169)

**TABLE 4.9** Authentic learning opportunities when creating a Geocache

| *Rubric for Assessing Authentic Learning* | | |
|---|---|---|
| Complex challenges in real-world context | Hiding a Geocache is a real-world activity involving complex and varied challenges. | ✓ |
| Learners exercise higher-order thinking | Creating a Geocache that challenges others involves higher-order thinking skills. | ✓ |
| Learners identify and define problems inherent in challenges | Creating a good, challenging Geocache needs creativity and imagination, and presents learning opportunities in various areas. | ✓ |
| Problems involve complex solutions rather than "right answers" | Hiding a Geocache, or creating a complex multicache that uses features in the environment as clues requires good problem-solving skills. There are many ways to create a good Geocache. | ✓ |

> Internet research, Edinburgh has a volcano in it very simple selection for an Earthcache, whilst researching that I found a mimetolith called the Grey Man of Merrick. I was so inspired about this face on a rock that I trekked out and found it and made that into an Earthcache. (Survey response 151)

However, this research is triggered by a wish to place a quality Geocache that will give pleasure and interest to those who seek it. Sharing information about a location is one of the ways of enhancing a Geocache. Creating a Geocache makes a significant contribution to the Geocaching community; the community wouldn't exist unless people were prepared to put the effort in to create and maintain Geocaches.

More explicit cooperative learning opportunities may occur when the Geocache creator is engaged in research that involves visiting the intended location for the Geocache, as illustrated by this quotation from case study 4:

> I went to the museum to do some research and met with the curator who was also a member of the local historical society. I explained to him all about Geocaching and he liked the idea and was happy to have the cache hidden in the garden at the front of the museum. He spoke about the town and described the places of interest that could be found. I then visited each of these sites and devised a safe walk around the town that took in some of the most interesting places. The historical society had erected information plaques around the town and I decided to make each waypoint rely on the collection of data from these plaques. (Case study 4)

Sometimes, the cache creator already possessed the subject-specific knowledge, yet collaborated as part of a group in order to create the Earthcaches for others:

> I did a degree in geology so I was very switched on to Earthcaches. I was part of the team who established the first Earthcache in the UK. This was at a place that I knew about from my geology studies and thought it would be good for other people to discover it too. I put together some questions which would hopefully make the cachers do a bit of web research and learn a bit more than they could from just a visit to the site. (Survey response 582)

This quotation does not mention any learning opportunities for the cache-creator, but the involvement of a team who "established the first Earthcache in the UK" suggests that there were collaborative learning opportunities available to others who might learn more about geology from survey respondent 582.

Table 4.10 illustrates how the learning opportunities presented when creating a Geocache for others to find map onto the criteria in Jonassen et al.'s rubric for assessing cooperative learning with technology.

**TABLE 4.10** Cooperative learning opportunities when creating a Geocache

| *Rubric for Assessing Cooperative Learning* | | |
| --- | --- | --- |
| Interaction with others in activities where collaboration results in success | Geocachers may create Geocaches without the help of others. However, when a group of Geocachers are involved, collaborative learning opportunities may arise. | ✓ |
| Interaction with experts | There may be interactions with experts, depending upon the type of research undertaken (e.g., talking to museum curators versus internet research). | ✓ |
| Social negotiation in which ideas of all members are valued | Researching in order to place a Geocache is usually an individual activity; however, if a group is working together, social negotiation is likely to take place. | ✓ |
| Acceptance and distribution of roles and responsibilities | Because Geocaching is voluntary, roles and responsibilities are not fixed and may be shared freely between individuals cooperating in the creation of a Geocache. | ✓ |

Table 4.10 illustrates how the learning opportunities encountered when hiding a Geocache as part of a group, as described by survey respondent 582, map onto the rubric for assessing cooperative learning with technology. However, a more typical Geocache created by an individual appears to present fewer cooperative learning opportunities.

The desire to give something back to the community, leading to deliberate informal learning efforts in a range of subjects, reveals a new angle on the relationship between community membership and informal learning opportunities.

> Caches have inspired me in two ways. First, in the clever methods of hiding and thereby to emulate the hide. More importantly, caches I have found in neat parks or locations I otherwise would not have visited inspired me to hide my cache in a place that was scenic and historic. (Survey response 248)
>
> I've done research on the background of ghost towns I discovered while caching, and often research areas in order to hide a cache there so I can educate others as well. (Survey response 246)

Creating a Geocache involves the individual (or team) choosing a location that has not been used in another cache and bringing together a range of external information resources to create a location-specific Geocache or Earthcache description. This description is then placed on the Geocaching website and made available to other Geocachers. This seemingly altruistic goal of learning in order to create stimulating and engaging learning opportunities for others is a facet of informal learning that is closely connected to community membership and collaboration.

## Conclusion

Informal learning is typically very difficult to measure. This study has provided substantial empirical data about informal learning and about how people are using mobile and social technologies to link up and learn together both online and offline. It has also applied a constructivist framework developed in a formal learning setting to assess learning with technology in an informal setting. The findings provide evidence of informal learning through membership of the Geocaching community and demonstrate that Jonassen et al.'s framework can be adapted as an effective tool for capturing evidence of informal learning.

Some elements in a framework developed in a formal learning context did not translate into the informal setting. For example, interaction with experts in a formal setting would refer to teachers and instructors. In an informal setting, although experts such as museum curators were sometimes involved, expertise more often lay with the members of the community. A Geocacher could be both a learner, when seeking a Geocache that someone else had hidden, and an expert, when, for example, collecting information to provide to other Geocachers through the Geocache description.

Collaborative opportunities presented through the virtual spaces of the internet were also difficult to characterise using the framework. This was because the framework for assessing constructivist learning with technology was originally developed in formal classroom settings where collaboration took place face-to-face. Also, at the time the framework was developed (2003), web-based social and learning networks and connected mobile technologies were still in their infancy, and so the learning affordances they now offer to both formal and informal learning did not yet exist.

A further characteristic of informal learning that was not well captured by Jonassen et al.'s framework was unintentional learning. Unintentional learning featured widely in the responses of Geocachers. Very few (4%, n=631) named learning as a specific reason for joining the community, yet a majority (89%, n=659) subsequently reported that they had learnt something as a result of Geocaching. This suggests that Geocaching membership presents unanticipated learning opportunities that occur as the individual participates in the activity of Geocaching.

In addition to the informal learning opportunities made possible by the act of Geocaching, specific technology-related informal learning opportunities emerged from using context-aware technologies. These technology-related learning opportunities can be sub-divided into effects *with technology* that amplify the users' cognitive powers during the use of the technology, and effects *of technology* that include cognitive spinoffs that occur without the technology (Perkins, 1993). The informal learning opportunities identified *with technology* included acquiring technology-related skills, for example, using GPS devices, connecting mobile devices to computers and using Web 2.0 applications such as web forums to communicate and upload photos to a website. This matches Gorard, Furlong, and Selwyn's (2004) finding that computer technology can be a "self-referential learning tool", with much of the informal learning opportunities arising out of the need to learn how to use it. Informal learning opportunities that occurred as a result *of technology* included the development of navigational and map-reading skills, understanding and using GPS, and learning techniques for accessing and using information relevant to location.

Prior to the arrival of the social web and GPS technology, people were already participating in location-based activities, such as orienteering and letterboxing, that combined some of the elements that were subsequently incorporated into Geocaching (for example, hunting for locations using a map and a compass and searching for hidden containers). Any informal learning opportunities that occurred as a result went largely unnoticed. However, the emergence of context-aware mobile technologies and Web 2.0 connectivity has added a new dimension to such location-based activities, allowing people to create and participate in informal learning opportunities for themselves and others. Not only does the technology present novel informal learning opportunities, it also provides methods for capturing evidence of those informal learning opportunities, thereby deepening our understanding of the mechanisms involved in informal learning with technology.

## References

Burbules, N.C. (2006). Self-educating communities: Collaboration and learning throughout the internet. In Z. Bekerman, N. C. Burbules & D. Silberman-Keller (Eds.), *Learning in places: The informal education reader* (pp. 273–284). New York, NY: Peter Lang.

Clough, G. (2010). Geolearners: Location-based informal learning with mobile and social technologies. *IEEE Transactions on Learning Technologies, 3*(1), 33–44.

Futurelab. (2006). Mudlarking in Deptford: Mini-report. Retrieved from http://archive.futurelab.org.uk/resources/documents/project_reports/mini_reports/mudlarking_mini_report.pdf

Gorard, S., Furlong, J., & Selwyn, N. (2004). How do adults learn at home. Presented at *British Educational Research Association Annual Conference*, University of Manchester.

Hine, C. (2005). *Virtual methods: Issues in social research on the internet.* Oxford: Berg Publishers.

Jonassen, D.H., Howland, J.L., Moore, J.L., & Marra, R.M. (2003). *Learning to solve problems with technology: A constructivist perspective.* Upper Saddle River, NJ: Merrill Prentice Hall.

Lave, J., & Wenger, E. (1991). *Situated learning: Legitimate peripheral participation.* New York, NY: Cambridge University Press.

Livingston, D. (1999). Exploring the icebergs of adult learning: Findings of the first Canadian survey of informal learning practices. *Canadian Journal for the Study of Adult Education, 13*(2), 49–72.

Perkins, D.N. (1993). Person-plus: A distributed view of thinking and learning. In G. Solomon (Ed.), *Distributed cognitions: Psychological and educational considerations* (pp. 88–110). Cambridge: Cambridge University Press.

Sprake, J., & Thomas, H. (2007). Transitional spaces: Mapping physical change. *International Journal of Art & Design Education, 26*(2), 167–176.

Tough, A. (1979). *The adult's learning projects*. Ontario: Ontario Institute for Studies in Education.

Wenger, E. (1998). *Communities of practice*. Cambridge: Cambridge University Press.

# 5

# LEARNING-THROUGH-TOURING

## A Methodology for Mobilising Learners

*Juliet Sprake*

## Introduction

My research practice, developed over several years at Goldsmiths with digital artist Peter Rogers, is concerned with building mobile platform services that facilitate testing out of what we think motivates people to discover new things about place (Sprake, 2009, 2012; Sprake & Rogers, 2011, 2013). We conduct experimental projects that push the boundaries of concepts-in-practice. In this way, we rework theoretically productive concepts through conceptual methods in practise to produce new insights and interpretations on the theory. This chapter highlights some of those concepts and methods that are relevant in the production of resources for exploring the urban landscape in alternative ways.[1]

Walking tours come in many different shapes and sizes, from guided tours in which visitors receive selected information about a specific site to self-guided tours instigated by people who want to discover a place for themselves. We can ascribe a level of risk to this spectrum of participating in walking tours; some kinds of tour are overtly 'low risk', where the expectations and experience are described in advance, whilst others make serendipity and happenstance the outcome. A common feature of taking and/or making a walking tour is participant interaction with published content, and therefore we can generally describe the experience in terms of how people are guided towards making connections between objects, people and places. Whether presented with a straightforward description of what is where or, conversely, with an intention to use everyday live occurrences as content for the tour, it is important that the participant trusts the guide. There is an implicit contract between guide and participant that is based on the guide earning that trust by providing engaging and trustworthy guidance, whether this is through face to face interactions, printed material or digital devices. This 'contract' may sometimes be described in terms of authenticity—for example, a guide may be described as authentic if he or she explicitly acknowledges the real-time actions of participants and everyday happenings of the location or appears as a perceived expert with specialist knowledge. In this way, the relationship between guide and participant has relevance for understanding that between teacher and learner.

Since 2005 we have been working through several projects to develop our understanding of participant generated content in tours of places that give voice to the visitor. In *Mudlarking in Deptford* in 2005 (Sprake, 2012), we tried to reimagine how the traditional guided tour could be designed as a participatory learning activity in which users fill in the gaps rather than receive a one-way flow of information. Collaborating with Futurelab and Hewlett Packard Labs, we created an application allowing images, sounds and text produced by 11–12 year old school students to be linked with their physical location. This content was mapped via interactive zones that were triggered by participants walking into or out of those zones with a GPS-enabled mobile device. This project highlighted emerging possibilities for non-experts to map and share local knowledge, stories and information in ways that allowed for more individual and personal content. *Transitional Spaces at the V&A Museum* in 2006 (Sprake & Thomas, 2007) focused on creating a tour of a national institution where the infrastructure was of primary importance. Again, school students (13–14 years old) seeded content into several separate threads of enquiry: 'untold stories', 'flooring and lighting' and 'material collage'. These threads created distinct but overlapping tours of the same location that provided alternate perspectives of the building. At the British Library in 2007, we were commissioned to work with students (14–15 years old) to develop audio-visual content for the *London: A Life in Maps* exhibition. We explored the building as a live space, and our students recorded their motion and emotions through that space. They developed ways of guiding others on an alternative walking tour of the location using the fabric of the building as markers (interestingly, their content illustrated how they felt watched and unwelcome as young people). In *Located Lexicon: Finding the Signal through the Noise* (Sprake & Rogers, 2011), we again explored "situated awareness" (Sprake, 2009, pp. 24–26; 2012, pp. 32–33), this time by using tools to extract and plot data from a mass of user generated content to see if we could detect environmental descriptions of place via geolocated devices. And most recently, in *Tall Buildings* (Sprake & Rogers, 2013) we investigated how height affected situated awareness of the city and how movement is important in developing our spatial perception. In this project users connect longitude, latitude and altitude points to make new paths along which to gather and publish new data.

In these projects, participants have learnt how to initiate an enquiry for making a tour, a tour that then involves others in generating content over a period of time. Understanding how to produce content that prompts others into making connections with what they are experiencing in real time and space is a creative skill that is relevant to anyone interested in making new discoveries about the built environment. Participating in these kinds of experiential learning requires confidence in taking a risk or following your own nose. Through these projects we have learnt that there has to be clear benefit for users to engage both as producers and recipients of content. There are validity issues when user-generated content is available alongside 'official' content. Who says what is right or wrong, and who is the expert? The methodology presented in this paper argues that the tour guide is expert in drawing on existing knowledge in ways that actively engage participants in generating new meanings, perspectives and understandings.

## Pedagogic Background to the Methodology

If we understand one way in which we learn is through embodied interactions with the physical environment, then the mobility of the learner and the geographical location are, simultaneously, *mobilising* elements in taking action to change or transform something. Learning environments are often described as formal or informal, indoor or outdoor, interactive or passive and so on, but rarely in ways that explicitly embrace the complexities of time and space. Educationalist Jan Nespor has focused specifically on relations between space and learning and considers how mobility and location may be important in transformative learning experiences (Nespor, 2004, pp. 309–326). He references the work of geographer Doreen Massey, who argues that space and time should be "thought together", in that "the imagination of one will have repercussions (not always followed through) for the imagination of the other and that space and time are implicated in each other" (Massey, 2005, p. 18). I argue that situated learning involves affecting a shift in thinking from site as geographical location to site as context for learning (Sprake, 2009). In this way a site is actively produced through interactions between learners and between learners and the live environment, rather than understood as a predetermined given. The expectations and formulae embedded within the notion of context as a geographical location make the learning situation dependent on the specifics of the traditional 'classroom' environment. We can consider the situatedness of the learner differently if we conceive of situation as an 'elastic environment' in which the social and spatial production of meaning situates the learner.

In this interpretation of mobile learning, site is understood as a subjective experience that embraces the complexities of defining place. Buildings such as schools, universities and museums that have traditionally been described as locations for learning may be reconceived as sites in this paradigm; the built environment is conceived as productive, unpredictable or unplanned through the actions of people. This means buildings that seem overtly planned and predicable in the ways we are expected to interact with them can be understood as being actively constructed and co-constructed by the people who use them in a multiplicity of ways. So situatedness, as an elastic environment socially and spatially produced through participation in mobile learning activities, provides opportunities for collaborative learner interactions in relation to their location. As tools, mobile devices are selected and utilised in terms of their capacity to orchestrate, mediate and guide those actions.

Edwards and Usher (2000) use the metaphor of (dis)location to help to frame this kind of pedagogical practise. They suggest that difference, dispersal and distance are forms of dislocation in a globalised world, and so the notion of fixed location is made necessarily problematic. Pedagogic space is no longer defined in terms of educational programmes and their attached environments, but in terms of the learner. Mobility of the learner and everyday environments are active elements in creating pedagogic space: "In this condition, new and multiple identities emerge from a multiplicity of centres and locations" (Edwards & Usher, 2000, p. 135). They argue that pedagogies of (dis)location are adaptable and learner-responsive, and may transgress traditional educational practises that seek to fix location for learning. Instead, Edwards and Usher (2000) suggest that the "ability to map different locations and translate between them, to shift and move and negotiate uncertainties and ambivalence" becomes the stimulus for learning (p. 141).

Moving between and around locations provides opportunities for learning through making connections by being mobile—simply defined as 'touring'. For example, physical and cognitive movement between trips to Eastern Europe and Singapore in 2004–2005 enabled me to thread together knowledge about experiences of occupation in two different countries during World War II. A sample of embroidered names and messages was displayed in a glass cabinet at the Museum of Occupation of Latvia observed during a visit to Riga in July 2004. Embroidering messages as a way for prisoners to communicate with loved ones represented an element of a history of mass deportation during the Soviet and Nazi occupations of Latvia between 1940 and 1944. Lists of names of people imprisoned in concentration camps were also on display at the museum.

During a subsequent visit in April 2005 to Changi Museum, the site of a former 'occupation prison' in Singapore, I noted a similar form of embroidered communication on display. This piece of embroidery was a quilt made by women internees to message men held in separate quarters of the prison. This connection between embroidered objects and occupation was further developed through noticing that the prisoner of war post cards also on display at Changi Museum used the same typeface as the lists in the museum in Latvia. The post cards were used by prisoners of war to communicate by typing up to 25 words per card.

The notion of officialdom generated by the typed words in both locations is simultaneously connected through a thread of 'communication during occupation'. Perhaps because the visits were separated by a year, the length of time was a factor in making such connections between different countries with histories of occupation. In making the connections, however, knowledge about occupation evolved through threading objects from different locations and involved shifting between small objects and wider histories. Considering ways in which bodily movement

**FIGURE 5.1** Making networks of association

may involve different kinds of spatial, temporal and social interactions in making networks of association in and between locations (Figure 5.1) can be understood as the beginnings of a methodology that mobilises learners. It would seem that negotiating uncertainty, ambivalence and risk is necessary for this kind of learning if participants are to develop confidence in this kind of pedagogical approach rather than fearing a loss of authority. With this in mind, we can start to sketch aspirational attributes of mobilised learners and possible implications for the design of mobile learning experiences and touring technologies (Sprake, 2012). These attributes continue to be probed and developed in the design of located learning activities—both in our research projects and teaching—and are presented here as theoretical ideas that underpin the methodology for Learning-through-Touring.

## Noticing

In learning to notice, participants experience a heightened sense of awareness in 'turning a corner' and finding something of interest that necessarily involves sensory interplay with the 'here and now' of the physical environment. Learners will draw on this sensory interplay to make imaginative associations between sites in order to make public spaces personal. Tour-guides who facilitate noticing enable participants to explore 'behind the scenes' of what is usually expected and/or presented for public view. Tours use sensory cues to prompt movement and action. These cues are designed to allow participants to differentiate between ambient sounds, smells and textures of the built environment—'environmental information'. Noticing is supported by technologies that compensate for 'deficiencies of the eye' by engaging other senses in finding objects. Technologies are designed as tools that act as view-finders, lenses or antennae to spot finds and glean information from them.

## Stumbling upon

In learning to stumble upon, participants develop confidence in 'following their nose' in moving from one place to another. They engage with location-based enquiries that involve them in asking questions, conjecturing and juxtapositioning to learn about the transitional nature of their environs. In stumbling upon, learners focus on making the invisible visible by making detailed recordings of transition and piecing these together to make new threads of enquiry (Sprake & Thomas, 2007). The tour-guide's capacity for facilitating stumbling upon can be explored through the way he or she stages authenticity, providing a narrative that supports participants in re-imagining that location and listening to the multiple 'voices' of the building. Participants will be able to recall previous events, experiences and knowledge in relation to the new stories and accounts being told on location. Technologies are used to make recordings of anomalies that evidence user and material transition (for example, using timelapse photography) and to organise, layer and share these recordings in nonlinear ways both during and after the activity.

## Connecting

In learning to connect, participants shift between personal finds and wider civic and urban issues of a place. As they tour, participants dynamically form a series of 'views' or perspectives that critique given authoritative information (such as a plan, map or seemingly factual visitor guide). The tour-guide can facilitate connections by using pauses later on in a tour to revisit content from earlier to build a series of perspectives. A tour that 'fills the gaps' is designed to draw on what participants bring to the event rather than what they take out and develops skills in negotiating and debating perceived 'truths' about a place. Technologies are employed to facilitate the production of alternative views, both physically (i.e., from an unusual viewpoint or position) and in connecting with authorities, sources of information and other participants on the tour as a platform for exchange and collaboration.

### Learning-through-Touring Methodology

These aspirational attributes of mobilised learners have informed the development of three pairings of theoretical concepts and practical methods on which to build a methodology for Learning-through-Touring (Table 5.1). The relationship between the concepts and methods in each pairing is an iterative one; one is informed and developed by the other in process-driven design of mobilised learning activities.

**TABLE 5.1** Framework of pairings for a Learning-through-Touring methodology

|   | *Productive Concept* | *Conceptual Method* |
|---|---|---|
| 1 | Subjective archaeology | Micromapping |
| 2 | Sensory interplay | Haptic referencing |
| 3 | Critical tour-guides | Ground untruthing |

## 1. Subjective Archaeology and Micromapping

Stewart Brand has explored what happens to buildings after they have been built, arguing that they change over time by adapting materially as "function melts form" through use. He suggests that buildings can be said to "learn" in their ability to change and adapt to external forces. This ability to learn can be seen in the changes to materials and use and how these processes are evidenced over time, and this thinking forms the basis of subjective archaeology. Brand visualises different rates of change by visualising layers to a building site—from the "stuff" frequently changing on the inside to the outer structure and skin (Brand, 1994, p. 13). Excavating in the urban built environment can be described as finding 'cracks in the concrete', a process that involves looking for transition and use in the built environment as a way of archiving found objects that don't normally belong there. As such, artefacts can be described as active in the way they are constantly recontextualised. Collecting and archiving evidence of 'cracks in the concrete' as a touring activity needs to incorporate methods of recording and storing content that may invite participants to juxtapose knowledge about original context with the object out-of-context. Learning about the built environment may involve collecting material evidence that connects with the social and spatial production of the built environment.

Micromapping involves making detailed recordings of transition in the built environment and piecing together these fragmented 'finds' into threads for a tour. The recordings are made using a handheld toolkit that should include both digital and non-digital tools. For example recordings can be made by taking rubbings using wax crayons and paper and castings using plasticine as well as using digital voice recorders to capture sounds. Micromapping creates opportunities for learning about transition in the built environment through finding the 'cracks in the concrete' or detecting anomalies using technologies as archaeological tools. Using digital technologies allows data to be layered and communicated in nonlinear ways. Reflecting on finds collected involves participants in mapping those recordings to identify threads of enquiry into a building or area. In doing so they move through a process of enquiry (Figure 5.2), from making descriptions to making associations, that involves:

Walking and recording finds

|

Producing threads of finds

|

Identifying patterns and layers of located finds

|

Inviting others to make conjectures

**FIGURE 5.2** A process of enquiry

This process develops what might be meant by learning-enabled buildings; the idea that a thread may be a personal and/or public repository for personal collections that may be evolved through participants tagging finds with location and date information so that others can identify when and where the find was made. The process also enables finds to be layered over time and across locations.

## 2. Sensory Interplay and Haptic Referencing

> Exploration provides the fine detail of a complex tactile world, communication establishes a participation or belonging to the world (and in a sense establishing our place in it) and simple contact continually maintains, often subconsciously, a connectivity with the physical world and our own bodies.
>
> (Rodaway, 1994, p. 45)

Paul Rodaway introduces the idea that being 'touched' and being 'in touch' are inextricably connected. Movement allows us to touch and to be touched by the physical environment—the body reaching out to the environment as well as the environment coming into contact with the body so that body and environment "touch and are touched" (Rodaway, 1994). He suggests that everyday haptic experiences involve us using and relating all three levels of reciprocity. "Simple contact" is literally two surfaces in contact with one another, whilst "exploratory activity" describes an active agent consciously investigating an environment. Although the environment does not "appear to register its own tactile sensation", the active agent can be said to absorb a "rich supply of information" from it. "Communication" involves an active agent making contact with another party, where each party responds to "tactile stimulations and messages are exchanged" (p. 45).

As we haptically perceive space, we come to know it through the "reciprocal nature of touch" in interactions between people, objects and places. This idea of reciprocity develops what we mean by learning through buildings—we are able to physically touch and be emotionally touched by the active, transitory nature of the built environment. And this now needs further discussion in terms of how technologies can help us to make sense of those sensations as learners. Can learners use mobile technologies to *amplify* awareness of the built environment? As we move, so we touch surfaces and extend our vision through touch:

> I reach my left arm up. I control the fountain. I press the button (sound of water). Put your left leg on the metal bar at the bottom of the sign. Take a couple of steps forward and turn to your right. You will see a cash machine. Try and press the numbers on the cash machine (sound of buttons being pressed). Stop and touch the opposite bar with your left foot and see on the wall on your right a light—touch it and try and not burn your hand. Go up the stairs and jump on every step (sound of jumping on steps). You are at the top and go towards where you can smell coffee. The smell of coffee is getting weaker.
>
> (Recorded by a 15-year-old guide using a
> digital voice recorder, *Transitional Spaces*, 2006.)

Steven Feld argues that the sentient subject hears and feels place, and there is a need to understand how we are "culturally attuned" in order to realise what the environment might offer (Feld, 2005, pp. 184–185). According to Feld, Western culture has placed too much emphasis on the visual senses, and it is the interplay of senses that produces a perceptual experience of place rather than the dominance of one sense over another. In my view, the more we recognise the role of cultural bias in producing sensory dominance, the greater the possibility for unblocking 'clogged' senses and experiencing a greater variety of environmental information.

Architectural writers David Littlefield and Saskia Lewis argue that buildings have 'voices' that can be heard in different ways. In the introduction to their book *Architectural Voices: Listening to Old Buildings*, Littlefield and Lewis (2007) suggest that stories and narratives are embedded within the fabric of old or 'elderly' buildings, some of which may be instinctively heard by visitors, whilst others may need to be explicitly amplified in order to be heard (p. 14). Placing Feld's argument that we are 'culturally attuned' alongside Littlefield and Lewis's idea that buildings have 'voices' creates an interesting way of approaching the design of learning activities that may be tuned into hearing such voices as well as the tastes, smells and textures of buildings. The synaesthesia of senses plays an important role in making connections between time and place.

Haptic referencing is broadly concerned with the production of nonvisual cues for participants to follow and respond to in making tours of the built environment. They may be involved in making connections between live and recorded sounds, plugging into what may be perceived as 'background' or ambient sounds, or orientating themselves in response to non-visual cues by locating reference points to ascertain their physical position ("standing here you can smell the coffee from the cafe"). Activities that prompt unexpected ways of 'being in touch' with a seemingly ordered environment can provide alternative physical experiences that heighten awareness of surroundings. Specifically, haptic referencing involves making movements that prompt noticing of this sensory-rich environmental information and provides opportunities for learning through making connections between the cue and the live happenings of the 'here and now'. Making movements and responding to nonvisual cues may be described in reciprocal terms in which participants engage in the interplay between live and recorded sounds in location-evoking intangible objects or stories that may be sensed in location.

Locating and developing haptic references that invite conjecture, juxtapositioning, questioning and orientating explicitly recognises the erosion of our perceptual sphere and works to slow down this erosion by noticing through listening, smelling and touching. In this way technologies may be employed as extensions to the body that act as antennae in locating and responding to cues. Haptic referencing focuses on developing personal antennae that sense sounds, smells and textures of the built environment that might otherwise go 'unnoticed'.

## 3. Critical Tour Guides and Ground Untruthing

Performance artist and writer Tim Etchells (1998) describes an "audience/witness distinction" in performance art, in which to witness means to "feel the weight of things and one's own place in them". He suggests that participation can be evidenced in the way participants will talk about an event afterwards as having left its "mark" in some way (p. 33, 35). The work of Wrights & Sites, Tim Brennan and PLATFORM are just a few examples of critical guiding practises that engage with this concept. The 'Mis-Guide' approach of Wrights & Sites is a practical one, a set of invitations that inspires an inclination to physically and emotionally experience urban environments (Hodge, Persighetti, Smith, Turner, & Weaver, 2003). In this way, the approach is a resource that supports a 'behind the scenes' experience of the built environment by trying out new things in both repetitive routines and 'one-off' activities. Tim Brennan's walking 'methodology' provides an alternative way of investigating the role of cues in guides that may support learners in 'stumbling upon' (Brennan, 1990). His 'walk/works' or 'manoeuvres' work in relation to the everyday environment; what happens to be happening is an integral element of the performance. Brennan's concept of 'manoeuvre' can be described as a walk that is guided by a narrative that is location-specific, in which there is an expectation that participants will engage in making imaginative associations between the guide and the location they are moving through. PLATFORM describe the act of walking as an important element in engaging with this kind of learning in that walking involves repositioning yourself "in the shoes of others" and in the "picture" of the environment, which enables the walker to learn through a process of "animation and implication" (Marriott & Trowell, 2000, pp. 76–82).

A guided walk led by Jane Trowell from PLATFORM in November 2005 followed the course of the Walbrook (Figure 5.3), an underground tributary of the Thames, through the City of London. The course of the Walbrook is hidden underground from public view, and the walk designed and guided by PLATFORM explores the connections between this concealed waterway and all aspects of the City of London above ground. The PLATFORM walk positioned participants physically and cognitively in considering tensions between global economic power structures and 'local' effects that supported participants in 'filling in the gaps'. The guide used the walk as a method to facilitate learning about history in sites visited whilst critically exploring contemporary issues.

Ground untruthing started as an antidote to GPS imaging linked with the term 'ground truthing'. Ground truthing describes a method for calibrating surface data collection (such as materials, human activity, environment samples) with satellite images of the area being studied. The distance between the satellite image and

FIGURE 5.3 The Walbrook, an underground tributary of the Thames

ground level data are used as a space to calibrate both sets of data in order to make the analysis as 'truthful' or accurate as possible. The resulting images can be colour enhanced to show different levels or regions of activity, and elevation images can also be drawn using radar-sensing technology. This interpretation of ground level 'truth' is based on determining a picture of ground level activity at a particular time and set of geographic coordinates using calibration with pixels captured using the same coordinates on the satellite image. Margins for error such as atmospheric interference are built into the system to maintain a high level of accuracy.

Ground untruthing is based on the principle that ground truth is always open to subjective interpretation and contestation depending on the author and the frame through which the analysis has been set and who conducted it. This method develops skills of critical enquiry through negotiating and debating perceived 'truths' about a place. Surveying an area of land to make it visible and intelligible through a process of rationalisation could be argued to be a never-ending task, as the real world is in a state of constant flux and change. The idea of learning about a place by surveying it as a critical enquiry, or ground untruthing, contributes to subjective constructions of topographical representations of urban landscapes.

## Conclusion

There are several findings emerging from our practice-led research that may be applied more widely in the design of tools and services for located learning activities:

* Understanding buildings as active rather than passive underpins what is meant by situated awareness. In this, the building operates as an interface between objects and people in which tools can be designed and used to find, record and publish details of the close-up fabric and users' conjecture about their identification and importance.
* Following on from this, involving participants (or visitors) in evolving an issue that has been identified as central to the initial enquiry or project brief can be done through engaging them in spotting and publishing everyday findings that are space-time specific and can be viewed, analysed and commented upon by others.
* In preparing for generating content for a tour of an unfamiliar location, we found that it was helpful to learn how to explore a well-known physical environment first and understand it as a dynamic situation. Skills in noticing how the physical built environment changes were then applied in generating content for a tour of an unfamiliar location. Drawing on from this, multiple visits to the same location created opportunities for participants to lead their own learning, creating threads of subject matter and content in response to the previous visit.

- Providing a clear framework for a focused enquiry and simple rules for generating content worked well in situations where each participant, in negotiation with others, could be led by their curiosity to make their own route through the project and, literally, the building, for example instructions such as walk the path, record observations and upload data to a shared map.

- We have realised that tools given to a user and/or the types of data captured will effectively prescribe how a user perceives using that service and, often in quite unexpected ways, will determine their activity and mobility. Our research has highlighted that metadata or associative data can be of more relevance to describing location, especially when mixed or augmented with other data sources, and the methodology encourages this. For a service to truly work, you must encourage unexpected augmentation of your data, including encouraging alternate ways of collecting data and visualising the results, with reassurance that the data gathered are not going to be used in a way that is unexpected or insecure.

- Mobile devices described as antennae to sense change and transition can be a helpful metaphor in utilising tools embedded in devices to heighten awareness and prompt motile activity in response to content designed in the form of cues.

- The speed at which walking happens, accelerations and decelerations, and different perspectives (from top-down viewpoints to immersive jostling) all affect the way in which people move through space, what they notice and where they go next.

User evolvement of seeded content has been the cornerstone of developing this methodology since our first project, *Mudlarking in Deptford*, in 2005. This has moved from creating initial content around a subject of interest that is designed in such a way as to prompt them to add to this in location, to creating services that can be utilised as tools for learning by users operating as instigators, experts, mashers and voyeurs (Sprake & Rogers, 2013). In this we have always been conscious of the need to present data through interactive maps and tools in ways that invite questions and further opportunities for learning. This journey has come to a point where we believe that a focused enquiry, event or project is important in generating meaningful located learning experiences that engage learners in developing situational awareness whilst on-the-move. This kind of awareness is valuable in developing a disposition towards active discovery and critical enquiry. I was once asked during a funding application interview at Futurelab in 2004 whether it was possible to develop situated awareness in others—i.e., could a personal way of 'seeing the world' be more widely applicable for public learning events and activities. The answer is yes. We have found that when a user really participates, it is the activity of discovery that literally propels them to do so. And this is what really encapsulates mobilised learning.

## Note

1 These are more fully articulated in *Learning-through-Touring: Mobilising Learners and Touring Technologies to Creatively Explore the Built Environment* (Sprake, 2012).

## References

Brand, S. (1994). *How buildings learn: What happens after they're built*. London: Viking.

Brennan, T. (1990). *Guidebook: Three manoeuvres by Tim Brennan in London E1/E2*. London: Camerawork.

Edwards, D., & Usher, D. (2000). *Globalisation and pedagogy*. London: Routledge.

Etchells, T. (1998). Valuable spaces: New performance in the 1990s. In N. Childs & J. Walwin (Eds.), *A split second of paradise* (pp. 31–40). London: Rivers Oram Press.

Feld, S. (2005). Places sensed, senses placed. In D. Howes (Ed.), *Empire of the senses* (pp. 179–191). Oxford: Berg.

Hodge, S., Persighetti, S., Smith, P., Turner, C., & Weaver, T. (2003). *An Exeter mis-guide*. Exeter, UK: Wrights & Sites. Retrieved from www.mis-guide.com

Littlefield, D., & Lewis, S. (2007). *Architectural voices: Listening to old buildings*. Chichester: John Wiley & Sons.

Marriott, J., & Trowell, J. (2000). 'Words which can hear': Educating for social and ecological art practise. In J. Carson & S. Silver (Eds.), *Out of the bubble: Approaches to contextual practice within fine art education*. London: Central St Martin's College of Art and Design.

Massey, D. (2005). *For space*. London: Sage.

Nespor, J. (2004). Educational scale-making. *Pedagogy, Culture and Society, 12*(3), 309–326.

Rodaway, P. (1994). *Sensuous geographies: Body, sense and place*. London: Routledge.

Sprake, J. (2009). Designing participant-generated context into guided tours. *International Journal of Mobile and Blended Learning, 1*(2), 19–38.

Sprake, J. (2012). *Learning-through-touring: Mobilising learners and touring technologies to creatively explore the built environment*. SENSE: Rotterdam.

Sprake, J., & Rogers, P. (2011). Located lexicon: A project that explores how user generated content describes space. In S. Sonvilla Weiss & O. Kelly (Eds.), *Future learning spaces: Designs on e-learning*. Helsinki: The School of Art, Design and Architecture, Aalto University.

Sprake, J., & Rogers, P. (2013). Crowds, citizens and sensors: Process and practice for mobilising learning. *Journal of Personal and Ubiquitous Computing, 18*(3), 753–764.

Sprake, J., & Thomas, H. (2007). Transitional spaces: Mapping physical change. *International Journal Of Art & Design Education, 26*(2), 167–176.

# 6

# TECHNOLOGY INTEGRATION IN NEXT GENERATION MOBILE LEARNING

*Teemu H. Laine and Eeva Nygren*

## Introduction

Imagine a learning system that is always with the learner, providing relevant learning content through a mobile device as she traverses across different contexts in daily life. The relevance of the learning content depends on her location and other aspects such as nearby people and objects, weather conditions, time of the day, states of the body and mind, previous knowledge, personal learning preferences, personal learning goals and abilities. Further imagine that the learning system is highly motivating because it knows what interests the learner and does its best to hide the fact that it is a learning system. It could be a game, for example; a game that uses a problem-solving approach to present challenges related to the learner's real life—challenges to ignite the intrinsic motivation in her. Boosting intrinsic motivation is possible by concentrating on the essential things that the learner is genuinely interested in and avoiding disturbances. This all sounds fantastic, but the best part of the system is that it can adapt to serve different types of users, regardless of their backgrounds and preferences, in unique, constantly changing situations.

The scenario described above would have been impossible some years ago when mobile devices were nothing but simple devices offering functions such as making phone calls, sending messages and playing games. In those days, a typical mobile learning system might have used SMSs for learning content delivery. Context-awareness was an unknown concept. Today, through the emergence of smartphones and context-aware technologies such as sensors and smart tags (e.g., RFID, QR code), the concept of *context-aware learning space* (CALS) has emerged as the next generation mobile learning. A context-aware learning space utilises the resources of the surrounding context to facilitate the learning process by combining physical and virtual realities. With modern technology we are closer than ever to building a CALS that would work like our imaginary system above. However, there are still considerable challenges to be solved. In this chapter we seek answers to one of the fundamental challenges:

> How can a mobile learning system provide contextually relevant learning experiences without disturbing the learner?

The amount of disturbances that a learning system inflicts on the learner can be expressed by *disturbance factors*, which are properties of a learning system that have negative effects on the learner. Examples of disturbance factors are a malfunctioning device, confusing user interface and poorly contextualised learning content. Sometimes disturbance factors can also facilitate learning. One example of this is the concept of conflictive animations in programming education—the learning content conflicts with the learner's ideas, thus stimulating a reasoning process (Moreno, Joy, Myller, & Sutinen, 2010). In many cases disturbance factors can be remedied by appropriate *technology integration*. Thus, to answer the aforementioned question, we explore the role of technology integration in CALSs.

As a case study, we present our experiences with the UFractions game, which combines physical fraction rods with a virtual story-based game on a mobile phone. The game was originally developed for and evaluated in the South African context (2009) but was subsequently tested in Finland (2010) and in Mozambique (2011). In these three different contexts, we explored technology integration in UFractions.

The information presented in this chapter can be utilised by educational tool designers who wish to incorporate context-awareness in their designs whilst minimising the disturbance factors. Whilst we present an evaluation of a single game, the same principles can be applied to other context-aware learning spaces as well.

This chapter is partly based on the doctoral dissertation of the first author (Laine, 2011). Authoring work was supported by the new faculty research fund of Ajou University (2012).

## Literature and Theoretical Background

### *Informal Learning and Games*

Mobile learning is often applied outside classrooms to complement formal educational systems. The role of mobile learning in supporting informal learning is important because it has been estimated that a majority of learning takes place in informal contexts (Livingstone, 1999; Tough, 1978). Experiential learning is a key characteristic of the informal end of the continuum of formality in learning (Dewey, 1938). Other characteristics include, but are not limited to, implicit, unintended, opportunistic and unstructured ways of learning and the absence of teachers (Eraut, 2004), as well as contextual (organisational) embeddedness, action orientation, non-routine conditions, tacit dimensions, and requirements for critical reflectivity and creativity (Watkins & Marsick, 1992).

In informal learning, the context in which the learning takes place is not solely dedicated to the purpose of learning, but learning takes place there as a secondary function. This aspect is different from formal classroom-based education where the primary function of the context is to foster learning and teaching. The richness of and the interest raised by the surrounding context may increase the intrinsic motivation of the learner (Cordova & Lepper, 1996). The involvement of the context also works as a catalyst for educators to implement alternative learning activities that are connected to real world resources. The next generation of mobile learning, context-aware learning (which we will discuss in the following sections), can be seen as an enabler in harnessing the contextual richness in informal learning settings.

Games are typically played outside school contexts as a leisure activity. Furthermore, games offer a great potential to learning, especially in increasing motivation of learners (Malone & Lepper, 1987). However, the captivating features of games have not been successfully incorporated into educational games, and the potential of games is still widely unexploited in the domain of learning (Egenfeldt-Nielsen, 2007; van Eck, 2006). In order to create more fun, engaging and effective mobile learning solutions, educators could learn from game designers about how they keep the player engaged (Prensky, 2002). The popular inducement used to explain enjoyment whilst playing games is the *flow theory* introduced by Csikszentmihalyi (1991). The concept of *flow* describes a person's preoccupation with the task at hand. Players often experience this heightened and improved state of mind whilst they are the most immersed in a game and performing at their best, thereby losing track of time and space. Good educational games can provide flow experiences to students (Rieber & Matzko, 2001).

## Context-awareness

Context-awareness can be interpreted in different ways depending on how the term *context* is defined. Abowd and Elizabeth (2000) define context with five W's: who, what, where, when and why. This definition can be applied also to non-computing contexts, but it does not cover details such as the user's previous knowledge, feelings and social contacts. Chalmers (2011) gives a more flexible definition but restricts it to computing environments, stating, "context is the circumstances relevant to the interaction between a user and their computing environment" (p. 69). Our definition of context is similar to that of Chalmers, but it also takes into account the temporal dimension. In this chapter, context is defined as a collection of interrelated *contextual entities*. A *situation* is defined as a snapshot of a context at a given moment of time. Contextual entities may be identified, for example, by knowing where the users are, what they are doing, how they are feeling, who else is with them, what resources are nearby, what time it is and what the parameters of the physical environment are. *Context-awareness* is a property of a system to recognise and act upon changes in consecutive situations (i.e., temporal snapshots of the context). In order for a system to be context-aware, it needs to utilise *context-aware technologies* such as object tagging (RFID, barcodes) and sensors for detecting location, movement and environment conditions.

Figure 6.1 illustrates how a context-aware system detects changes between two consecutive situations in a context and then adapts learning resources accordingly. The system detects changes ($\Delta_1$ and $\Delta_2$) in *contextual resources* (Entity$_1$ and Entity$_2$), which form a subset of all contextual entities that can be observed by a given set of context-aware technologies and then utilised by the system. In contrast, Entity$_3$ is not a contextual resource because it is not detectable. *Context-free resources* (e.g., theory of a topic) are not dependent on the context. By being aware of changes in contextual resources, a system can adapt both the contextual and context-free resources to fit the user's current situation. As a result, the system provides the user with *context-sensitive resources* (i.e., learning materials and activities) with high relevance to the user's situation. A typical example is a context-aware museum or gallery system (see Heumer, Gommlich, Jung, & Mueller, 2007; Islas Sedano, Sutinen, Vinni, & Laine, 2011; Lonsdale, Beale, & Byrne, 2005) that detects objects that are near the visitor and provides content relevant to those objects.

## Context-aware Learning Space (CALS)

Context-aware learning utilises resources of the surrounding context in the learning process. Context-aware learning typically takes place in informal learning settings where the contexts are rich in terms of learning possibilities. It builds on the foundations of mobile learning (m-learning), where the learners with mobile devices have time- and location-independent access to learning resources

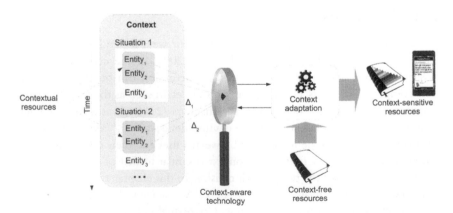

**FIGURE 6.1** Change detection and context adaptation in a context-aware system

(Eschenbrenner & Nah, 2007; Naismith, Lonsdale, Vavoula, & Sharples, 2005; Sharples, Milrad, Arnedillo Sánchez, & Vavoula, 2009). A major challenge in traditional m-learning is that the same learning material can be studied at home, at school, in a bus or in a park, but the surrounding context is disregarded. In such learning situations, the learner's attention is likely to be focused on the mobile device's screen (Goth, Frohberg, & Schwabe, 2006). As a remedy for ignoring the contextual relevance in m-learning, context-aware learning integrates the contextual resources into the learning content. A mobile device delivers context-sensitive learning content to the learner and provides relevant feedback upon the learner's actions. Because of context-sensitiveness of the learning content, the learner is encouraged to interact with surrounding objects and phenomena.

A learning environment that makes use of a context-aware system is referred to as *context-aware learning space* (CALS). The term *learning space* in this case refers to a combination of physical and virtual realities in which the learning takes place. A typical CALS comprises a number of mobile devices (clients), wireless connectivity, a server, a set of context-aware technologies and a collection of learning content and activities. A selection of CALSs is presented in Table 6.1. Context-awareness is most commonly achieved by detecting the learners' and objects' locations within the context, but more advanced technologies have also been used such as sensors.

## Technology Integration in CALSs

The term *technology integration* refers to the process by which a technology (typically digital) is introduced into a classroom for pedagogical purposes. Technology integration in formal education has been researched extensively (Becker, 1994; Ertmer, 1999; Levine & Wadmany, 2008; Means et al., 1993; Staples, Pugach, & Himes, 2005; Strudler & Wetzel, 1999). Koehler and Mishra (2008) have introduced the TPCK (technological pedagogical content knowledge) framework for technology integration in formal education. The TPCK framework is based on Shulman's PCK (pedagogical content knowledge) model, which suggests that a competent educator should master both knowledge of pedagogy and knowledge of content (Shulman, 1987). Koehler and Mishra added the component of technology to the PCK model to meet the requirements of technology-enhanced pedagogical practises.

The importance of proper technology integration is high in CALSs where the technology plays a big role in contextualising the learning experience. Without proper technology integration, the learning process may be disturbed. For example, a badly integrated technology may disrupt the user experience (Kaasinen, 2002), or the system simply does not work because of a lack of technical maintenance skills.

The iterative process of technology integration in a CALS is illustrated in Figure 6.2. The idea is that the first version of a CALS is placed under an evaluation

**TABLE 6.1** Examples of context-aware learning spaces

| CALS | Purpose | Context-awareness |
|------|---------|-------------------|
| Ambient Wood (Rogers et al., 2004) | Support contextualised scientific enquiry during school field trips in forests | Light and humidity sensors, GPS positioning |
| Augmented Knight's Castle (Hinske & Langheinrich, 2009) | Facilitate children's playing and learning by technologically augmented toys | Tagged objects (RFID) |
| GreenSweeper (Hui-chun, Liu, & Sambasivan, 2008) | Increase awareness of green areas in an urban environment through a game similar to Minesweeper | Manual user location, camera for detecting greenness |
| Microlearning environment (Beaudin, Intille, Tapia, Rockinson, & Morris, 2007) | Learn second language vocabulary through interaction with everyday objects | Object usage sensors, water flow sensors, accelerometers, RFID |
| Cyberguide (Abowd et al., 1997) | Provide a context-sensitive tour to the visitors of a research laboratory | Infrared positioning |
| Environmental Detectives (Klopfer & Squire, 2007) | Support learning of environmental science through a multiplayer real-world simulation game | GPS positioning |
| JAMIOLAS (Hou et al., 2010) | Learn Japanese mimicry and onomatopoeia through context-aware learning activities | Wearable and wireless sensors, RFID positioning |
| LieksaMyst (Islas Sedano et al., 2011) | Learn about lives in the past in a living museum. | Tagged objects (codes) |
| LORAMS (Ogata, Matsuka, El-bishouty, & Yano, 2009) | Learn and share everyday tasks through context-aware videos | Tagged objects (RFID) |
| Nottingham Castle Museum gallery (Lonsdale et al., 2005) | Receive context-sensitive information on paintings in a gallery | Ultrasound positioning |
| REXplorer (Ballagas et al., 2007) | Support tourist game-based context-aware exploration of Regensburg city | Motion detection, GPS |
| Via Mineralia (Heumer et al., 2007) | Explore a mineral collection through a treasure hunt game | Tagged objects (RFID) |

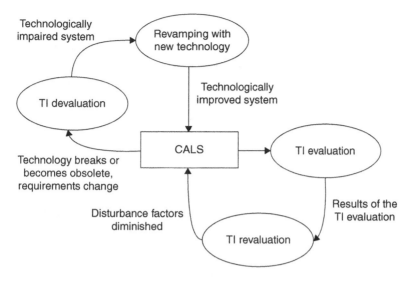

**FIGURE 6.2** Technology integration cycle

of technology integration. The results of the evaluation are utilised in the *devaluation* process, which diminishes the disturbance factors discovered in the evaluation. The revaluation process aims at increasing the pedagogical and motivational value of the CALS. *Devaluation* may take place when a technology breaks or becomes obsolete, or when requirements change. In this case, *revamping* the CALS with a new technology is needed. After revamping, new evaluation should be performed to ensure successful integration.

Technology integration can be divided into passive and active components according to the roles of technology in the integration process:

- *Passive integration*: technology *must be integrated* into the CALS so that it becomes subtle and unobtrusive to the learner and to the context. In other words, technology is the object of integration.
- *Active integration*: technology *must integrate* the contextual resources and context-free resources into the CALS and make the system adaptive to the changing situations of the context, including users within. In other words, technology is the subject of integration.

This division is necessary in order to manage technology's direct and indirect influences on the learning experience. Figure 6.3 presents an updated version of Figure 6.1 with passive and active integration that is driven (or restrained) by available resources such as technology, money, time and context-free resources. Passive integration aims at achieving unobtrusiveness of the technology from the learners' and the context's perspectives. The integrated unobtrusive technology provides context-awareness to the active integration process via contextual resource detection. The goal is to establish a context-sensitive environment through adaptation

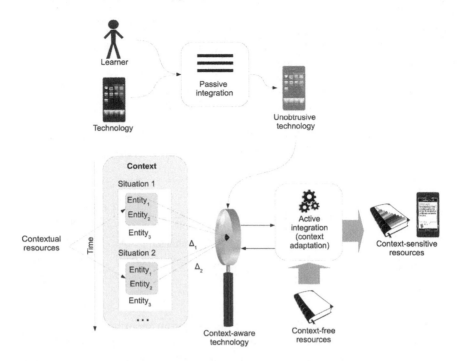

**FIGURE 6.3** Passive and active technology integration

of contextual resources and the context-free resources to the learner's situation. It is worth noting that passive integration should always precede active integration. Finally, the concepts of disturbance factors as well as active and passive technology can be applied to both high-tech and low-tech learning systems.

## Technology and Contexts

### UFractions

UFractions is a game-based CALS that was developed in 2009 to help the children at rural South African schools learn fractions and become motivated towards mathematics (Turtiainen, Blignaut, Els, Laine, & Sutinen, 2009). We later translated game content to Finnish and Portuguese and evaluated UFractions also in Finland (2010) and in Mozambique (2011) to discover the effect of context change. UFractions combines physical fraction rods with a story-based game running on a mobile device. The story features fraction problems that must be solved by the player using the rods. The intention of combining the fraction rods, mobile phone and story-telling game was not only to motivate the children to learn but also to create a connection between the virtual world (story, fraction theory) and the real world (mobile phone and fraction rods).

In the beginning of the game, the player meets Mother Leopard and her newborn cub, Senatla. Raising the cub entails challenges such as finding food to eat, learning how to hunt, avoiding enemies and finding sources of fresh water. The player's task is to help the leopards to meet these challenges by solving fraction problems with the fraction rods. Every time the player solves a problem, he or she is rewarded with points. After a wrong answer the player may retry, but the point value of the problem is decreased. If the player needs scaffolding aids, they can request hints from the leopards after unsuccessful answers.

The fraction problems were designed so that the players must gain an understanding of the problem and the concept of fractions in order to be able to find the correct solutions. Furthermore, the game content is organised in three levels with increasing difficulty. The leopards interact with the player through the mobile phone screen. Through this interaction, the player gains information on the lives of the leopards and fraction theory. The aim of wrapping an appealing story around the pedagogical content was to make the players feel as if they would be playing and helping the leopards, not learning.

The story is presented through the means of text, images and sound (Figure 6.4). The fraction problems require either multiple choice or exact numeric answers, and the fraction rods are referred to using short codes mapped to the colours (e.g., 'W' for white, 'BL' for blue). The leopards' discourse with the player is represented by speech bubbles in comic style. The content for the game was created with help of South African cultural and pedagogical experts.

UFractions allows the players to identify and record evidence of fractions from the everyday living environment by taking pictures and adding comments to the pictures. The evidence is posted to the game's website, which also displays scores, guestbook entries and real-time status of the leopards' and the players' struggle against hunger and enemies.

UFractions is based on client-server architecture where the Java-based server pushes game content to Java-based clients in XML (extensible markup language)

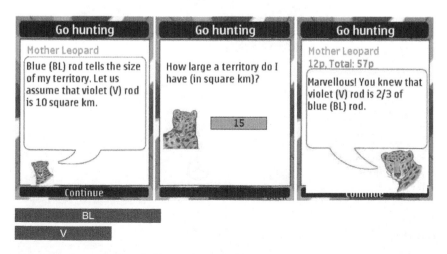

FIGURE 6.4 An example of a UFractions problem

format over a network connection. One advantage of this content delivery model is that if the content is modified, the clients do not need to be upgraded. Another advantage is that the player's status is stored on the server, so the game can be resumed after a period of absence or device crash. Mobile phones running the client software are connected to the game server over a wireless network such as WLAN or 3G (Figure 6.5). During evaluations we used Nokia N95 and N80 phones that connected via a WLAN to the UFractions server running on a laptop. Using a low-latency WLAN ensured that the players experienced the gameplay as if the entire game was running on the mobile device.

In addition to a mobile device, another technology that can be directly observed by the player is a set of fraction rods. These rods have different lengths, which are mapped to different colours. For each fraction problem, the game tells the player the colours and codes of the associated fraction rods. After this, the player uses the rods to calculate an answer. In some cases the players employed auxiliary tools such as pens, papers and calculators to solve the problems. These auxiliary tools were not designed to be part of the game.

UFractions utilises some other contextual resources in addition to fraction rods. Time stamps are used for organising game results and guest book entries. The learner's background is considered through game levels that provide challenges of increasing difficulty to match various skill levels of the players. The story and game characters were designed for the South African context with an assumption that the leopard characters would be appealing for pupils of the same age in other contexts as well. The game does not need to track the player's position, as they remain stationary. However, the positions of intelligent fraction rods are detected

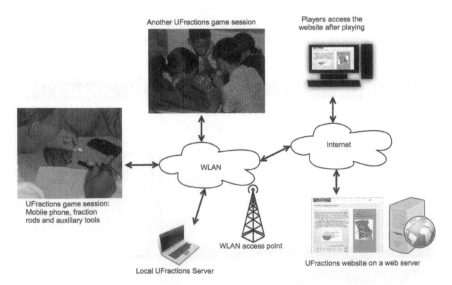

**FIGURE 6.5** Technological setting of UFractions

in the latest version of the game (Smith & Laine, 2011), but this technology was not ready during the evaluations.

### Contexts: South Africa, Finland and Mozambique

South Africa has a complex and diverse population of more than 47 million people. The major ethnic groups include Africans (79.5%), whites from mixed European descent (9.2 %), coloured from mixed African, European and Malaysian descent (8.9%) and Indians (2.5%). Education is compulsory for all South Africans aged 7–15, and general education includes grades from R to 9. Both local and international measures of learning achievements show that South African learners perform poorly, especially in mathematics and literacy (OECD, 2008).

About 38% of South African schools provide access to computers for their grade eight students, and only about 15% of mathematics and science teachers use ICTs in their teaching (Blignaut & Els, 2010). In contrast, South Africa is amongst the fastest growing mobile phone markets in the world. Especially the youth in South Africa are avid users of mobile phones (Kreutzer, 2008). According to the study, playing mobile games is a popular activity: over 50% of the grade eleven students in a poor urban township school play mobile games daily.

The Finnish population is about 5.4 million people, and the official languages are Finnish and Swedish. Finnish students start their compulsory education at the age of seven and continue until they are aged 17 or have passed nine grades. Basic education is free of charge, and teachers are highly qualified. Finnish students' performances have been consistent in OECD's PISA tests, and there are only small differences between the best and poorest results, as well as by schools and regions (OECD, 2010).

The use of ICT in Finnish schools is fairly high, as the level of computer access is 100%, the level of internet access is 100%, and over 70% of schools had fewer than 10 students per computer. However, only 61% of science teachers and less than 48% of mathematics teachers make use of ICT during the school year (Kankaanranta & Puhakka, 2008).

The Mozambican population is almost 23 million people. Whilst 14 languages are spoken, Portuguese is the official language. After gaining independence, the Mozambican government focused on developing education (Gapminder, 2013). Primary school enrollment has increased, but school construction and teacher training enrollments still leave room for improvement.

The Ministry of Education and Culture policies emphasise the use of ICT, especially at the secondary level. Currently there is a general understanding that computers are important resources to facilitate teaching activity, and teachers are being trained to use these technologies (Matavele & Camundimo, 2009). Projects such as SchoolNet Mozambique, NEPAD eSchools, and EPCI aim at increasing the use of ICT at schools in Mozambique (Farrell, Isaacs, & Trucano, 2007).

## Evaluation of UFractions

### Evaluation Settings and Instruments

UFractions was evaluated using a mixed-method strategy in five schools in South Africa, four schools in Finland and two schools in Mozambique during March 2009, March 2010 and May–June 2011, respectively. In each country we targeted eight middle school pupils, but in some cases allowed students of other ages to play if their instructors considered the content to be of appropriate level. Table 6.2 presents key figures related to the evaluation settings. The total numbers of participants were 105 in South Africa, 104 in Finland and 70 in Mozambique. One distinctive feature of the Mozambican data set is that the participants were of 24 different nationalities, whereas in South Africa and in Finland the participants were almost entirely locals. Furthermore, the participants at Polana Secondary in Mozambique were members of Kids Club—a technology club for children.

In all contexts the test procedures were as follows. Before evaluations the researchers acquired necessary permission letters from the schools' and children's representatives. In evaluations the participants were first asked to form teams of two to four. The researchers explained the purpose of the evaluation and shortly introduced the game's story and the usage of fraction rods. The participants then individually filled in the first part of a questionnaire. After this, the teams played the game for approximately 30–45 minutes. During the gameplay, the researchers made observations and gave guidance to the participants when required. Upon finishing the game, the participants completed the second part of the questionnaire.

**TABLE 6.2** Evaluation settings

|  | Sample (m/f) | Mobile phone ownership | Median age |
| --- | --- | --- | --- |
| *South Africa* |  |  |  |
| Alabama Secondary | 21 (8/13) | 38% | 14 |
| Lebone II | 22 (11/11) | 77% | 13.5 |
| Seiphemelo Secondary | 16 (6/10) | 25% | 14 |
| High School Zeerust | 27 (11/16) | 78% | 14 |
| Zinniaville Secondary | 19 (8/11) | 84% | 13 |
| *Finland* |  |  |  |
| Arppen Koulu | 32 (14/18) | 100% | 14 |
| Lieksan Keskuskoulu | 31 (16/15) | 100% | 14 |
| Joensuun Normaalikoulu | 18 (9/9) | 100% | 14 |
| Tietäväisen koulu | 23 (14/9) | 100% | 14 |
| *Mozambique* |  |  |  |
| Kids Club at Polana Secondary | 16 (11/5) | 50% | 15.5 |
| Maputo International School | 54 (32/22) | 61% | 11 |

Afterwards, the researchers interviewed three to five volunteer participants from each evaluation group.

## Instruments in South Africa and Finland

The questionnaire included open-ended and multiple choice questions with the Likert scale. The first part of the questionnaire collected demographics and background information such as mobile phone usage and feelings towards mathematics. The second part of the questionnaire measured the participants' perceptions on motivation, usability, game activities, game/learning experience, challenges and relevance to normal mathematics classes.

The participant interviews aimed at gaining a deeper insight into participants' motivation, as well as their perceptions on using the game as a learning tool and playing games in general.

## Instruments in Mozambique

The primary aim of evaluating UFractions in the Mozambican context was to test technology integration. To achieve this aim, we developed a technology integration evaluation tool (Laine, Sutinen, Joy, & Nygren, 2011) for CALSs. The evaluation tool is grounded in the critical factors of context-awareness, unobtrusive technology and available resources. It also uses the concepts of affordances and constraints from the TPCK (technological pedagogical content knowledge) framework (Koehler & Mishra, 2008). The tool follows a mixed-method approach and consists of questionnaires and interviews for both students and their teachers. These instruments measure aspects such as likes, dislikes, surprising elements, suggestions for improvement, usability, difficulties, motivation and applicability of UFractions to other contexts. We aimed at evaluating the attractiveness of UFractions as a learning tool both from the learners' and the educators' perspectives. Furthermore, the qualitative data (open questions, interviews) aim at identifying disturbance factors, which have a negative effect on the learners' experiences.

The technology integration evaluation tool retains some of the components from the instruments used for evaluating UFractions in South Africa and in Finland. Specifically, demographics, background, usability and motivation meters are similar.

## Technology Integration Evaluation

As we defined earlier, the disturbance factor is a property of a learning system that has a negative effect on the learner. Thus, we can improve the system by identifying and diminishing disturbance factors related to active and passive technology integration. To identify disturbance factors in UFractions, we first analysed qualitative data from South Africa and Finland (Laine et al., 2011), which revealed 16 disturbance factors. We later used the technology integration evaluation tool in the Mozambican context to uncover 22 disturbance factors. These included all but one of the previously discovered 16 factors. Table 6.3 presents the 22 disturbance factors, together with integration type (*I*, active or passive) and evidence samples. ZPD stands for Vygotsky's zone of proximal development (Vygotsky, 1978).

## Discussion and Conclusions

In this chapter, we have introduced context-aware learning spaces as an example of the next generation of mobile learning. A CALS enhances traditional location-agnostic mobile learning by providing contextually relevant learning experiences to the learners. The utilisation of context-awareness to supercharge mobile learning should be done without disturbing the learner. To tackle this challenge, we presented the concept and an evaluation of disturbance factors that may inflict negative effects on learning experiences. Through identification and elimination of disturbance factors, a CALS could be brought one step closer to becoming an unobtrusive next generation learning tool.

In the evaluation of UFractions, we identified 22 disturbance factors that were indicated by a few players. Conversely, there were many players who very much liked the game and did not report anything negative about it. We cannot state that the discovered disturbance factors render the game useless, but it is important to pay attention to these aspects in future development to ensure the game's fluent operation in all situations. It is very difficult or even impossible to please everybody at all times, but the system should be able to adapt the learning content, through active technology integration, to be suitable for a good majority of the learners. The tradeoff between available development resources and achieved benefits ensures that a system (be it a game or any other application) can be sensibly improved only to a certain extent.

Whilst most disturbance factors are negative, some of them could have positive effects as well. For example, disturbing content can stimulate cognitive curiosity by raising questions in the learner's mind. Another example is conflicting content, which may cause the player to critically compare their own idea against the game's idea. Even though these positive disturbances were not sought after in the game design, they are significant outcomes that require further studying.

The heterogeneity of the three evaluation contexts is important for the contextual generalisability of the results. The next step is to develop a CALS design tool that would warn about potential disturbances in an early design phase (Figure 6.6). Inputs for this predictive tool would include parameters of the target context (e.g., culture, indoor or outdoor, informal or formal, environment), learning content and presentation (e.g., subject matter, story, quiz, multimedia modality), types of learning (e.g., individual, group-based, game-based, problem-based), applied technologies and target group (e.g., age, knowledge level, learning preferences). Based on these inputs, the tool would output warnings of disturbance factors that are likely to emerge with a given set of inputs and what features are

**TABLE 6.3** Disturbance factors identified in UFractions

| Disturbance factor | I | Evidence |
| --- | --- | --- |
| Game too long | A | "The game is very big. It must have been a bit shorter." (M13, Indian) |
| Game too short | A | "I thought they could have a bit . . . maybe a bit longer the game." (M12, Mozambican) |
| Beyond ZPD | A | "There were some fractions that were difficult to solve." (M13, Mozambican) |
| Below ZPD | A | "For learning purpose maybe you should make it a little harder." (M12, Indian) |
| Wrong age group | A | "Maybe it would be better for younger kids because it's this story of two leopards, so it would be from 8 to 11." (F13, Indian) |
| Lack of scaffolding | A | "Sometimes when you were doing a question and you keep on not understanding I think there should be like where you can go to the next question if you can." (M11, Mozambican) |
| Conflicting content | A | "I was surprised because I had some answers that I was sure were correct but somehow they were wrong." (M11, English) |
| Too much story | A | "Too much reading and after a while it gets boring." (F13, Mozambican) |
| Monotony | A | "A part that I didn't like was that it was always about leopards. If we had lots of settings with maybe gorilla and rhino we could all learn the lives of lots of animals which show you lots of different facts. (M11, Irish) |
| Too educational | A | "It was nice but the thing is like it's not something I wanna do on a weekend or something. Maybe if you're bored . . ." (M12, Indian) |
| Harassment | A | "It was difficult to concentrate on the tasks when other people in the group were fiddling with the phone." (F14, Finnish) |
| Lack of peer support | A | "Disadvantage is that maybe no one would be there to explain to you." (F13, Indian) |
| Disturbing content | A | "The story of Senatla is not very good because the father of Senatla did not care for Senatla." (F17, Mozambican) |
| Punishment | A | "[I disliked] When we got questions incorrect." (M11, Mozambican) |
| Lack of animation | P | "I'd just say more animations into the story, kind of hide the fact that it's about fractions." (M12, Indian) |
| Inappropriate graphics | P | "The screen was a bit too . . . all the colors around it and . . . it kind of . . . not too many colors but all the colors around it were kind of distracting. It could be one plain color maybe." (M11, Irish") |
| Inappropriate sounds | P | "Make it more lively with sound." (M13, Mozambican) "If someone has troubles reading it you should have voice over." (M12, Indian) |
| Inconvenient interaction with rods | P | "I wouldn't advise to use them because sometimes they make it complicated." (F15, Mozambican) |

*(Continued)*

**TABLE 6.3** (*Continued*)

| Disturbance factor | I | Evidence |
|---|---|---|
| Inconvenient interaction with phone | P | "One thing that I really didn't find that much interesting was using the phone. [...] I think it would be easier if you use something like maybe a calculator or something." (M11, Mozambican) |
| Technical faults | P | "It quit by itself but then we were on track again." (M11, Irish) |
| Small screen | P | "The phone's screen was a bit too small so I couldn't see." (F11, Korean) |
| Unclear instructions | P | "I didn't like some parts because I didn't quite understand some questions." (M12, Mozambican) |

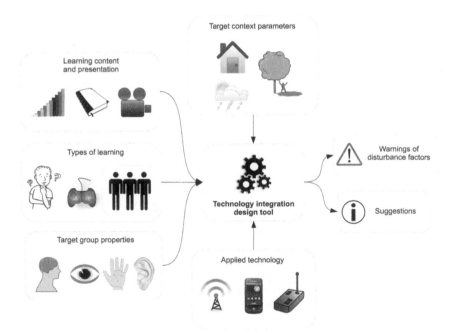

**FIGURE 6.6** CALS design tool concept

the most vulnerable for disturbances. The tool would also suggest how the disturbance factors could be diminished. Before this tool can be created, we need more information on the generalisability of the results presented in this chapter. Additionally, taxonomies of topics such as learner types, task types, technologies and disturbance factors are needed. This requires evaluations and analyses of different types of context-aware learning spaces because not all of them are non-competitive story-telling games with low technical complexity.

In the beginning of the chapter, we envisioned a next generation mobile learning system that would be highly adaptable to the learner's context and his or her personal properties. If we would design a CALS for a single learner with that learner in that learner's context, we might be able to make it near-perfect, without disturbance factors. Unfortunately, all learners and contexts are different, so it is impossible to create a one-size-fits-all learning space. The results of this chapter shed some light on the difficulties that CALS designers must meet to avoid and diminish disturbance factors. Hope remains in the future intelligent tools that are capable of automatically identifying the possibilities and pitfalls already in the design phase, thus enabling next generation mobile learning systems that provide contextual learning experiences without disturbing the learner.

## References

Abowd, G., Atkeson, C., Hong, J., Long, S., Kooper, R., & Pinkerton, M. (1997). Cyberguide: A mobile context-aware tour guide. *Wireless Networks, 3*(5), 421–433.

Abowd, G., & Elizabeth, M. (2000). Charting past, present and future research in ubiquitous computing. *ACM Transactions on Human-Computer Interaction, 7*(1), 29–58.

Ballagas, R.A., Kratz, S.G., Borchers, J., Yu, E., Walz, S.P., Fuhr, C.O., ... Tann, M. (2007). REXplorer: A mobile, pervasive spell-casting game for tourists. Proceedings from the *CHI Conference on Human Factors in Computing Systems* (pp. 1929–1934). San Jose, CA.

Beaudin, J.S., Intille, S.S., Tapia, E.M., Rockinson, R., & Morris, M.E. (2007). Context-sensitive microlearning of foreign language vocabulary on a mobile device. Proceedings from *The 2007 European conference on Ambient intelligence* (pp. 55–72). Darmstadt: Springer-Verlag.

Becker, H.J. (1994). How exemplary computer-using teachers differ from other teachers: Implications for realizing the potential of computers in schools. *Journal of Research on Computing in Education, 26*(3), 291–321.

Blignaut, A.S., & Els, C.J. (2010). Not yet where we want to be: South Africa's participation in SITES 2006. *US-China Education Review, 7*(2), 55–66.

Chalmers, D. (2011). *Sensors and systems in pervasive computing: Engineering context aware systems.* London: Springer.

Cordova, D.I., & Lepper, M.R. (1996). Intrinsic motivation and the process of learning: Beneficial effects of contextualization, personalization, and choice. *Journal of Educational Psychology, 88*(4), 715–730.

Csikszentmihalyi, M. (1991). *Flow: The psychology of optimal experience.* New York, NY: Harper Collins.

Dewey, J. (1938). *Experience and education.* New York, NY: Collier Books.

Egenfeldt-Nielsen, S. (2007). Third generation educational use of computer games. *Educational Multimedia and Hypermedia, 16*(3), 263–281.

Eraut, M. (2004). Informal learning in the workplace. *Studies in Continuing Education, 26*(2), 247–273.

Ertmer, P. (1999). Addressing first- and second-order barriers to change: Strategies for technology integration. *Educational Technology Research and Development, 47*(4), 47–61.

Eschenbrenner, B., & Nah, F.F. (2007). Mobile technology in education: Uses and benefits. *International Journal of Mobile Learning and Organisation, 1*(2), 159–183.

Farrell, G., Isaacs, S., & Trucano, M. (2007). Survey of ICT and education in Africa (Vol. 2). Retrieved from http://www.infodev.org/en/Publication.354.html

Gapminder. (2013). Gapminder world. Retrieved from http://www.gapminder.org

Goth, C., Frohberg, D., & Schwabe, G. (2006). The focus problem in mobile learning. Proceedings from *The Fourth IEEE International Workshop on Wireless, Mobile and Ubiquitous Technology in Education* (pp. 153–160). Athens.

Heumer, G., Gommlich, F., Jung, B., & Mueller, A. (2007). Via Mineralia—A pervasive museum exploration game. Proceedings from *The 4th International Symposium on Pervasive Gaming Applications (PerGames 2007)* (pp. 159–160). Salzburg.

Hinske, S., & Langheinrich, M. (2009). An infrastructure for interactive and playful learning in augmented toy environments. Proceedings from *The IEEE International Conference on Pervasive Computing and Communications* (pp. 1–6). Galveston, TX.

Hou, B., Ogata, H., Miyata, M., Mengmeng, L., Liu, Y., & Yoneo, Y. (2010). JAMIOLAS 3.0: Supporting Japanese mimicry and onomatopoeia learning using sensor data. *IJMBL— International Journal of Mobile and Blended Learning, 2*, 40–54.

Hui-chun, L., Liu, K., & Sambasivan, N. (2008). GreenSweeper: A persuasive mobile game for environmental awareness. Proceedings from *The Ubicomp 2008 Workshop on Ubiquitous Sustainability: Citizen Science and Activism*. Seoul.

Islas Sedano, C., Sutinen, E., Vinni, M., & Laine, T.H. (2011). Designing hypercontextualized games: A case study with LieksaMyst. *Educational Technology & Society Journal, 15*(2), 257–270.

Kaasinen, E. (2002). User needs for location-aware mobile services. *Personal and Ubiquitous Computing, 7*(1), 70–79.

Kankaanranta, M., & Puhakka, E. (2008). Kohti innovatiivista tietotekniikan opetuskäyttöä; Kansainvälisen SITES 2006-tutkimuksen tuloksia (The results of an international SITES 2006 comparison). University of Jyväskylä: Institute for Educational Research.

Klopfer, E., & Squire, K. (2007). Environmental detectives—The development of an augmented reality platform for environmental simulations. *Educational Technology Research and Development, 56*, 203–228.

Koehler, M. J., & Mishra, P. (2008). Introducing technological pedagogical content knowledge. In AACTE Committee on Innovation and Technology (Ed.), *Handbook of technological pedagogical content knowledge for educators* (pp. 3–29). New York, NY: Routledge.

Kreutzer, T. (2008). *Assessing cell phone usage in a South African township school*. Presented at e/merge 2008, Cape Town.

Laine, T.H. (2011). *Technology integration in context-aware learning spaces* (Doctoral dissertation). University of Eastern Finland, Joensuu.

Laine, T.H., Sutinen, E., Joy, M.S., & Nygren, E. (2011). *Rapid improvement of technology integration in context-aware learning spaces*. Presented at IEEE Africon 2011, Livingstone.

Levine, T., & Wadmany, R. (2008). Teachers' views on factors affecting effective integration of information technology in the classroom: Developmental scenery. *Journal of Technology and Teacher Education, 16*(2), 233–263.

Livingstone, D.W. (1999). Exploring the icebergs of adult learning: Findings of the first Canadian survey of informal learning practices. *Canadian Journal for the Study of Adult Education, 13*(2), 49–72.

Lonsdale, P., Beale, R., & Byrne, W. (2005). Using context awareness to enhance visitor engagement in a gallery space. Proceedings from *The HCI05 Conference on People and Computers XIX* (pp. 101–112). Galveston, TX.

Malone, T.W., & Lepper, M.R. (1987). Making learning fun: A taxonomy of intrinsic motivations for learning. *Aptitude, Learning, and Instruction, 3*, 223–253.

Matavele, J., & Camundimo, V. (2009). PanAfrican research agenda on the pedagogical integration of ICTs. *Mozambique Report*. Retrieved from http://www.ernwaca.org/panaf/pdf/phase-1/Mozambique-PanAf_Report.pdf

Means, B., Blando, J., Olson, K., Middleton, T., Morocco, C.C., Remz, A.R., & Zorfass, J. (1993). *Using technology to support education reform*. Washington, DC: US Government Printing Office.

Moreno, A., Joy, M., Myller, N., & Sutinen, E. (2010). Layered architecture for automatic generation of conflictive animations in programming education. *IEEE Transactions on Learning Technologies, 3*(2), 139–151.

Naismith, L., Lonsdale, P., Vavoula, G., & Sharples, M. (2005). Literature review in mobile technologies and learning: NESTA Futurelab Series.

OECD. (2008). *Reviews of national policies for education: South Africa*. Paris: OECD.

OECD. (2010). PISA 2009 results: Executive summary. Retrieved from http://www.tuac.org/en/public/e-docs/00/00/07/FB/document_doc.phtml

Ogata, H., Matsuka, Y., El-bishouty, M., & Yano, Y. (2009). LORAMS: Linking physical objects and videos for capturing and sharing learning experiences towards ubiquitous learning. *International Journal of Mobile Learning and Organisation, 3*(4), 337–350.

Prensky, M. (2002). The Motivation of Gameplay. *On The Horizon, 10*(1).

Rieber, L.P., & Matzko, M.J. (2001). Serious design of serious play in physics. *Educational Technology, 41*(1), 14–24.

Rogers, Y., Price, S., Fitzpatrick, G., Fleck, R., Harris, E., Smith, H., . . . Weal, M. (2004). Ambient Wood: Designing new forms of digital augmentation for learning outdoors. Proceedings from *The Third International Conference for Interaction Design and Children (IDC 2004)* (pp. 3–10). College Park, MD: ACM Press.

Sharples, M., Milrad, M., Arnedillo Sánchez, I., & Vavoula, G. (2009). Mobile learning: Small devices, big issues. In N. Balacheff, S. Ludvigsen, T. de Jong, A. Lazonder & S. Barnes (Eds.), *Technology enhanced learning: Principles and products* (pp. 233–249). Dordrecht: Springer.

Shulman, L.S. (1987). Knowledge and teaching: Foundations of the new reform. *Harvard Educational Review, 57*(1), 1–12.

Smith, A. C., & Laine, T. H. (2011). An intelligent fractions learning system: Implementation. Proceedings from the *IST Africa 2011* (pp. 1-9). Gaborone.

Staples, A., Pugach, M.C., & Himes, D. (2005). Rethinking the technology integration challenge: Cases from three urban elementary schools. *Journal of Research on Technology in Education, 37*(3), 285–311.

Strudler, N., & Wetzel, K. (1999). Lessons from exemplary colleges of education: Factors affecting technology integration in preservice programs. *Educational Technology Research and Development, 47*(4), 63–81.

Tough, A. (1978). Major learning efforts: Recent research and future directions. *Adult Education Quarterly, 28*(4), 250–263.

Turtiainen, E., Blignaut, S., Els, C., Laine, T.H., & Sutinen, E. (2009). Story-based UFractions mobile game in South Africa: Contextualization process and multidimensional playing experiences. Proceedings from *The Second Workshop of Story Telling and Educational Games*.

van Eck, R. (2006). Digital game-based learning: It's not just the digital natives who are restless. *EDUCAUSEreview*, March/April, 16–30.

Vygotsky, L.S. (1978). *Mind in society: The development of higher psychological processes*. Cambridge, MA: Harvard University Press.

Watkins, K.E., & Marsick, V.J. (1992). Towards a theory of informal and incidental learning in organizations. *International Journal of Lifelong Education, 11*(4), 287–300.

# 7

# EXPLORING THE POTENTIALS OF MOBILE LEARNING FOR STROKE PATIENTS

## RehabMaster Mobile

*Ahreum Lee, Jieun Kim and Hokyoung Ryu*

## Introduction

The ageing of the population has become an enduring phenomenon that could have major consequences and implications in the future for society, especially with regard to social care systems and healthcare services. It is thus becoming essential to find innovative ways to help increasingly elderly populations to maintain an active lifestyle and delay the need for institutionalised care. The same applies to the patients affected by stroke and many other age-related diseases who need long-term rehabilitation in both mental and physical activities.

Yet, the uptake and diffusion of ICT (information and communication technology) remains a significant challenge for many governments, health managers, healthcare practitioners and system developers. For instance, The National Program for Information Technology in England's National Health Service (NHS) was established in 2005 to provide integrated electronic records; however, the evaluation of the program reported that its adoption was very slow, labour intensive and technically very challenging, and was unable to show any direct evidence of societal innovation or benefits for relevant stakeholders (Greenhalgh et al., 2008). Notwithstanding, the increasingly prevalent availability of interactive consumer health information, especially through the internet or mobile devices, is reflective of major developments providing people with the means to take on more responsibility for their own health (Eysenbach, Sa, & Diepgen, 1999; Jadad, 1999). Often described as 'consumer empowerment', this trend represents an endeavour to enhance an individual's ability to satisfy their own needs and control their own lives (Gibson, 2006). According to Curran (2005), healthcare consumers are no longer deemed to be submissive contributors to their wellbeing, but are now expected to be active participants in their healthcare with the ability to choose the degree of control they wish to exercise over care decisions that affect their health.

Yet, there have been surprisingly few studies that have drawn together and reviewed the evidence concerning a range of health information technology applications, particularly those related to the management of chronic diseases. To date, only tentative steps have been made to increase our understanding of how patients actually engage with e-health information and the circumstances in which they do so (Kelly, Jenkinson, & Ziebland, 2013; Tustin, 2010; Wicks et al., 2012; Ziebland & Wyke, 2012).

That said, within the purview of this book, we set out to undertake an interpretative review of healthcare information sharing for stroke patients to examine existing users' requirements for mobile learning, the circumstances in which it can be used and community implications involved with its diffusion.

## Supporting Stroke Patients

As the trend of increasing patients with age-related illness shows, nearly three-quarters of all stroke patients are over the age of 65. A stroke causes difficulty with speaking, seeing, sensing or walking. As expected, a stroke brings enormous changes to the patients and the life of their family members. Hence, various support groups are both physically and mentally needed as a valuable means of working through fear of long-term disability by sharing detailed stories, gaining a positive outlook and seeking practical information (Lasker, Sogolow, & Sharim, 2005). As a similar example, Alm et al. (2004) developed a community-based learning program called CIRCA (2015), facilitating communication amongst people with dementia and helping them to take control of the lack of social interaction.

However, significant barriers to engagement of stroke patients still remain. Many stroke patients who need a long rehabilitation process depend not only on their physical and psychological capabilities, but also the demands that the interaction with technology makes on them (as one can identify in CIRCA case studies). In order to develop an effective health-supporting community for the stroke patients, we first need to understand how they might be able to engage with technology and what interests can be leveraged to rehabilitate their willpower to recover.

## Mobile Learning as a Community Involving Medium for Stroke Patients

The increasing spread of mobile devices is dramatically affecting people's daily lives. Arguably, mobile technologies, particularly the increasingly sophisticated mobile phone, combine both ubiquity and utility. This phenomenon has given rise to opportunities to employ mobile technologies more broadly than just as communication tools. In this sense, for learning design with mobile technologies,

Park, Parsons, and Ryu (2010) claimed that mobile learning is not limited to delivering educational materials onto stakeholders' mobile handsets, but also encompasses public information or even commercial information on lifestyle choices and health promotion.

In particular, health practitioners see the advantages of mobile learning environments in providing personalised content via the mobile phones that have become so pervasive in recent years (see Kikunaga, Tin, Ishinashi, Wang, & Kira, 2007; Whittaker, Bullen, Lin, McRobbie, & Rodgers, 2009). Klemm and Nolan (1998) analysed the messages from a cancer support group on the web and found that the participants sought and gave information, encouraged one another and used personal experience and prayer in their communication. Several other studies consistently reported the use of information technology to effectively support chronic patients and their caregivers (Ahern, Woods, Lightowler, Finley, & Houston, 2011; van der Eijk et al., 2013; Yellowlees, Nesbitt, & Cole, 2011).

In a similar vein, the stroke population also experiences isolation as a result of the chronic nature of the illness and may find internet (or mobile) communications to be a strong link to others beyond institution-based treatments and information access. Of course, this is not suggesting that information seeking from institutions has less special and important frames of reference for what constitutes learning. However, as learning activities begin to escape these frames, there are some important questions that need to be addressed about whether traditional approaches can meet these rising challenges and opportunities. One consequence of this is an increasing interest in the potentials of mobile learning to share information amongst patients (or their caregivers) and between the patients and the healthcare professionals. In particular, it is vital to understand the meaning of their communication activity (e.g., emotional support, empathy, praying or cheering-up).

In this chapter we describe the design of a learning space with mobile technologies in order to lay out some important concepts and themes that will provide a context for how the stroke patients might be supported by mobile learning, in conjunction with the rehabilitation system, by exploring their interests, activities, characteristics and needs of community-based expansive learning.

## Community-based Rehabilitation: Mobile-mediated Communication

Apart from individual learning activities, many researchers (such as Beckman, Argote, & Epple, 1990; Collier, 1980; Slavin, 1983) have also identified that socially constructed learning is more effective when people can converse or learn with each other by interrogating and sharing their descriptions of the world. This has been epitomised in the work of Vygotsky (1978) and other educational professionals (see Tudge, 1992), who believed that education's role is to give people experiences that are within their zones of proximal development, thereby encouraging and advancing their individual learning activities. Indeed, both the capabilities of mobile devices and their wide context of use contribute to their propensity to foster collaborative learning activities whether they are intentional or incidental. This draws upon the essential benefits of the collaborative learning space provided by mobile technologies.

Creating a collaborative learning space can obviously be a rewarding opportunity, but it is also full of challenges and dilemmas. In particular, motivating people to actively participate is not easy, and information seeking and sharing in collaborative settings bring many tensions between the process of learning and content coverage. Nonetheless, this learning experience is widely believed to give people an insight into a sharing learning community via their own mobile devices, mutually building up strong social bonds in their own community. Moreover, it has been seen that patients and their caregivers are experiencing their own zone of proximal development, mutually working towards a common goal and elaborating a unique community-based synergy in the collaborative learning environments.

Situated learning theory (Lave & Wenger, 1991) well describes this context-based learning activity from others that can provide a barometer to guide and support the learner. To model situated learning activities for the stroke patients and, in particular, to understand what tensions or contradictions might hinder the community-based learning, we chose activity theory (AT) (Bendy, Seglin, & Meister, 2000; Engeström, 1999; Leont'ev, 1978) as our theoretical foundation, as it can effectively explain situational and contextual circumstances that are linked to one's learning activity (Bertelsen & Bødker, 2003). Furthermore, many previous studies (such as Kurti, Spikol, Milrad, Svensson, & Pettersson, 2007; Sharples, Taylor, & Vavoula, 2007) showed evidence that it is a comprehensive conceptual framework to describe the structure, development and context of tasks that are to be supported by a mobile learning system.

## RehabMaster: A Rehabilitation Program for Stroke Patients

As part of a core rehabilitation program for stroke patients, we designed Rehab-Master (shown in Figure 7.1). This commercial project aimed to treat physically impaired patients in their own homes. RehabMaster progresses in two stages for rehabilitating the patients. In the first stage, physiatrists (or rehabilitation physicians) who specialise in non-surgical physical medicine and rehabilitation for patients with physical disabilities or impairments resulting from disease or injury offer the training set to the patient depending on the patient's status. Based on the physiatrist's diagnosis, patients do certain RehabMaster programs guided by the occupational therapist at hospital; otherwise they are given the home-based training program. The training programs consist of 36 types of motor skill exercises, and the patient's performance through the exercises is applied to the game-based training exercises in the second stage. The game-based rehabilitation programs

**FIGURE 7.1** RehabMaster: a rehabilitation program for stroke patients

comprise different types of physical exercises, but they are entertaining ones such as goalkeeping and swimming with dolphins. These are specially designed to help motivate the stroke patients to complete the physical rehabilitation with fun. The performance and training data collected by the system are sent back to the phys-iatrists to monitor the conditions or states of the patients. As part of the grand U-Health project in Korea, RehabMaster is now being introduced to the stroke patients at several Hanyang University Hospitals and the patients' homes, and around 75% of the stroke patients hospitalised completed their training program with it, using it for at least around half an hour per day.

However, at present, no communication activity between the physiatrists and the patients through RehabMaster is implemented, which would limit an effective home-based rehabilitation program. This lack of communication dis-couraged the participants of this pilot project and slowed their rehabilitation progress. Hence, the last stage of the project considered a new artefact that is able to support communication activity and emotional supports from other users of RehabMaster, which falls into the realm of learning technology. In so doing, we applied activity theory (AT) to figure out how the current work practices might be changed by the new artefact called RehabMaster Mobile as a key module for RehabMaster.

# Activity Design for RehabMaster Mobile: Mobile Learning for Stroke Patients

## Current Work Practice Analysis

The current work practices and activities can be summarised as shown in Figure 7.2. The activity systems are committed to articulate how a new work context would change current work practices, and what contradictions or tensions might be resolved with use of RehabMaster Mobile.

The key to success in rehabilitation is exercising properly and getting helpful information. At this point, information needed means not only the stroke-related information, but also emotional encouragement that has an effect on the patient's motivation to further participate in the training sessions with RehabMaster. At present, RehabMaster is installed in two different sites (i.e., hospitals and homes). The differences in the two activity systems arise from who constitutes the community in collaboration. As to the hospital-based activity system, the patients and their caregivers might easily get some advice or information from physiatrists or occupational therapists. In contrast, this would not be the common case at home except as they are able to directly communicate with them over the phone. The lack of communication between the patient and physiatrist at the home-based rehabilitation program is seen as a driving force to make the stroke patients (or their caregivers) look for the information from others, which is depicted in Figure 7.3. Of course, this conversely leads us to develop a mobile-based online community for the home-based RehabMaster users.

In the sense that the communication between the physiatrist and patient has a profound impact not just on the relationship between them but also on the outcomes of care (Roter & Hall, 1992), the possible contradictions should be removed. However, simply providing an online community for the *RehabMaster*

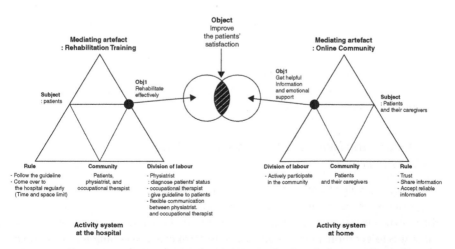

FIGURE 7.2 Current work practices and activities involved with the use of RehabMaster

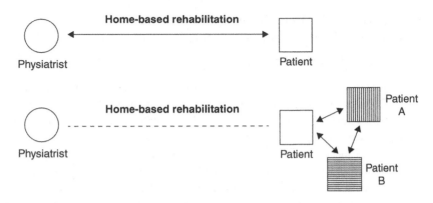

**FIGURE 7.3** How stroke patients seek information from others

users would not be good in that the information to be shared might not be legitimate or reliable. To deal with this, the immediate inclusion of professionals in the community might not be a proper solution either. Our reconnoitering observation on several disease-related online communities in Korea revealed that the community consisting of only patients and their family members seemed to be much more active than others (12 major bulletin boards were observed for three months, and it was found that only one bulletin board had a strong involvement with the healthcare professionals). These current work practices have to be considered in designing RehabMaster Mobile.

## New Work Practices with RehabMaster Mobile

Based on the understanding of the current activity systems in the relevant contexts, as above, we conceptually situated a new artefact (here, it is a new mobile-based social networking service) in the context of the current activity systems by identifying whether the other entities or nodes (i.e., users, communities, environments, activities and rules) would be affected by the introduction of this new artefact and, more importantly, whether users' intrinsic activities in which the typical tasks are supposed to be embedded would differ from the current activity systems. The procedure for the contextualisation of our social networking service system is outlined in Figure 7.4.

### Understand the New Activities in Using the Proposed Mobile Application

In delivering RehabMaster Mobile to the RehabMaster users, it can be seen that the patients (or their caregivers) may be geared to finding the information for their own rehabilitation courses at home. From the patient's perspective, he or she wants to get more practical information, particularly matching his or her own cases from either the physiatrist or other users with similar symptoms.

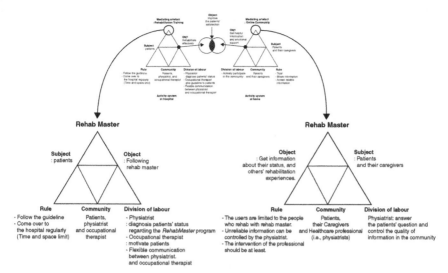

**FIGURE 7.4** Procedure for the contextualization of the proposed social networking service system

## Understand Whether the Proposed Mobile Application Would Support the Users' Intrinsic Activities

The caregivers are oriented to getting the best and most effective practices. For this reason, they will search best cases or ruggedised information, contact the persons who post the information and understand how they did it with Rehab-Master. The outcomes of the sequence of actions will also obtain the best possible practises, dietary information and so forth. Conversely, the persons who post their own experiences want to share their feelings or success stories, so they will post the details (e.g., photos or video clips) of their practises and something important to share. The mobile application proposed here would enhance this information sharing process without changing the intrinsic activities. However, from the physiatrist's perspective, some information shared in the online communities might not be legitimate; hence, the healthcare professionals who have a strong interest in using RehabMaster can monitor information and intervene on a regular basis.

## Consider Rules of the New Activities for Analyzing Contradictions or Tensions

When the existing mediated artefact (i.e., online community) is changed to RehabMaster Mobile, based on the analyses above, the current activity system becomes unstable and needs to find renewed stability thanks to the rule-producing activities. As shown in Figure 7.5, the activity system draws a context for the stakeholders (patients, patients' caregivers, healthcare professionals such as physiatrists) who will join the community-based mobile learning system. In principle,

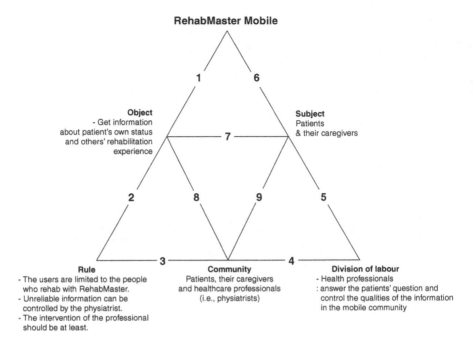

**FIGURE 7.5** Context map for stakeholders who will join the community-based mobile learning system

the three groups of participants would use one mediating artefact, RehabMaster Mobile, and this makes them have a strong community.

The mediating artefact-producing activity includes the intrinsic communication activities amongst the group members. Using RehabMaster Mobile, the patients and their family members or caregivers can get information about the RehabMaster-based rehabilitation program (the triangle with arrows 1, 6 and 7 in the above figure). They could ask questions or look for the relevant information via the mediating artefact (arrows 1 and 6), and connect with other patients or their caregivers or the physiatrists from the community (arrows 8 and 9). Developing their rehabilitation stories or other supporting messages from other patients (or their caregivers) in the community (arrow 8) can propagate some untruthful or unreliable information. Hence, it has to be controlled by the healthcare professionals (the rule-producing activities, the triangle with arrows 2, 8 and 3). Perhaps the primary contradiction from this triangle would be that the rule-producing activities discourage the participation of the users.

Finally, the communication between the caregiver and the physiatrist also requires a lot of effort (the triangle with arrows 9, 5 and 4). The second contradiction arising from this triangle might be how effectively the responsibilities and roles of the physiatrist can be divided. In particular, the physiatrists might be heavily asked to report their own answers back to the caregivers and to control the quality of the information in the community, which is not that easy.

**FIGURE 7.6** Artifact design of RehabMaster Mobile™

In sum, the two contradictions based on activity theory should be reduced in the design of a mobile learning activity, also focusing on socially constructed learning amongst the stakeholders. The artefact design of RehabMaster Mobile is shown in Figure 7.6.

## Reflections and Food for Thought

Whilst applying activity theory to the design of RehabMaster Mobile, we were able to derive several important characteristics required for community-based mobile learning specifically related to the health service. Building a learning community for stroke patients generates a lot of information that can be shared by the stakeholders. However, the reliability of the information is a key to the sustainability of the community. Especially for sensitive health (or medical) issues, community-based information sharing without an intervention by the healthcare professionals tends to include unreliable information that might cause negative effects. Therefore, the intervention of healthcare professionals (e.g., physiatrists) is of great necessity. For instance, within the RehabMaster Mobile community, the physiatrists are asked to filter out non-medical treatments or untruthful information. That is, the physiatrists could edit or delete the unreliable information to support the collaborative learning community. It would be of great value for caregivers, in particular, to use the right health information to support their patients.

Though this way of system operation could contribute to improving the quality of information, it asks a lot from the physiatrists. Initially, the physiatrists did not want to keep receiving a lot of questions via the mobile community (arrows 2, 8 and 3 in Figure 7.5 above). Even if they do their job perfectly, it might deactivate the patients' and caregivers' participation in the community because of their interventions. Hence, a higher level of information integrity can be maintained alongside the first-hand information by the caregivers, which establishes a positive feedback loop within the RehabMaster Mobile community.

The potential learning benefit of RehabMaster Mobile is also supported by Nonaka and Takeuchi's SECI theory (1995, pp. 73–83). The theory points out that the success of knowledge creation is dependent on several enabling conditions— "organizational intention", "autonomy", "fluctuation and creative chaos", "redundancy" and "requisite variety". The organisational intention in RehabMaster and RehabMaster Mobile is to ensure stroke patients are effectively treated. This is also a strong driving force for the stroke patients to overcome their hardships. In such cases, autonomy would be the strongest force to lead and motivate patients to use RehabMaster, and then RehabMaster Mobile would help them create diverse information or emotional supports that the healthcare professionals would not be able to present. In fact, through this process, fluctuation and creative chaos of their current knowledge might take place in the communication and information being shared, so evaluating the assimilation of the general methods that result from solving the given learning activity is essential. The design of Rehab-Master Mobile thus focuses on how to resolve this issue by generating several rule-producing activities.

Although the stroke patient's potential to create his or her own knowledge formed from active community participation is commonly regarded as inappropriate, it does occasionally break through and become visible. Engeström's expansive learning theory (2001) predicts such learning processes in which the very subject of learning can be transformed from an individual to a collective activity system. Initially, individuals begin to question the existing order and logic of their activity (e.g., the knowledge of how to use RehabMaster at home). As more actors join in (e.g., via RehabMaster Mobile), a collaborative analysis and modelling of the zone of proximal development are initiated and carried out. The theory of expansive learning sees the mechanism of transition in the stepwise evolution of contradictions (e.g., the heavy intervention from the physiatrists in RehabMaster Mobile discourages the participation of the patients and their family members) inherent in the object of learning—that is, in the activity that is being transformed. In different phases of the expansive learning process with RehabMaster Mobile, contradictions may also appear as emerging latent primary contradictions within each and any of the nodes of the activity system, as openly manifest secondary contradictions between two or more nodes, and as external contradictions between the newly reorganised activity and its neighbouring activity systems, which are shown in Figure 7.4.

In particular, dilemmas and conflicts should be also analysed as manifestations of the contradictions (Engeström & Sannino, 2011). That being said, a new work practice to disseminate meaningful information should be the primary purpose of the questions and answers posted through mobile learning. Patients and their caregivers used RehabMaster Mobile as a resource to question each other about issues that arose whilst living with their general illness and disability. Because the users in RehabMaster Mobile assumed the participants in the community all had a similar experience with strokes, the advice was sought from people they trusted.

Also, sharing personal perspectives indicates the willingness and tendency of the users to divulge views of their experiences and their personal feelings. For instance, caregiver A asked what training program could be most motivating for his father to exercise pleasantly on the RehabMaster Mobile. Just a few hours later, someone replied, "The training program, named swimming with dolphin, might be fun to play. When my mother tried that game, she loved it very much. I bet your father will like it." This is not just applied to practical problems with the rehabilitation problem, but also for emotional support. Through sharing their thoughts and feelings, caregivers could gain a sense of belonging and affirmation from someone who had been there before. For instance, caregiver B posted about her concern: "After my mother suddenly has a stroke in a day, she feels depressed a lot. She always says that she do not want to be a burden for me. In this situation, I could not say anything to make her feel better . . . " All the replies to the post were about cheering up caregiver B, and this helped to relieve her concern. It seems that the community could be a psychiatrist for the RehabMaster users, providing the place to express their thoughts and worries. The postings could give background knowledge for others to find commonalities to gain a sense of camaraderie. The RehabMaster Mobile users almost have the same value: be healthy and return to community living. The commonality made them empathise, and as a consequence this made them easily tell their own stories on the mobile.

Finally, supportive interaction describes a type of interactive communication between users that offers support and understanding of common experiences. Users mutually communicate with each other. Over time, they could follow each other's stories and often gave updates on what was happening in their lives (e.g., described a new test and suggested effective training programs). The users also posted cheerful messages and positive feedback to encourage one another through times of depression and uncertainty. For example, patient A was very active in the RehabMaster Mobile community. Through the community, he got helpful information and cheerful comments. He wanted to cheer up others in the community just like others had cheered him up before, so he posted a blue sky photo with a message that read "Cheer up, we will be better than ever", and people who saw the message replied to the posting with many thanks.

One pattern would emerge that links all the aforementioned relational themes together. *Therapeutic connection* describes the ability of persons with strokes to use RehabMaster Mobile as a supportive source for information, as a forum to share personal perspectives and stories and as a place to interact with people with similar problems. In effect, in designing a learning space for patients, storytelling was one of the key elements, which could facilitate the communication by setting a context for the common ground of the group and instil credibility. Information seeking, giving encouragement and sharing personal experiences are the main reasons people would use RehabMaster Mobile to obtain support from others with similar conditions, and our mobile learning research also aimed to support these work practises.

Stroke patients seek support to cope with the psychological effects of living with any level of disability. The ability to use mobile communication to seek support from persons with similar experiences opens up a new avenue for support that transcends the barrier of traditional care. However, the healthcare professionals should also maintain an open connection with their patients to clarify any questions their patients may have from the discussions, and studying how to help them to intervene would be another important project. For the healthcare professionals to facilitate help–seeking in this way, they need to further understand, through future research, this type of communication and its meaning to the participants, as well as the type of people who use this informal medium for support.

As healthcare with the help of ICT is emerging, many healthcare systems are suggested. However, these are more focused on the healthcare providers' perspectives in terms of monitoring the patients' status and giving them some feedback. As discussed in this chapter, providing the medical information related to the patients' illness would not be enough to empower patients to self-motivate. Instead, sharing rehabilitation experiences with other patients would be further able to support one's own rehabilitation. That is, the ways in which mobile learning can promote emotional support and empathy with other similar patients and/or caregivers might be key to further study. This requires a change in current work practises and a reengineered new practise that capitalises on current technology.

## Acknowledgement

This work was supported by the National Research Foundation of Korea grant (NRF-2014R1A2A2A01002583).

## References

Ahern, D.K., Woods, S.S., Lightowler, M.C., Finley, S.W., & Houston, T.K. (2011). Promise of and potential for patient-facing technologies to enable meaningful use. *American Journal of Preventive Medicine, 40*(5), S162-S172.

Alm, N., Astell, A., Ellis, M., Dye, R., Gowans, G., & Campbell, J. (2004). A cognitive prosthesis and communication support for people with dementia. *Neuropsychological Rehabilitation, 14*(1.2), 117–134.

Beckman, S. L., Argote, L., & Epple, D. (1990). The persistence and transfer of learning in industrial settings. *Management Science, 36,* 140–154.

Bendy, G. Z., Seglin, M. H., & Meister, D. (2000). Activity theory: History, research and application. *Theoretical Issues in Ergonomic Science, 1*(2), 168–206.

Bertelsen, O. W., & Bødker, S. (2003). Activity theory. In J. M. Carroll (Ed.), *HCI models, theories, and frameworks: Toward an interdisciplinary science* (pp. 291–324). Los Altos, CA: Morgan Kaufmann.

CIRCA. (2015). Retrieved from http://circaconnect.co.uk

Collier, G. K. (1980). Peer group learning in higher education: The development of higher order skills. *Studies in Higher Education, 5,* 55–62.

Curran, V. R., Lockyer, J., Kirby, F., Sargeant, J., Fleet, L., & Wright, D. (2005). The nature of the interaction between participants and facilitators in online asynchronous continuing medical education learning environments. *Teaching and Learning in Medicine, 17,* 240–245.

Engeström, Y. (1999). Activity theory and individual and social transformation. In Y. Engeström, R. Miettinen & R. Punamaki (Eds.), *Perspectives on theory* (pp. 19–38). Cambridge: Cambridge University Press.

Engeström, Y. (2001). Expansive learning at work: Toward activity-theoretical reconceptualization. *Journal of Education and Work, 14*(1), 133–156.

Engeström, Y., & Sannino, A. (2011). Discursive manifestations of contradictions in organizational change efforts: A methodological framework. *Journal of Organizational Change Management, 24,* 368–387.

Eysenbach, G., Sa, E. R., & Diepgen, T. L. (1999). Shopping around the internet today and tomorrow: Towards the millennium of cybermedicine. BMJ. Retrieved from: http://www.bmj.com/cgi/content/full/319/7220/1294

Gibson, C. H. (2006). A concept analysis of empowerment. *Journal of Advanced Nursing, 16,* 354–361.

Greenhalgh, T., Stramer, K., Bratan, T., Byrne, E., Mohammad, Y., & Russell, J. (2008). Introduction of shared electronic records: Multi-site case study using diffusion of innovation theory. *British Medical Journal, 337,* 1040–1044.

Jadad, A. R. (1999). Promoting partnerships: Challenges for the internet age. *BMJ, 319,* 761–764.

Kelly, L., Jenkinson, C., & Ziebland, S. (2013). Measuring the effects of online health information for patients: Item generation for an e-health impact questionnaire. *Patient Education and Counseling, 93*(3), 433–438.

Kikunaga, S., Tin, T., Ishinashi, G., Wang, D. H., & Kira, S. (2007). The Application of a handheld personal digital assistant with camera and mobile phone card (Wellnavi) to the general population in a dietary survey. *Journal of Nutritional Science and Vitaminology, 53,* 109–116.

Klemm P., & Nolan, M. (1998). Internet cancer support groups: Legal and ethical issues for nurse researchers. *Oncology Nursing Forum, 25,* 673–676.

Kurti, A., Spikol, D., Milrad, M., Svensson, M., & Pettersson, O. (2007). Exploring how pervasive computing can support situated learning. Proceedings from the *Workshop of Pervasive Learning* (pp. 19–26). Toronto: Massey University.

Lasker, J. N., Sogolow, E. D., & Sharim, R. R. (2005). The role of an online community for people with a rare disease: Content analysis of message posted on a primary biliary cirrhosis mailing list. *Journal of Medical Internet Research, 7*(1), E10.

Lave, J., & Wenger, E. (1991). *Situated learning: Legitimate peripheral participation.* Cambridge: Cambridge University Press.

Leont'ev, A.N. (1978). *Activity, consciousness and personality*. M. J. Hall (Trans.). Englewood Cliffs, NJ: Prentice-Hall.

Nonaka, I., & Takeuchi, H. (1995). *The knowledge-creating company*. New York, NY: Oxford University Press.

Park, J., Parsons, D., & Ryu, H. (2010). To flow and not to freeze: Applying flow experience to mobile learning. *IEEE Transactions on learning technologies, 3*, 56–67.

Roter, D. L., & Hall, J. A. (1992). *Doctors talking with patients, patients talking with doctors: Improving communication in medical visits*. Westport, CT: Auburn House.

Sharples, M., Tayplor, J., & Vavoula, G. (2007). A theory of learning for the mobile age. In R. Andrews & C. Haythornthwaite (Eds.), *The Sage handbook of elearning research* (pp. 221–247). London: Sage.

Slavin, R. E., & Madden, N. A. (1983). Mainstreaming students with mild academic handicaps: Academic and social outcomes. *Review of Educational Research, 53*, 519–569.

Tudge, J. (1992). Vygotsky, the zone of proximal development, and peer collaboration: Implications for classroom practice. In L. Moll (Ed.), *Vygotsky and education: Instructional implications and applications of sociohistorical psychology* (pp. 155–172). Cambridge: Cambridge University Press.

Tustin, N. (2010). The role of patient satisfaction in online health information seeking. *Journal of Health Communication, 15*(1), 3–17.

van der Eijk, M., Faber, M.J., Aarts, J.W., Kremer, J.A., Munneke, M., & Bloem, B.R. (2013). Using online health communities to deliver patient-centered care to people with chronic conditions. *Journal of Medical Internet Research, 15*(6), E115.

Vygotsky, L. S. (1978). *Mind in society: The development of higher psychological processes*. Cambridge, MA: Harvard University Press.

Whittaker, R. B. R., Bullen, C., Lin, R. B., McRobbie, H., & Rodgers, A. (2009). Mobile phone-based interventions for smoking cessation. *Cochrane Database of Systematic Reviews, 4*, 1–22.

Wicks, P., Keininger, D.L., Massagli, M.P., la Loge, C.D., Brownstein, C., Isojärvi, J., & Heywood, J. (2012). Perceived benefits of sharing health data between people with epilepsy on an online platform. *Epilepsy & Behavior, 23*(1), 16–23.

Yellowlees, P., Nesbitt, T., & Cole, S. (2011). Telemedicine: The use of information technology to support rural caregiving. In R. C. Talley, K. Chwalisz & K. C. Buckwalter (Eds.), *Rural caregiving in the United States* (pp. 161–177). New York, NY: Springer.

Ziebland, S.U.E., & Wyke, S. (2012). Health and illness in a connected world: How might sharing experiences on the internet affect people's health? *Milbank Quarterly, 90*(2), 219–249.

# 8

# ANALYSING CONTEXT FOR MOBILE AUGMENTED REALITY PROTOTYPES IN EDUCATION

*Brenda Bannan*

## Introduction

The learning context is a highly complex and multi-layered environment where multiple factors may influence learning and are difficult to tease apart for the purposes of instructional design and educational research. Context in learning has been defined through a learner perspective as something that is engendered in the individual and manifests through that person's interactions in the world (Luckin, 2010). Context has also been addressed from the designer perspective in software design and development and applied design research methods such as utilising applied research methods of contextual analysis (Goodwin, 2009). Finally, context has been described through learner-generated activities as a learner-centric ecology of resources that are deliberately deployed by learners to meet their needs (Luckin et al., 2005).

Complementary to these various perspectives on defining context in learning, this chapter attempts to address the designer-generated analysis of the learning context for the purposes of mobile application design and development to attempt to best meet learners' needs implementing applied design research methodologies. Certainly, an argument could be articulated that designer-generated analysis of context could coexist or be co-created with learner-generated contextual factors, but that is a topic beyond the scope of this chapter. Notwithstanding, the basic premise of this chapter is that if designers can provide more sensitivity to their analysis and definition of the mobile learning context, then we may be able to improve learning experiences through more informed mobile design and design research. To do this well requires a learner-centred or human-centred design perspective that incorporates design research methodologies that are described in detail later in this chapter.

## Mobile Learning and Context

Broadening the definition of context beyond traditional conceptualisations is important when addressing the analysis of the context of mobile learning. Mobile learning provides new pedagogical and technological affordances for learning that blur the lines between formal and informal settings, as well as employ the combination of user-generated and teacher-directed learning goals. Recent work on research in mobile learning states that an inter-, multi- or transdisciplinary approach and/or diversity of research methods are desirable in order to fully understand the unique pedagogical affordances of the use of mobile devices for learning (Vavoula, Pachler, & Kukulska-Hulme, 2009). Yet, at the same time, there is also a need for a common set of underpinning research and theoretical directions for the field of mobile learning that aims at specific research questions, data collection and methods for improved articulation of processes for learning technology researchers (Bannan, Pashler, Cook, & Bachmair, 2011). Design research may be able to address these competing demands.

## Context and Design Research

Assuming a broader view of context involves more than environment and technological tools, as it involves interactions amongst persons (motivations, knowledge, perception, directed attention, etc.), content (learning goals, selection, representation, delivery, integration, etc.), learning context (learning environment, analysed conditions for generating features) and functionality (trying out prototype in-situ, what works, what does not, how to revise, etc.) In his book related to design research and learning, Dai (2012) discusses how person, content and context issues need to be integrated and addressed simultaneously as the challenge is:

> . . . a) how to leverage students' knowledge, abilities and motivations while addressing potential constraints at the individual and interactive levels (person); b) how to direct attention and thinking to engender proper content representations in the service of overall learning goals (content); c) how to orchestrate important design elements of classroom teaching (pedagogical tools, technological support, social organization of learning) to enable optimum learning conditions for intellectual growth (context). (p. 26)

Dai (2012) also states that it is important that the social-contextual, interactive factors (activities learners are engaged in) and psychosocial variables (learner intentions and motivations) in a learning situation are defined, substantiated and operationalised for enactment and execution in educational design research. As Akman and Bazzanella (2003) state that context is a difficult construct to analyse and fully understand, it follows that educational researchers, mobile designers and design researchers need some methodology for examining or analysing learning contexts for mobile learning for the purposes of integrative design and research. The central question of this chapter is how mobile design researchers can better understand contextual factors through analysis in order to engineer, promote and improve learning design that may incorporate contextual awareness in particular settings. Context awareness then, from the mobile learning design researcher perspective, takes on a new meaning beyond the technology itself.

## Analysing Context in Design Research

**Design Research Process—Integrative Learning Design Framework (ILDF).** Design research provides a particularly useful methodological approach to investigate and uncover emergent learning phenomena, theory and applied technology where little theory or understanding about a particular learning context exists (Kelly, 2009). Design research can be described as integrating analysis, design and development processes with applied or empirical research cycles for the purposes of generating knowledge about the teaching, learning or training context whilst simultaneously working towards producing a useful learning innovation or intervention. Design research processes also involve leveraging data collection and analysis of user/learner participation or co-construction of curriculum, artefacts or digital components with learners to inform the design researcher's understanding about the learner's experience and knowledge of content or process for integrative design and research purposes (Bannan, 2013).

With the expanded view of context articulated above and afforded by current mobile technologies, the mobile design research effort can present pronounced pedagogical and research challenges. The cases described below attempted to address these challenges through graduate students employing a design research approach to investigate specific learning contexts through the design of contextually aware mobile learning augmented reality (AR) prototypes in education. A systematic process was employed using applied and user research methods to gather and analyse data for designing a mobile AR application. The design research approach was based on the integrative learning design framework (ILDF) that has been employed in multiple studies across disciplines and technology development (Bannan-Ritland & Baek, 2003; Bannan & Baek, 2008; Bannan, 2012; Martínez-Álvarez & Bannan 2013; Evmenova & Bannan, 2013).

The ILDF provides a four-phase, systematic process incorporating various applied and empirical methodologies appropriate to each phase (see Figure 8.1).

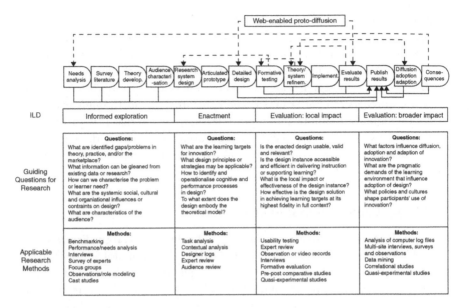

**FIGURE 8.1** Integrative learning design framework

The framework is not necessarily linear but recursive in its application, moving from the informed exploration phase, where a design problem context is investigated, framed and clearly articulated, to the enactment phase, where the insights from prior analyses are enacted into a prototype design with clear learning targets and a theoretical framework. Subsequently, the prototype progresses through multiple revisions and formative testing in the local impact phase in smaller group settings to finally move to the broad impact phase, where the locally tested mobile prototype is scaled up to larger numbers of participants and diverse settings. Design research has been employed in research involving many different technology-based learning environments, such as game-based learning, virtual worlds and eLearning applications, but to this point has had more limited reporting in the literature related to mobile learning applications. This chapter describes two cases of the application of design research methods to the mobile learning context, particularly focusing on the design and prototyping of two context-aware applications to demonstrate the importance of analysis of contextual factors for mobile design. The methods incorporated in the ILDF design research approach are described below by phase and methods incorporated within each phase and then illustrated by each of the two cases. The methods are varied representing both applied and empirical methods but are not exhaustive, as diverse methods and integrated cycles of data collection and analysis are characteristic of design research and rely on the selection of the methodology that best fits the design situation.

# Informed Exploration Phase

## *Problem Identification and Definition*

Problem finding, framing and solving in learning technology settings may be facilitated by systematic design research. Design research contexts have been characterised as interacting ecological systems rather than isolated factors or a collection of activities (Cobb, diSessa, Lehrer, & Schauble, 2003). In complex learning settings, it is essential to clarify the problem focus for design research as it relies on clear articulation of an identified gap in theory, practise and/or the marketplace to attempt to engineer designed solutions. Mobile technologies can add to the challenge of problem identification in complex learning settings as their use can blur the lines between formal and informal education in regard to who and what is facilitating learning and where (e.g., user-generated, socially shared, location-aware technologies), as well as employing the powerful combination of in-situ, real-world and virtual data (e.g., augmentative reality applications or digital layering of real world information in real time) (Bannan, Pachler, Cook, & Bachmair, 2011). However, applied and basic design research methods, such as identifying, defining and framing the problem, may be used to attempt to progressively provide increasing clarity on the design problem, setting and participants and interaction amongst these factors that comprise the learning context. Jackson (2001) refers to this process as locating and bounding the problem in software development by stating, "When you set about analyzing and structuring a problem, it's fundamental to determine what it is about—that is, where the problem is located, and what parts of the world it concerns" (p. 20).

**National Zoo Case: Problem Identification and Definition.** A design research team enrolled in a learning technologies graduate program at a university outside of Washington, DC identified a problem for mobile learning design at one of the area's most popular tourist destinations—the National Zoo. Their initial analysis revealed one important component of the zoo's mission statement is education; however, the zoo targets educational programs only for children from three to 14 years of age (preschool to middle school levels in the US). The team initially interviewed a zoo education specialist who stated that older teenage visitors (high school students) are an underserved population for involvement in educational programs at the National Zoo and attracting this population to the zoo is a challenge. The National Zoo staff indicated that their organisation is very interested in the potential of mobile AR to expand their targeted learning outcomes and provide educational experiences within the zoo for older high school students.

**Mount Vernon Case: Problem Identification and Definition.** Another graduate design research team identified an informal learning problem related to Mount Vernon—George Washington's estate, museum and gardens in northern Virginia. The team's initial analysis determined that Mount Vernon is one of the most popular historic estates in the US, encompassing 500 acres with 20 structures and 50 acres of gardens maintained as they existed in 1799. The team identified and targeted a problem related to improving the visitors' informal educational experience, which does not currently include educational or historic information related to the outdoor part of the mansion, grounds or outbuildings on the estate. The team also identified the related problem of the museum only offering tours in English with no support of other languages despite a diverse visitor population.

These two cases identified and defined formal and informal learning problems in complex learning settings or ecologies that could potentially be addressed through mobile technology. Framing the problems helped to begin to define the parameters of the design research efforts by ". . . capturing the characteristics and interconnections of the parts of the world it is concerned with, and the concerns and difficulties that are likely to arise" (Jackson, 2001, p. xii). Next, the analysis of the context continued with the incorporation of performance and needs analysis methods.

### Performance and Needs Analysis

Once the problem is framed, performance analysis permits analysis of the learning situation that goes beyond mere problem definition to attempt to begin to determine the parameters of the potential mobile solution. The performance analysis involves interacting with actual users, target audience members interacting directly with the design researcher immersing himself or herself in the actual setting, if possible, to best understand the learning context to improve design. Performance analysis involves gathering information quickly and efficiently from people involved, observing their environment, analysing workflow or process, as well as accessing existing reports, documents or research (Rossett, 2009). Needs analysis presents an opportunity to go more in-depth, after an initial understanding of the situation is established through the performance analysis, by collecting targeted data through interviews, focus groups or other qualitative or quantitative methods to inform the design researcher's understanding of the problem and form the foundational need that the design will address. When implemented, performance and needs analyses can provide in-depth information on the social, cultural and learning context, which is imperative for mobile learning design and for successful implementation of context-aware mobile applications as evidenced in the cases described below.

**National Zoo Case: Performance and Needs Analysis.** In understanding the problem and context related to high school students' educational experiences at the National Zoo, the design team conducted additional analyses of the context, employing performance analysis and needs analysis processes. The team identified a private high school that participated in a yearly educational trip to the National Zoo for their freshman class (14–15 year-olds). They interviewed the high school students and their teachers to gain an understanding of their experience at the zoo. The teachers and students stated that whilst it was an enjoyable field trip involving exposure to the animals, their habitats and environments, the experience was not a very structured one and was lacking in pedagogical value. The interviews with teachers revealed that they were interested in deliberately connecting science taught in the classroom with the zoo field trip to: spark students' curiosity about biological science, encourage students to work in teams, and guide students in developing critical thinking about science content. The team visited the National Zoo to conduct observations, interviewing the staff as well as the high school students who had visited the zoo previously, and demonstrated the potential of AR to these potential target audience members. The interview data revealed that zoo staff, teachers and the students were all very interested in employing interactive technology, such as mobile AR and context-aware features, to deliver a more engaging educational experience at the zoo. The detailed information from these multiple interviews and observations of the setting helped to better define the social (e.g., high school students operated in groups at the zoo), cultural (e.g., game-based designs were appealing) and organisational influences and constraints (e.g., engaging more with educational content) of the potential design features. The team then clearly articulated the initial parameters of the design research effort in a design brief. The design brief defined the design parameters to develop a mobile AR application prototype that provides an engaging, challenging and mature educational experience through a narrative quest that would incorporate high school level cross-disciplinary educational information and data using the exhibits at the National Zoo as anchor locations for the experience.

The design research team integrated existing learning theory in their efforts as well by reviewing associated literature and research that aligned with the design direction—in this case, prompting students to construct meaning in a self-directed manner to potentially result in improved learning outcomes (Bruner, 1996). The team also reviewed literature related to a technology-based game quest approach, potentially with AR features that could engage the target audience in transformative learning experiences (Hoge & Hughes, 2010; Squire & Klopfer, 2007). As part of the needs analysis, the team integrated their literature review with survey data from the freshman class who had recently visited the zoo. The results from these surveys were used to enquire into what activities the students considered important and their perspective on how to create an engaging educational field trip to this location. The results indicated that the social aspects of the trip, including being with friends, bonding with new friends, participating in group activities and learning together, were most important to this audience for inclusion in the design of the experience. Knowing where their friends were located in the zoo and competing in teams were also mentioned as potential features for the application. The analysed data from all these efforts combined served as the foundation for later design of the AR mobile learning prototype.

**Mount Vernon Case: Performance and Needs Analysis.** The design research team involved in the Mount Vernon project tapped into existing documents and data for their performance analysis effort. The team identified the overall demographics of the visitor population from ticket sales data. Data from a prior visitor survey of 226 participants showed that most visitors were female (61%), possessed a bachelor's degree (76%), earned between $50,000–$99,000 per year and traveled more than 100 miles to visit Mount Vernon. The adult age demographic broke down into percent of all visitors by age as: 7% (18–24 years old), 10% (25–35 years old), 19% (35–44 years old), 31% (45–54 years old), 26% (55–64 years old) and 7% (65–74 years old). This extant or existing data was useful in characterising the target audience as part of the contextual analysis of this design problem.

Additionally, interviews were conducted with visitors at Mount Vernon as part of the needs analysis to attempt to get more in-depth information as to their perceptions of problems or barriers to the educational experience at the estate. Analysis of the interview data revealed that visitors would have liked to have had more historical information and explore content and locations beyond the traditional tour that included areas they did not have access to such as the outbuildings and parts of the garden. The visitors interviewed indicated that a half-day experience at the museum was difficult to manage as there is a great deal to see and the maps were difficult to use with few signs available for guidance. The visitors would have also liked to personalise their educational visit according to their own interests. Direct observation of visitors on the estate grounds by team members supported these findings. At this point and based on the data reviewed, the design research team definitively decided to direct their efforts towards designing an educational experience that incorporated an estate tour mobile device application integrating AR features to provide an interactive, personalised and enhanced user experience that allowed the visitor to design his or her own personalised historical tour of the outbuildings and gardens in different languages.

As Dai (2012) indicates in any design research effort, person, content and context issues need to be integrated and addressed simultaneously. The performance/needs analyses for the two cases described and simultaneously integrated information about: high school students' and estate visitors' general knowledge, motivations and social and psychosocial factors, observations of the learning settings (i.e., zoo and estate), and applicable learning theory integrated with teacher perceptions and visitor demographics, perceptions and experiences. This initial level of analysis largely contributed to the design research team's deep understanding of the context of their learning situation to more clearly define, articulate and substantiate their intended mobile learning design.

## Benchmarking and Competitive Analysis

Benchmarking and competitive analysis are complementary methods to the analyses described above that attempt to provide a wider perspective on the broad context or marketplace, examining related solutions or applications that address similar problems or opportunities to the intended design. Benchmarking is defined as, "The process of continually measuring and comparing an organization's business processes against business leaders or organizations identified as best in class to gain information that will help the organization improve its performance" (Barksdale & Lund, 2001, p. 167). In software design and development, this process is referred to as competitive analysis or comparative evaluation that reviews the marketing landscape to determine a potential product's viability in the marketplace and can " . . . pit two or more products or concepts against one another" to evaluate an existing or potential design" (Goodwin, 2009, p. 650). These methods entail examining organisational best practises or individual learning technology product competitors' features and functionality for analysis of the market landscape or business context to determine a design niche or gap to potentially provide an alternative solution or an improved learning process or solution. In this manner, benchmarking or competitive analysis provides a broad view of context complementary to the deep view of the learning context provided in early methods.

**National Zoo Case: Benchmarking and Competitive Analysis.** The National Zoo project design research team undertook a competitive analysis early on in the project in order to determine what mobile apps may exist that relate to zoo contexts. The team identified that, at the time of this analysis, the following national and international zoos had mobile applications designed to help enhance a user's experience during their visit: Cincinnati, Detroit, Philadelphia, Dallas, Houston, Lincoln Park (Chicago, IL), Memphis, Columbus, Cleveland Metroparks, Woodland Park Zoo (Seattle, WA) and Tiergarten Schönbrunn (Vienna, Austria). In a cross-case analysis of these applications, the majority seemed to be primarily more informational applications in nature rather than educational and designed for a wide range of ages from children to adults. The animal information presented was limited to those animals found at the zoo (including their names, feeding habits, etc.), as well as highlighting programs or initiatives underway to save specific habitats or species. More structured learning experiences represented in their sample were found to be significantly limited or mostly unavailable and provided a sound case for this design direction.

**Mount Vernon Case: Benchmarking and Competitive Analysis.** In this level of analysis, the design research team interviewed employees at Mount Vernon who indicated that two other Virginia historical museums were considered to be significant competitors: President Thomas Jefferson's home, Monticello, and Colonial Williamsburg. A search online of tourism sites presents two additional museums that were similar in nature: President James Madison's home, Montpelier, and President James Monroe's home, Ash Lawn-Highland. All of these 'living history' museums offer visitors opportunities to learn about colonial American history and the lives of founding fathers and early US presidents through exploration of original buildings, grounds, exhibits and interpreters.

In a more in-depth, competitive analysis view of mobile learning in these contexts, it was uncovered in that the Montpelier historical museum estate offers an audio tour using the Acoustiguide system for a self-guided tour of the museum's gardens and grounds. Neither Monticello nor Ash Lawn-Highland offers any hand-held audio tours. Colonial Williamsburg does offer mobile phone apps for download off its website. At the time of this analysis, there were four different apps available: 'Visitor Information Center', which is a menu-driven list of information useful for a visit; 'Photo of the Day', which is a single static image; 'Word of the Day' and 'Today in the 1770s'. Colonial Williamsburg also offers visitors the opportunity to rent three different audio tours: 'Highlights of the Historic Area', 'Reading the Restoration Architecture' and 'Voices of the Revolution'. At the time of the analysis, none of Mount Vernon's competitors offered mobile phone AR exhibits or enhancements. However, over the past 10 years, different technologies have been tested and used in several different types of installations in museums around the world. Early adopters incorporated static touchscreen videos in exhibition rooms, which allowed museum visitors to interact with the content. In another example (Baltimore Museum of Art, 2005), visitors were able to 'handle' virtual objects and view and zoom in on different elements of the room configurations through a larger screen whilst also having access to additional textual curatorial notes on the items.

In their research, the team identified Cone Collection at the Baltimore Museum of Art that provided one example of a successful interactive AR museum experience. In addition, from 2005–2007 the Kärner Landesmuseum in Austria offered a test case for a mobile AR interactive game geared towards young teenagers who were asked to play the role of detective within the museum by searching out clues found in AR components of museum objects on display. These cases demonstrated the ease of use, power of engagement and potential for learning that AR can have in museums. In addition the analysis uncovered that the Stedelijk Museum in Amsterdam has recently deployed AR in two different ways: using the Layar AR browser with 3D works of student art and the Quick Response (QR) system, which 'reads' markers next to objects so that visitors can display curatorial information on their mobile phones whilst also viewing the museum objects. Plans for developing future AR installations that link up visitor experiences in the museum with related sites around town were being implemented according to the information located online about this effort (Rieland, 2012). The comparative analysis of these sample AR museum projects suggests design implications that for American 'living history museums', mobile AR apps could connect visitors to figures and events in history as they walk around locations or cities such as Alexandria, Philadelphia or Boston, where so much American history took place. This broader analysis of the wider context of museum and app competition greatly informed the progression of the design research direction in the Mount Vernon case.

## *Audience Observations, Role Modelling and Personas*

Typically in learning technology design projects, the designer gathers target audience information often limited to primarily demographic information in order to design for a particular population. This standard practise is limited in terms of thoroughly understanding the learners and learning context for the purposes of design research. Other applicable design research methods exist to generate a rich representation of the audience in a mobile learning setting such as observational research (O'Grady & O'Grady, 2006), role modelling (use in context) and personas (Goodwin, 2009). All three methods require an immersion in the learning context, interaction with the learners and observation of their behaviour or activities and are based on the design researchers' direct experience with the potential users of the design. The resulting data collection may involve analysis of the target audience or user's mental model, environment, any tools that are used, processes employed, materials or resources, as well as direct interaction with the audience members through interviews or talk-aloud protocol studies to understand their perspective on the problem or process as well as their frustrations and encountered obstacles. The design research teams utilised personas, which are defined as ". . . archetypes that describe the various goals and observed behavior patterns among your potential users and customers" (Goodwin, 2009, p. 229). The personas represent a composite of cross-case analysis of user experiences and data to employ as an anchored description for a human-centred approach to defining and designing the mobile learning solution as well as communicating requirements, building consensus and evaluating the mobile design.

**National Zoo Case: Audience Observations, Role Modelling and Personas.** The design research team working on the National Zoo project elected to represent their experience with teachers, zoo staff and high school students as important personas for their AR mobile learning designs. To create the personas, the team leveraged their earlier data collection, personal experience at the zoo with the staff, and focus groups with teachers and high school students to gain insight into their concerns, goals, behaviours and mental models, as well as demographic variables such as environment and tools that might impact behaviours. The result was three personas that attempted to capture and represent characteristics of potential stakeholders (e.g., zoo staff) and users of the AR mobile learning design (e.g., high school students and teachers) experience at the zoo, which greatly informed later design and evaluation of the prototype. One of the three personas (the high school student persona) is presented here as an example (see Figure 8.2) that was leveraged for design.

**Mount Vernon Case: Audience Observations, Role Modelling and Personas.** Based on the audience analysis from existing surveys of visitors as well as direct interaction with visitors at the Mount Vernon estate, the design research team was able to articulate several personas to work towards a mobile design. The

**Age: 14**

Siobhan's interests include history and English. She is a strong science student even though she does not particularly like science. Her writing ability is clear in her lab reports, and she has a creative way of thinking about how parts of our environment affect the other parts. Siobhan plays field hockey and is learning to play the guitar. She wants to be a writer. She is hoping to attend the University of Notre Dame. *"Apps have to be fun. If it's not fun, then it's boring and I won't want to do it."* Siobhan's father is a computer programmer and has taught Siobhan several programming languages.

| Technical Competence | |
|---|---|
| **Internet Browsing** | Competent |
| **PC Capabilities** | Competent; limited troubleshooting skill |
| **Internet Applications (e.g., Google Docs)** | Competent. Maintains her own website. She is a member of the school's robotics team. |
| **Program Competencies** | • Competent with Microsoft Word, Excel, PowerPoint, BlackBoard, Excel and Google Docs<br>• Competent with 3D architecture, Alice<br>• Limited HTML knowledge<br>• Programs in C++<br>• Uses a Wii to play games on a regular basis<br>• No troubleshooting skills other than very basic |
| **Mobile Devices** | Has owned a cellular phone since she was in third grade. Regularly accesses Facebook, Twitter and MySpace. Uses an iPod daily. |
| **Needs** | • Fun, engaging and interesting<br>• Quick action. Slow moving games are boring<br>• Needs to know what the goal is, no ambiguous time-wasters<br>• Must be realistic in appearance<br>• Colourful and witty with good quality audio |

**FIGURE 8.2** High school student persona for zoo project

visitor demographic and survey information revealed an adult population with language and disability diversity as well as children and professionals who visited the estate each with their own motivations and expectations. The team attempted to capture this diversity through a fatherly figure persona (see Figure 8.3), along with a professional with disabilities, an adult Spanish speaker, a teacher, and a high school and a middle school student, a group representative of some of the actual

## Personal Information

Ross Thompson is a married man with two children: Michael, age 10 and Olivia, age 8. He is an accountant at a large corporation based in Missouri. Ross has been looking forward to the time when his children would be old enough to appreciate a trip to Washington, DC to learn about the founding of the country and to enjoy all that the nation's capital has to offer. He visited DC once several years ago and has never been to Mount Vernon.

> "I can't wait to pass along my love of American history to my children during this trip."

His son Michael is "all boy", and enjoys learning about anything mechanical and taking part in active, hands-on activities. Olivia enjoys these activities as well and also has a love for animals. Ross's wife, Amanda, works in the IT field. She enjoys their vacations, but Ross typically takes the lead on planning because he enjoys it so much. Her goal for their yearly vacations is to spend time with her family and see the sites.

Ross has a lifelong passion for American history, particularly the Revolutionary War period.

The History Channel is one of his favourites, and he always downloads the latest history book that interests him to his Kindle. He definitely considers himself a technology-forward guy, as he loves having the "latest and greatest" and playing around with its capabilities. He purchased an iPhone when the first version came out and has upgraded as each new version has been released. He is looking forward to taking advantage of the iPhone's capabilities for planning during their trip. However, because of his busy work and family schedule, Ross has limited time for planning. The iPhone alleviates this problem, as it allows him to take advantage of little snippets of time during the day.

ROSS THOMPSON

**Age: 40**

**Description:** College educated professional. Married 12 years, Ross and his wife have two children, ages eight and 10. The family only goes on one major vacation a year, and Ross enjoys planning these trips.

**Technical Comfort:**

**PC:** Comfortable

**Internet:** Comfortable

**Mobile Devices:** Comfortable. Has had a smartphone since they came out and has upgraded as newer versions have been released.

**Other:** Uses technology in his profession, but also enjoys feeling like he is on top of the latest technologies for his personal use.

**Needs:**

Access to visit-specific engaging learning resources.

Tools to organise his family's visit for time and for interest priorities.

**FIGURE 8.3** Mount Vernon persona

demographics of the visitor population. The team arrived at their personas based on a synthesis of the existing data as well as the obtained focus groups, interviews and observational data. The inclusion of persons with disabilities and languages other than English was deliberate to consider diversity in the visitor population, and therefore the subsequent mobile learning design.

The crafting of personas based on synthesis of actual data to represent an archetype of actual users or target audience members of the intended learning technology design is a technique that maintains the fidelity of context through a human-centred design perspective. Personas preserve the behavioural, cognitive, attitudinal and environmental attributes, as well as demographic contextual characteristics, of the target audience to continually sensitise and resensitise the design research team to specific designs and affordances that are deliberately structured to match the intended users' needs and context. This design research method provides and maintains a rich, human-centred perspective on important contextual factors related to the user or target audience for the purpose of enacting a learning design in a specified context for a specified learning purpose, which will be discussed in the next section.

## Enactment Phase

### Target Learning Goals and Priorities for Instruction

Contextual analysis, design and enquiry involve a user-centred process to determine learning goals and priorities for instruction for design research. Contextual analysis has been described above in integrating diverse sources of information from practise, the literature, existing data and research to deeply analyse and understand the learning context for design purposes. Contextual enquiry is a similar term involving the collection and analysis of data from individuals in the field or learning context to uncover their perspectives, tools they use and problems they encounter to begin to determine how a potential learning design takes shape (Kuniavsky, 2003). Contextual design processes may involve determining learning targets and priorities, modelling of the learning task or flow, representation of learning patterns or strategies and functional and system requirements that parlay into a prototype (Holtzblatt, Wendell, & Wood, 2004). These techniques are particularly appropriate for mobile learning design, as the mobile learning context can incorporate both informal and formal learning activities and experiences requiring deep understanding of how, when and where the intervention may be used cross-context. Therefore, determining mobile learning targets or goals based on deep contextual analysis or understanding of these complex environments is crucial to then articulate specific learning targets, goals or priorities, and an important first step in the design, modelling and enactment phase.

To determine learning goals in design research, Sandoval (2004) captures the importance of consideration of context: "Designed learning environments embody design conjectures about how to support learning in a specific context that are themselves based on theoretical conjectures of how learning occurs in particular domains" (p.215). The design researcher begins with theoretical conjectures about how learning may occur in the context based on experience, prior research or observations in the content area and environment. These conjectures then manifest into more formal learning targets reflecting priorities for instruction and design that serve as the foundation for later testing and evaluation of the learning system. An embodied conjecture is a conjecture about how learning occurs or is supported within designed learning environments through the integration of available tools, how learning tasks are organised and the social participation structures in the experience (Sandoval, 2004). Learning conjectures, goals and priorities were established as the beginning of the design process in the enactment phase for the two design research cases.

**National Zoo Case: Target Learning Goals and Priorities for Instruction.** The National Zoo design research team attempted to integrate what they had learnt in their contextual enquiry into learning targets and priorities for the educational experience. The team's analysis revealed teachers' and students' desire to make the experience pedagogically engaging, but also specifically address the developmental level of the high school audience. The team decided their embodied conjectures were that involving high school students in learning about African grassland biomes in-situ at the zoo through a developmentally appropriate collaborative game may engage the students in learning about biomes and improve the pedagogical value of the zoo experience. The learning target was based on a constructivist learning theoretical approach of employing a group-directed, open activity structure that incorporated challenge and competition to correctly answer geolocated questions regarding the specific animal and habitat information related to the nearby animal zoo exhibits (e.g., the African grasslands biome). The challenge was further elaborated to incorporate developmentally appropriate behaviour of teenage groups by leveraging their articulated 'herding' behaviour into the game through group identification, but also by capitalising on the target audience's stated preference in analysis that they want to interact in groups with their friends when visiting the zoo.

**Mount Vernon Case: Target Learning Goals and Priorities for Instruction.** The contextual analysis of the Mount Vernon estate, leading to the targeted learning goals and priorities for a visitor informal educational experience, began with close examination of the estate's mission statement to uncover organisational values, norms and cultural expectations to help guide the learning design focus. This information was supplemented by existing visitor demographics and interviews with museum stakeholders, staff, master interpreters and visitors. Integrating this information helped to articulate an embodied learning conjecture that posited that supporting visitors through a self-guided experience with visual pathways and revealing geolocated information throughout the grounds and outbuildings of Mount Vernon would promote an enhanced informal educational experience. The specific learning targets for design were to provide interactive and personalised learning paths based on location and preference for visitors including translation for multiple languages. The theoretical conjecture or proposition was that utilising the self-directed mobile AR application would promote increased engagement, interest and satisfaction through user-generated and self-selected informational paths through the grounds and outbuildings that were not currently accessed in the estate experience.

The theoretical conjectures or propositions for design research efforts at both the National Zoo and Mount Vernon involved the reliance on geolocated digital layering of information to improve pedagogical value and engagement in specific outdoor educational experiences. The contextual analyses of the environment, stakeholder perspectives, target audiences and organisational values, amongst other factors, led to theoretical conjectures about how these educational experiences might be improved to facilitate formal and informal learning, which then led to formal learning goals. In these settings, the tools (i.e., mobile AR), the activity structure or how the task was organised (i.e., challenges to correctly identify biome information whilst in a related area of the zoo or expand the experience and information provided to make invisible historical information more visible in a personalised manner) and the social participation structures (i.e., capitalising on herding behaviour of animals in content and teenagers in social roles at the zoo and desire for an individualised and customised estate visitor educational experience) reified the theoretical conjectures or propositions in initial targeted design concepts to support learning and engagement. Contextual analysis plays a crucial role in integrating information about learners, setting, organisation and available technological tools to inform and articulate theoretical conjectures and learning targets for design research. The next section speaks to iterative development of the intervention that ultimately contributes to aligning and testing these conjectures about learning in context.

## Iterative Prototyping and User-Centred Design

The iterative prototyping or user-centred design process employed in design research can refine the intervention as well as the theoretical conjectures, as the conceptual design is articulated with embedded learning goals into a prototype that can be tested in-situ. The iterative design process attempts to uncover information related to agency and social and cultural aspects that manifest in mobile learning as well as usability and feasibility of the design. According to Obrenovic (2011), design research as a method of contextual enquiry advances our knowledge, specifically about: the problem we are solving, the process we are following and the solution we are building. The build and evaluate iterative process generates valuable knowledge about the use and viability of the learning design. The iterative prototyping process based on a user-centred approach also provides a window into contextual factors related to learning such as the learner's knowledge, abilities and motivations; obstacles or drivers related to the setting or learning environment; and how to direct attention and thinking to attempt to best engineer the desired learning outcome in context.

**National Zoo Case: Iterative Prototyping and User-Centred Design.** The design research team began to operationalise the theoretical conjectures and learning goals into a concrete design. The iPad mobile learning devices were selected deliberately to provide an important connection and crossover between the in-class learning about biomes and habitats with portability for an outdoor zoo field trip. The mobile platform with digital layering of geolocated information through AR applications provided the opportunity for the high school students and teachers to engage with the zoo environment. To flesh out the theory and design, the team generated a game concept that required each high school group to select an animal avatar (e.g., zebra) as part of a herd of animals and answer geolocated questions correctly in order to try to maintain the status of the group's food, water and size of herd. The game would be collaborative in that all of the high school student groups would be able to view competing 'herds' and their statuses whilst at different locations in the zoo. Taking advantage of natural herding behaviour in teenage groups, the team leveraged this behaviour and the zoo environment to provide an insightful activity structure that incorporated game-based competitive features and specific social structures targeted for this age group. In this manner, the in-depth contextual analysis was crucial to the subsequent design in order to best promote engagement and target specific learning goals in this setting. The game evolved through multiple versions of prototypes and was subsequently evaluated with student groups described in the next major section of this chapter.

**Mount Vernon Case: Iterative Prototyping and User-Centred Design.** The Mount Vernon estate design research team integrated information about the identified problem of the lack of educational information and unrealised informal learning experiences surrounding the outbuildings, mansion and grounds of Mount Vernon. George Washington was a notable horticulturalist with over 8,000 acres of land, which could provide valuable insight into the historical information and processes of the time. Given the targeted learning goal and based on interviews with guests at the estate, the design team generated an initial mobile learning design prototype planned for the iPhone using marker-based, GPS and point of interest (POI) AR technologies. These technological capabilities would allow for a custom and predesigned walking tour of the grounds of Mount Vernon as well as improve the information services (e.g., directions or signage to direct visitors at the estate). The marker scan features would provide more curatorial information on exhibit items throughout the estate. These features were a direct outcome of the contextual analysis and interview data, where guests stated they would have liked to personalise their visit to have been able to explore content beyond the traditional tour and elaborate on areas to which they did not have access, such as closures due to renovation. The prototype design provided a personalised solution for touring, additional educational information, signage, language and storable data on use and deployment of a mobile enhanced museum experience. The prototype was put through two rounds of testing in the next phase of local impact.

## Local Impact Phase

The local evaluation phase begins to uncover what happens when the design intervention is placed in the actual learning context to learn more about the learners, the learning environment and contextual factors connected to the stated learning conjectures. This is akin to a multiple phase process, including analysis of the context to determine theoretical learning conjectures, targeted design to enact these conjectures with sensitivity to the learner and context, and concluding with placing the designed intervention back into the analysed context. This yields different types of information related to usability of the intervention, as well as the enactment of the theoretical conjecture in-situ, through a concrete design that can reveal expected and unexpected information about the learners, setting and interaction between these factors. Dai (2012) states that it is important that social-contextual, interactive factors (activities learners are engaged in) and psychosocial variables (learner intentions and motivations) in a learning situation are defined, substantiated and operationalised for enactment and execution in educational design research. The two design teams involved in the National Zoo project and the Mount Vernon project attempted to conduct two rounds of local evaluation testing with resulting revisions.

**National Zoo Case: Focus Groups, Interviews and Usability Testing.** To demonstrate the application of contextual local evaluation techniques in an iterative design research process, the zoo team's testing cycles and subsequent revisions of the prototype revealed important information related to the learners and learning context. The learning target of high school students engaging in a developmentally appropriate and engaging collaborative AR mobile game learning experience whilst in the African grassland exhibit of the zoo provided several ways to test and iteratively expand the design whilst also gaining important contextual knowledge about this goal. The team initially wanted to gather feedback and more input on their initial design, so they implemented a focus group with high school students as an initial local evaluation cycle. A small group of 10 students were shown the budding prototype in their classroom once all the way through the experience and then again one screen at a time, when they were encouraged to freely share their thoughts on the prototype design, scenario, appearance, attractiveness and logical flow. Results recorded and qualitatively analysed by theme indicated that the students needed: clear instructions on how to play the game; questions, explanations and answers to be colour coded to distinguish; information regarding the potential benefits and losses in the game (e.g., size of herd, food supply, etc.) before answering a question; and visual alerts when food, water or herd size decrease. This feedback from representatives from the target audience for the design resulted in specific revisions of the intervention to better suit the audience (see Figure 8.4).

Interviews were also conducted with three game design professors. These interviews revealed that an interactive explanation of the game and tutorial were needed. Additional areas of competition were needed between the groups in

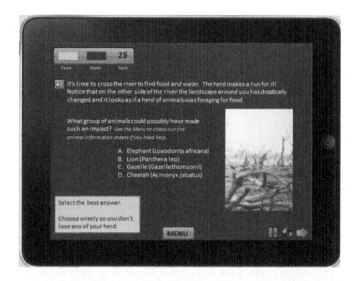

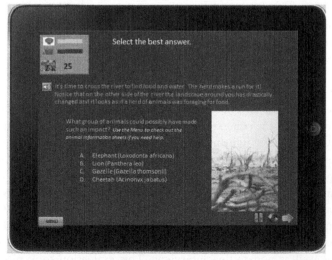

**FIGURE 8.4** Initial and revised zoo mobile AR prototype from focus group data

the game, so creating an achievement system and a map with progress checking was suggested. In addition, more user control was suggested so that teams could know where the other high school student teams were located in the zoo to add information whenever possible, as well as a timer to help the kids keep track of time.

Finally, the prototype was tested in the zoo with several high school students. Results indicated that there was a need for an interactive help guide for additional instructions to operate in the game. Elaborated visual information was needed to clarify interactions, as well as reducing the amount of text and placing key information in the centre of the screen to improve the prototype's readability on the iPad. It was also suggested that the size of the penalty should reflect the gravity of the error in the game. The testing within the zoo context or in-situ emphasised the need to allow additional time in the learning experience for students to take pictures and to take in the contextual information about the animals they encounter on the quest.

The local impact testing of the prototype with the high school students and game design professors and use of the prototype in the zoo provided a rich contextualised view of how the target audience and expert designers could progressively improve the prototype in design research cycles. The use of the intended prototype revealed strengths and weaknesses of the design prior to implementing it in the setting as well as in the zoo context experience. The AR mobile game prototype has much potential, as it has been positively received and designed in an iterative manner through focus group testing and revision. This limited testing with target audience members, experts and in context at the zoo revealed additional revisions, as well as motivations of the audience (e.g., wanting to see what other teams were doing and where they were located) and needs and behaviours that emerge (e.g., pacing of the game within zoo experience, perception of the size of the penalty or wrong answer being equitable with error in the game). Each design research cycle of analysis revealed a new slice of information related to the target audience and expert and situated or contextualised feedback to improve the design. The integrated design and research processes sensitised researchers to important perspectives or potential variables within the particular learning experience and context to greatly inform design direction. Diving deeply into the context, collecting data and analysing that data also adds to what we know about informal learning contexts for particular groups and settings, like high school students and zoo field trips integrated with an AR mobile game experience.

**Mount Vernon Case: Usability Testing and Interviews.** The local evaluation phase of the Mount Vernon project involved several cycles of usability testing. Initial usability testing involved five Mount Vernon staff members using the prototype with a script protocol recording their comments and observations, as well as post-testing interviews. This evaluation took place on the grounds of Mount Vernon to focus on initial reactions to and usability of the prototype and revealed some confusion about button names and functionality, desire for more visually appealing route marker overlays with the AR features, and additional instruction on marker scanning, POI markers and AR embedded in the prototype.

The testing also revealed that the users had difficulty visualising how the technologies would work together, as they were not fully functional at this point (particularly the marker scan and GPS-dependent features of the prototype). Overall, however, the Mount Vernon staff members were very receptive to the intervention, stating positive perceptions about this intervention for the target audience's informal learning experiences, such as that they: enjoyed the capability of obtaining more context-aware information about points of interest along a directed, customised path; thought the design was professional and the app idea had overall value and merit for estate use; felt the opportunities for contextualised audio would work especially well for teacher-chaperoned school groups or vision-challenged visitors; and felt the app combined information in palatable and manageable amounts to select the information a user wanted and "help people get from point a to point b" at the estate. These findings resulted in not only changes to the prototype, but changes in the usability protocol for the second round of testing to learn even more about this setting of design research.

The second round of testing involving the same participants took place off-site due to attempts to better simulate the full functionality of the phone application on a web browser. As the participants had already experienced a more limited version in the actual context, the goals of this test were to provide more detailed feedback on the function and flow of the majority of features (without the language feature) that the application would provide. The prototype was expanded and revised based on prior testing to include embedded information in two QR code markers for participants to scan using Zxing, NeoReader or other marker scanning apps available on their phones. One marker provided a link to Mount Vernon's website and a text welcome message. The redesigned prototype used Hoppala and Layar software to create a functional overlay that would allow users to download an AR Mount Vernon smartphone application for their use. The application, along with the functionality of Hoppala and Google Maps, provided a visual list of all the points of interest (POIs) within a specified range of a Mount Vernon location and allowed the selection of each option to customise a path to view information, related resources and/or videos. The prototype enabled the user to see nearby geolocated points of interest via radar graphic overlay and to have information pop up on screen for the user to see when in range. In the revised version of the prototype and in response to feedback from testing, the user employed the new 'take me there' feature to have Google Maps navigate the user towards a specified POI, using the walking directions option.

The participants were walked through a scenario of using the prototype at Mount Vernon whilst demonstrating the revised intervention. Verbal feedback was transcribed and participants were asked to complete a Likert scale related to their overall impressions. Results from this testing indicated that the participants responded positively to the interface changes, rating the visual appeal as 4.8 out of five. The participants also stated (four out of five respondents) that they would use the application and its functionality would improve the informal educational experience at Mount Vernon. One participant suggested that she wouldn't necessarily rely on a turn-by-turn guide as demonstrated but related that the overhead map of the estate with indicated points of interest would be enough for her to customise her own tour. Reminders and alerts were suggested to better manage the time effectiveness of the tour, highlighting planned and featured exhibits with digitally overlaid information. Overall, the revisions and second round of testing were successful in establishing the participants' positive reactions that the enhanced prototype would provide visitors with a more complete learning experience as a result of information provided at their disposal and customised to their needs. The intervention seems to be able to appeal to multiple audiences and make invisible information on the grounds and outbuildings visible and accessible to enhance informal learning about the estate.

## Broad Impact

Unfortunately, this 16-week graduate course design research experience did not afford time to further test the prototypes. Additional testing would be structured to involve additional participants increasingly scaling the prototype to more users. The broad impact testing would also attempt to better identify or characterise specifically how students' learning happens in these contextually-based information situations, specifically in these two environments based on the identified learning targets. However, much information related to the learning context was mined from the contextual analysis that would directly inform empirical mobile research methods.

## Conclusion

Despite the inability to progress to the broad impact phase given time constraints, the implemented design research approach progressed through three of the four ILDF phases and provided significant information and generated knowledge about the interaction of target audience members, the task and the setting that can greatly inform both design and research for context-aware mobile applications.

As Dai (2012) points out, the social-contextual and interactive factors as well as psychosocial variables and person, content and context issues need to be integrated and addressed simultaneously in design research. These factors take particular prominence in the design of mobile, context-aware applications such as the two cases described above. A systematic approach to analysing context for the purposes of design research has been presented through the integrative learning design framework and various methodologies employed in each phase in order to uncover valuable information related to contextual factors for context-aware mobile design. The analysis and design methodologies presented in these two cases attempted to reveal and leverage the target audience's existing knowledge, abilities and motivations to direct attention and thinking towards appropriate content representations in the generated prototype in order to best engineer and evaluate contextual conditions within the designed setting that may contribute to learning. Context-awareness in analysis as well as design is then, crucial, to attempt to create effective context-aware mobile applications. It is hoped that mobile designers may benefit from sharing these methodologies and an approach for their context-aware application design and research. Design research may provide a valuable approach to attempt to uncover information related to agency, social and cultural aspects that manifest in mobile learning, such as user/learner constructed content or participatory design experiences, and sensitise the designer to important contextual factors for improved design and research outcomes.

## Acknowledgement

Members of graduate student design teams contributed to the above described analyses and prototyping including: Mount Vernon case example team members—Deborah Baker, Matt Dworsky, David Lord, Jane Scharankov and Windy Schneider and the National Zoo case example team members—Mimi Corcoran, Beth Krause, Lisa Ogonowski and Jennifer Saville.

## References

Akman, V., & Bazzanella, C. (2003). The complexity of context: Guest editors' introduction. *Journal of Pragmatics, 35,* 321–329.

Baltimore Museum of Art. (2005). Virtual tour: Cone sisters' apartments. Retrieved from http://www.irc.umbc.edu/2005/10/01/cone-sisters

Bannan, B. (2013). GO inquire—geological observational inquiry: Cycles of design research in inquiry-based geological reasoning. In T. Plomp & N. Nieveen (Eds.), *Educational design research: Introduction and illustrative cases* (2nd ed., pp. 113–140). Enschede: SLO Netherlands Institute for Curriculum Development.

Bannan, B. (2012). Design research and twice exceptional children: Toward an integration of motivation, emotion and cognition factors for a technology-based intervention. In D. Y. Dai (Ed.), *Design research on learning and thinking in education settings: Enhancing intellectual growth and functioning* (pp. 53–84). Mahwah, NJ: Lawrence Erlbaum Associates.

Bannan, B. (2009). The integrative learning design framework: An illustrated example from the domain of instructional technology. In T. Plomp & N. Nieveen (Eds.), *An Introduction to educational design research* (pp. 73–87). The Netherlands: Enschede.

Bannan, B., Pashler, N., Cook, J., & Bachmair, B. (2011). *Pedagogically-oriented mobile learning research—the case of design research: A framework and examples.* Presented at *The Annual Conference of the American Educational Research Association,* New Orleans, LA.

Bannan-Ritland, B. (2003). The role of design in research: The integrative learning design framework. *Educational Researcher, 32*(1), 21–24.

Bannan-Ritland, B., & Baek, J. (2008). Investigating the act of design in design research: The road taken. In A. E. Kelly, R. A. Lesh & J. Baek (Eds.), *Handbook of design research methods in education: Innovations in science, technology, mathematics and engineering* (pp. 299–318). Mahway, NJ: Taylor & Francis.

Barksdale, S., & Lund, T. (2001). *Rapid evaluation.* Alexandria, VA: The American Society for Training and Development.

Bruner, J. (1996). *The culture of education.* Cambridge, MA: Harvard University Press.

Cobb, P., Confrey, J., diSessa, A., Lehrer, R., & Schauble, L. (2003). Design experiments in educational research. *Educational Researcher, 32*(1), 9–13.

Evmenova, A., & Bannan, B. (2013). ACTIV—adapted captioning through interactive video: Cycles of design research. In T. Plomp & N. Nieveen (Eds.), *Educational design research: Introduction and illustrative cases* (2nd ed., pp. 253–276). Enschede: SLO Netherlands Institute for Curriculum Development.

Goodwin, K. (2009). *Designing for the digital age: How to create human-centered products and services.* Indianapolis, IN: Wiley Publishing, Inc.

Hoge, B., & Hughes, F. (2010). The pedagogy behind the new century energy game: The potential for transformative PBL. *Journal of Technology Integration in the Classroom, 2*(3), 11–22.

Holtzblatt, K., Wendell, J. B., & Wood, S. (2004). *Rapid contextual design: A how-to guide to key techniques for user-centered design.* San Francisco, CA: Morgan Kaufman.

Jackson, M. (2001). *Problem frames: Analyzing and structuring software development problems.* London: ACM Press.

Kelly, A. E. (2009). When is design research appropriate? In T. Plomp & N. Nieveen (Eds.), *An introduction to educational design research* (pp. 73–87). The Netherlands: Enschede.

Kuniavsky, M. (2003). *Observing the user experience: A practitioner's guide to user research.* San Francisco, CA: Morgan Kaufman.

Luckin, R. (2010). *Redesigning learning contexts.* London: Routledge.

Luckin, R., du Boulay, B., Smith, H., Underwood, J., Fitzpatrick, G., Holmberg, J., . . . Pearce, D. (2005). Using mobile technology to create flexible learning contexts. *Journal of Interactive Media in Education, 22,* .

Martínez-Álvarez, P., Bannan, B., & Peters-Burton, E. E. (2013). Effects of strategy instruction on fourth grade dual language learners' ability to monitor their comprehension of scientific texts. *Bilingual Research Journal, 35*(3), 331–349.

Obrenovic, Z. (2011). Design-based research: What we learn when we engage in design of interactive systems. *Interactions, 5*(18), 56–59.

O'Grady, J., & O'Grady, K. (2006). *A designer's research manual: Succeed in design by knowing your clients and what they really need.* Gloucester, MA: Rockport Publishers, Inc.

Rieland, R. (2012, August 14). Augmented reality livens up museums. *Smithsonian.com.*

Rossett, A. (2009). *First things fast: A handbook for performance analysis.* San Francisco, CA: Pfeiffer.

Sandoval, W. A. (2004). Developing learning theory by refining conjectures embodied in educational designs. *Educational Psychologist, 39*(4), 213–223.

Squire, K., & Klopfer, E. (2007). Augmented reality simulations on handheld computers. *Journal of the Learning Sciences, 16*(3), 371–413.

Vavoula, G., Pachler, N., & Kukulska-Hulme, A. (2009). Researching mobile learning: Frameworks, methods and research designs. Oxford: Peter Lang.

Yun Dai, D. (2012). *Design research on learning and thinking in educational settings: Enhancing intellectual growth and functioning.* New York, NY: Routledge.

# 9

# MAKING SENSE OF CONTEXT FOR MOBILE LEARNING

*Mike Sharples*

## Introduction: Vignettes of Context for Mobile Learning

Children at an elementary school in Taiwan are engaged in an activity to reflect on reading (Figure 9.1a). On each child's desk are a small netbook computer and a stack of books that he or she has read during the past week. Working in silence, the child gives each book a star rating, types a short personal review and draws a picture with a stylus on the computer screen to illustrate the book's content. These are saved to the school's website, where children and teachers can view the ratings, reviews and illustrations.

A group of friends visiting the Long Gallery art collection at Nottingham Castle are clustered round a painting (Figure 9.1b). A context-aware handheld multimedia guide is giving a commentary on the painting that depends on movement, location and time. When the visitors first walk up to the painting, the guide announces its title and artist. As they linger, the guide speaks further information about the genre, style and content of the work. A little later it shows an interactive image of the painting on the screen, with regions that can be clicked to show text offering more detail of the characters and scenes in the painting. One person in the group reads the description and the others peer at that part of the painting, leading to a lively discussion on representation in Victorian art.

A team of students is on a geology field trip to the Newlands Valley in the English Lake District. They have been given the task of evaluating five technologies for providing visitors with an enhanced experience of interacting with the landscape: computer generated acetates that can be held up in front of a view showing labels that describe landscape features; a custom-designed application to make notes about views and locations; a GPS multimedia guide triggered by moving into a location; Google Earth running on a tablet computer; and a head-mounted immersive

(a)

(b)

(c)

**FIGURE 9.1** Contexts for mobile learning: a) personal reading in a classroom, b) discussing a painting in a gallery, c) exploring a landscape

display showing the landscape as it was 20,000 years ago with glaciers carving out the valleys. On a windy patch of grass halfway up the mountain, the students film each other describing the experience of operating the devices (Figure 9.1c).

Each of these vignettes illustrates an aspect of context for mobile learning. In the Taiwan classroom, the setting is tightly constrained. The children sit at near-identical desks in a traditional classroom with a single teacher moving through the rows inspecting the work. Through the mediation of a netbook computer, each child experiences a subtly different learning activity, based on a personal choice of book, and produces outcomes to be shared with peers and the teacher. This depiction of context matches the ecology of resources model proposed by Luckin, where context is "centred around an individual" (Luckin, 2010, p. 155) who manages a variety of resources (e.g., books and computer software) within a carefully-constructed surrounding environment that contains tools and resources to enable focused and productive learning.

The visitors to the art gallery are free to wander at will, but in actuality they keep to the lines of red carpet on each side of the Long Gallery. The handheld technology acts as a cyberguide, where "knowledge of the user's current location, as well as a history of the past locations, are used to provide more of the kind of services that we come to expect from a real tour guide" (Abowd et al.,

1997, p. 421). This notion of context matches Cole's (1996) context as container model, where the learner is embedded in a surrounding environment that orients, informs and constrains the unfolding activity. But the group is also generating its own context through interaction and conversation: commenting on the audio narrative, pointing to parts of the painting and discussing the artistry in relation to their own knowledge of Victorian art. Together, the visitors create a temporary 'micro-site' for learning in front of the painting, out of their immediate environmental, technical and social resources (Vavoula & Sharples, 2009). The context is a continually evolving relation between people, locations, objects and resources.

The geology students have been set a task to evaluate mobile guide technologies, taken to a location and provided with relevant resources. For the morning, they are free to wander the hillside, exploring how the different devices could assist tourists in interpreting the landscape. The students are not only situated within a location, they are also deliberately trying to make sense of their surroundings (landmarks, rock formations, glaciation) through visual inspection aided by location-aware mobile technology (Priestnall, Brown, Sharples, & Polmear, 2009). By viewing the landscape, testing mobile technologies to support sense-making and discussing their findings with peers and teachers, they are able both to improve their understanding of the landscape and to evaluate the tools for learning.

From these three exemplars of the management and experience of learning, we can extract very different conceptions of context that correspond roughly to *learning through context*, *learning in context* and *learning about context*. From the perspective of *learning through context*, the learner experiences context as a means to satisfy learning goals by deliberately or implicitly creating and augmenting interactions with people, environments and materials. So, the children in the Taiwan classroom are given the learning goal of recording their responses to books, and they are provisioned by a school-provided context of books, technology and environment to carry out their work in an efficient manner. For *learning in context*, the learner is aware of being situated within an environment that is fashioned to enable learning. Each movement through the physical space of the gallery is also a movement through conceptual space, from one work of art to another, where these are deliberately arranged to support an interpretation. This congruence of physical and conceptual space is exploited by the handheld museum guide that turns motion into information: it automatically records the user's physical movement and current location so as to provide relevant information about relations between the current painting and ones that the user has seen previously. For *learning about context*, the natural surroundings become the object of learning. Whereas the Taiwan classroom filtered out the surrounding world to focus on personal learning and the Long Gallery created a world of art within the confines of a single room, the concern of the students on the field trip is to employ mobile technology to interpret the rich natural world in all its "blooming, buzzing confusion" (Nardi, 1996, p. 70).

## Related Work: Conceptions of Context

Early work in context-aware computing was largely directed towards support-ing learning in context by integrating and abstracting data from environmental sensors (e.g., absolute and relative time and the user's physical location), as well as features indicating the user's current activity, preferences and social surround-ings (e.g., the availability of other users nearby or accessible online) (see Want, Hopper, Falcao, & Gibbons, 1992; Abowd et al., 1997). This approach considered the environment as a 'shell' encasing the user, described by scalar properties such as current time, location (positioning coordinates) and a list of available objects, technology users and services (Schilit, Adams, & Want, 1994; Yang, 2006). The work led to successful demonstrations, providing context-based content and ser-vices (Oppermann & Specht, 2000; Cheverst, Davies, Mitchell, Friday, & Efstra-tiou, 2000; Dey & Abowd, 2000). For example, researchers at the University of Birmingham developed mobile technology to provide location-dependent ser-vices that adapted to whether the user was walking, standing or sitting (Bris-tow, Baber, Cross, Knight, & Woolley, 2004). The MOBIlearn project developed a context-aware subsystem using ultrasonic indoor positioning, described in the gallery vignette (Lonsdale, Baber, & Sharples, 2004).

The problem with this approach is that it models the user as receiving data from an environment rather than interacting with it. The 'environment as shell' approach does not acknowledge the dynamics of interaction between people and their environment, for example as we move or modify objects around us to cre-ate a supportive workspace or form an ad hoc social network out of people with shared interests either in the immediate location or available online (Dourish, 2004). Furthermore, if we regard context as a negotiated construct between com-municating partners in the world, then it is likely that context as acquired by auto-mated sensing mechanisms might not match the continually evolving negotiation. Thus, the experience of learning in context may be most relevant when a single learner has a strong sense of time and place, for example when a lone visitor inter-acts with a multimedia guide in the surroundings of a museum or heritage site.

When people gather together to make sense of their world through conversa-tion (whether the semiotic world of books or the physical world of a gallery), then they not only experience context but also create it through mutual interaction. As Nardi states, "People consciously and deliberately generate contexts (activities) in part through their own [objectives]; hence context is not just 'out there'" (Nardi, 1996, p. 76). This generation of context through shared objectives relates to the puzzle of intersubjectivity: If we each have a personal experience of the world, how do we reach a mutual understanding? The answer to this longstanding philo-sophical conundrum is that we have a shared culture and language that allows us, when we meet, to rapidly establish a common accord. Even when we meet people from different backgrounds and nationalities, we share a sense of identity in the world and an ability to negotiate. That process of reaching mutual agree-ment, or productively recognising and exploring differences, can be enhanced by *contextual tools*: technologies that help us to interpret and share context. Consider a small group of people standing at a painting interacting with a multimedia guide. The guide directs the visitors' attention towards a part of the painting, providing enough information about the artist's technique and symbolism to establish a shared frame of reference so that people in the group can then discuss the work and contribute with their own knowledge of art and history.

## Context as an Explanatory Concept

Thus, context is an important explanatory concept in mobile learning. If we see learning as a mobile activity that can occur anywhere, supported by a wide variety of physical, technical and social resources with or without a teacher, then understanding the ever-changing context of learning becomes a central concern. Even in a school, students move from one classroom to another, shifting topic and teacher, but always within a predesigned structure. Outside the constraints of classroom and curriculum, we have to examine how people, individually or together, can create conditions for learning. A central research challenge is to reconcile the three perspectives of *learning through context*, *learning in context* and *learning about context*. Rather than regarding these as conflicting models of context, we should understand the interplay between them to produce a rich picture of contextual mobile learning. We are perpetually *in a context*, situated in a location at a particular point in time enveloped by persons, objects and resources, we *create context* through interactions with our surroundings, by holding conversations, making notes and modifying nearby objects, and we come to *understand context* through interpreting our environment, supported by guides and measuring instruments. Also, a learning activity can only be fully understood by taking an historical perspective (Engeström, 1996) to examine how it has been shaped and transformed by previous ideas and practises. This is particularly true of mobile learning, where both the immediate history of physical movement and the wider historical process of coming to know merge to create new understandings.

We offer an analogy of context as an ever-playing movie, a continually unfolding interaction between people, settings, technologies and artefacts (Figure 9.2), consisting of a seamless flow of scenes representing specific points in time, space or sequence of learning goals. Each scene of current context (e.g., visitors viewing a painting) progresses from earlier ones, and within the scene some elements are emphasised as relevant to the focus of learning and level of awareness of the surroundings. The entire movie provides a resource for learning. But this is a movie continually being constructed by its cast, moment to moment, as they share artefacts and create mutual understanding through dialogue and physical interaction. To understand mobile learning, we need to examine how people create meaning within and from their surroundings and how they carry that learning from one setting to another.

The children in the Taiwan classroom have been trained to ignore distractions from their physical surroundings (even when a group of visitors with cameras

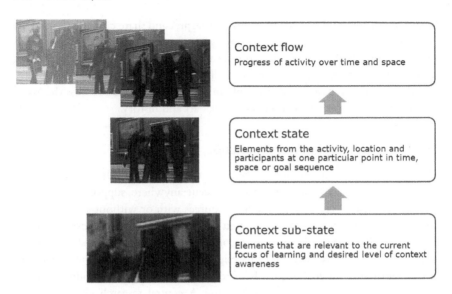

**Context flow**
Progress of activity over time and space

**Context state**
Elements from the activity, location and participants at one particular point in time, space or goal sequence

**Context sub-state**
Elements that are relevant to the current focus of learning and desired level of context awareness

**FIGURE 9.2** A framework for explaining context in mobile learning (based on Lonsdale, Baber, & Sharples, 2004)

entered the room, they barely glanced up and none spoke) and to focus exclusively on their interactions with their personal computers and library books. This creates the current context, providing a means to learn through reflective writing on the screen derived from the history of their previous book reading.

For the group at the gallery, each person has an individual timeline of previous appreciation of art, filtered through classroom teaching and personal interest, and these intersect as they collectively gaze at the painting. Fortunately, their shared culture and language is sufficiently predictable for the developers of the mobile guide to provide a human-computer interaction that enhances their context substate, indicating elements from the painting that enable shared learning.

The students in the Lake District have been prepared in advance of their situated learning experience by being shown the technologies they need to evaluate and being introduced to the location of the visit. Although they are free to choose the context state, this is guided by their shared history as geology students in a specific course and on a field trip. Theirs is the most demanding task, as they are simultaneously navigating within the context of the Newlands Valley, creating the context of a comparative evaluation of mobile devices, and as part of that activity using these devices to interpret the landscape.

## Implications for Teaching and Learning

As mobile devices become more widely adopted for learning within the classroom and outside, so teachers will need to understand context as a component of education alongside curriculum, pedagogy, assessment and resources. The screen draws attention from the teacher and the immediate surroundings, connecting learners to a world of interactive digital media. It forms a physical and conceptual barrier between the learner and the teacher and poses a challenge to the traditional teacher-led lesson. The science teacher in our Personal Inquiry project (Anastopoulou et al., 2012) found difficulty in capturing the attention of a class of children with netbook computers, eventually telling them to close the lids and concentrate on the lesson. At the other extreme, the Taiwan teacher had prepared a lesson where the focus was entirely on the screen, and she was available only when a child asked for assistance. The computer materials were filtered to provide just the educational context required for the lesson.

Between these extremes we have the current confusion of introduction of mobile devices into formal education. Rather than seeing this as an intrusion of technology or a problem of maintaining discipline, it may be better to regard it as an issue of context. How can teachers create new and productive contexts for learning? What filters are required to enable rather than restrict productive learning? How can children be educated to switch seamlessly between learning through, in and about differing contexts?

The MyArtSpace project (Vavoula, Sharples, Rudman, Meek, & Lonsdale, 2009) was an example of successful cross-contextual learning. Its aim was to support children for enquiry-based learning between the school classroom and a museum visit. For a period of a year, over 3,000 children used the MyArtSpace service at three UK museums. Typically, a class teacher introduced children to the aims of the museum trip. Then, collectively they formed one or more questions to ask on the visit. At the museum the children were handed mobile phones preloaded with the MyArtSpace software. Working in pairs, the children gathered evidence from the museum to address the question. For example, on a visit to the D-Day museum in Portsmouth (that commemorates the Allied landings in Normandy during World War II), a typical question might be "Were the landings a success or a failure?" Some museum exhibits had labels with two-letter codes (e.g., AX), and the children could type the code into the phone to view a multimedia presentation. They could also create their own interpretation by typing notes, taking pictures or making voice recordings. These were automatically sent to a personal web space for each child. Then, back in the classroom the children could review their evidence and produce a group presentation to address the question.

From the perspective of contextual mobile learning, the MyArtSpace project employed connected mobile and desktop technologies to re-present the materials collected within the museum environment in a form that could provide evidence for a classroom assignment. Whilst this addressed a well-known limitation of traditional school museum trips, that the museum activity is disconnected from the classroom learning, it also brought problems of classroom management. Generally, the children had no difficulty in operating the phones in the museum and were able to collect rich and relevant evidence. But back in the classroom, material was stripped of its context so that the children were sometimes unable to recall where and why they had created a picture or recording. Often the children had collected many more items than they could use in a presentation, requiring them to sort and select the material on the basis of a fading memory of the visit. For the teacher, there was the challenge of managing a semi-improvised lesson based on turning the children's collections into coherent presentations. Teachers on the Personal Inquiry project (Anastopoulou et al., 2012) faced a similar issue of improvising a lesson around data the children had collected at home or outdoors. This is unlike a typical homework assignment, where the teacher might assess the work produced at home but not try to integrate it into a classroom lesson.

The issue might be addressed by structuring the collection process so that the materials children bring into the classroom are pre-organised and described to assist the lesson, with the teacher having access to metadata (such as where and when each item was collected plus a title or short description). But this is one example of a more general problem of students failing to apply knowledge and skills gained in one context to other situations. Perkins and Salomon (1988) discuss how to address the problem of transfer of knowledge through a process of 'bridging', where learners are supported in making abstractions from their contextualised experience so that knowledge gained in one specific setting can be applied broadly across many contexts. In the museum example, that might involve the teacher guiding the students to be careful in capturing only materials that are relevant to the initial question and to elaborate these with notes about when, where and why they were collected and how each collected item relates to the initial question. Then, back in the classroom the teacher might ask groups of children to organise their collections around themes or different responses to the question. For other outside contexts, such as field trips, the technology may make a greater contribution by logging the time and location or providing additional tools to help students in connecting and reflecting on their findings in the field (Brown, 2010).

## Implications for Design of Mobile Learning

Implementing new technologies to support learning within and across contexts is now a major concern of mobile learning. Well-designed applications could help learners to plan a sequence of activities across times and locations, collect and elaborate information in the field, share the data with other learners and teachers as it is being acquired, set up micro-sites to reflect on the contextualised learning, and enable their knowledge and experience to flow from one context to another.

As part of the MOBIlearn European Commission 5th Framework project (IST-2001–37187), we developed and implemented an interactional model of contextual learning (Lonsdale, Baber, & Sharples, 2004), whereby learners create context through continual interaction with technologies, other people, artefacts and surroundings. A similar approach was adopted by Kurti (2008), who describes a context model of interaction between learners and services based on the three axes of location/environment, activity/task and personal/interpersonal attributes. Kurti's model was implemented in the AMULETS project for children to learn about environmental sciences by combining classroom and outdoor activities (Spikol, Kurti, & Milrad, 2009).

Figure 9.3 shows the abstract hierarchical model of context that was developed for the MOBIlearn project. Context is represented as a dynamic process of interaction with historical dependencies. For example, family members visiting a museum create context by interacting with the exhibits, the museum space, themselves and other visitors. Their current context is influenced by previous visits, routes and activities. A context state is a snapshot of a particular point in this ongoing process of generating context through interaction. A context substate is the set of those elements from the context state that are directly relevant to support of the current task and activity and that can be explicitly modelled. Lastly, context features are the individual, atomic elements found within a context substate, and each refers to one specific aspect of interaction in context (e.g., the current location, the time, the closest exhibit or another person within communication range).

Contextual information can be represented as XML documents, and Figure 9.3 shows the interaction and flow of data between components. Contextual metadata (1) is either acquired automatically (from sensors or other software subsystems) or constructed from patterns of existing context data, or input directly by the user (see Chan, Sharples, Vavoula, & Lonsdale, 2004). This metadata is integrated to form context feature objects (CFOs) that represent the user's setting, current and previous activity, device capabilities and so on to derive a context substate

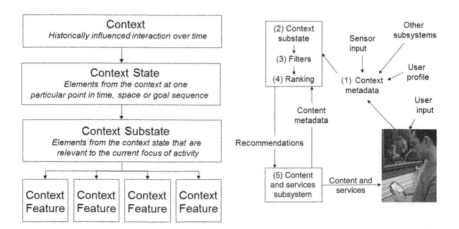

**FIGURE 9.3** The MOBIlearn implementation of a model of context for learning (Lonsdale, Baber, & Sharples, 2004).

(2). This context substate is first filtered (3) to exclude any unsuitable content (e.g., high-resolution images that cannot be displayed on the mobile device) and to then rank the remaining content (4) to determine the best options. The ranked set of options is sent to the content and services subsystem (5) to activate appropriate content, services or interface presentations to the user. CFOs are created at runtime from a set of definitions provided by the designer of the context-aware experience for which the system is being employed. These definitions specify values for the parameters such as the relative salience values for different CFOs and the links between them. To achieve more complex interactional modelling of content, CFOs can be linked together so that their function can depend on the state of other context feature objects. Link objects are used to send to other context features either the values of context features or the time they have held that value. Criteria associated with each link determine what action should be taken.

To give a simple example, a player of an outdoor educational game is standing in front of an unusual object with a context-aware mobile device. The device is continually updating a model of the context, based on the player's profile (skill level, objects successfully identified, etc.), location, routes, resources (virtual and physical) and the availability of other players. The CFOs of all current players are linked so that each person's context subsystem can detect similarities of context and opportunities for proposing content (such as hints) and services (such as asking another player for advice, or forming a team to solve a particular distributed problem). The players can continually modify their profiles, either implicitly through activity (such as finding an object) or by making explicit changes to their parameters through the interface.

There are many research challenges associated with each stage of the process. Deriving a context substate involves a process of data merging and abstraction to produce a problem-oriented representation of the user's current context. Employing the context features to enhance human experience requires an investigation of the costs (in time, disturbance and resources) to construct context features against the possible benefits from more direct support for activity and interaction.

A more general issue for designers of mobile learning to consider is whether there is value in developing technologies that implement explicit models of context (as with the MOBIlearn project) or whether it would be more cost-effective to develop more generic 'awareness and reflection' tools such as dynamic maps showing the location of oneself and others, note-taking applications and probes to sample the environment. Technology designers need to work within a set of trade-offs between simplicity and complexity of the interface and between context-specific and generic tools for learning. We are only beginning to understand how to design for learning within and across contexts.

## A Broader Notion of Context

So far, this chapter has kept within a somewhat restricted notion of context: as a physical, social and semiotic environment that learners, individually or collectively, are situated within, create through their interactions and understand through probes and reflections. Now we take the luxury of extending that notion to consider the broader contextual implications of mobile learning. Learning is historically and culturally contextualised: what is considered appropriate to learn, and how that learning should be conducted, differs across countries, cultures and periods in history. We tend to become fixated on our own historical and cultural context such that it seems natural to teach or learn in a particular style, with other methods appearing difficult or alien. In an interconnected world of rapidly changing technologies and intermingling cultures, such differences inevitably produce tensions that mobile technologies can exacerbate—by providing personal devices designed and manufactured in one particular country for use worldwide, by promoting software applications for a global market and by enabling users to carry their learning and leisure activities with them wherever they go.

Mobile learning is already conceived differently across national contexts, for example with a focus on personalised learning and just-in-time instruction in the United States, on classrooms equipped with 'one-to-one' technology in Taiwan and on learning between school and home in the UK. Each of these notions of mobile learning brings its own context-oriented issues and opportunities. Personalised learning must confront the problem of adapting instructional content and delivery to the learner's needs and location.

Goodyear (2011) frames this problem of enabling personalised learning within a global education system in terms of two shifts in educational research. The first is to understand how learning activity is distributed across differing contexts, with the implication not only that learning and teaching should adapt to context but also that learners and teachers continually shape their environments to meet changing needs. The second is to embed the practise of design into education so that teachers and educational leaders do not just react to innovations in technology and pedagogy, but take an active role in designing new ecologies for learning. Teachers are best placed to understand the opportunities afforded by children bringing their personal technologies into the classroom and to design activities that connect learning in the classroom, at home and outdoors.

There is neither a simple solution to the tensions and disruptions of mobile technology nor a guaranteed way to enhance learning by providing access to educational content anywhere, anytime. But by examining context as a construct that enables learners to make sense of the surrounding world and to carry an abstracted version of that sense-making to other locations and social situations, we may come to an expanded notion of mobile learning that embraces not only the three vignettes at the start of this chapter, but also the many other settings, activities and technologies, already existing and still to be invented, that constitute mobile learning.

## References

Abowd, G.D., Atkeson, C.G., Hong, J., Long, S., Kooper, R., & Pinkerton, M. (1997). Cyberguide: A mobile context-aware tour guide. *Wireless Networks*, *3*(5), 421–433.

Anastopoulou, A., Sharples, M., Ainsworth, S., Crook, C., O'Malley, C., & Wright, M. (2012). Creating personal meaning through technology-supported science learning across formal and informal settings. *International Journal of Science Education, 34*(2), 251–273.

Bristow, H.W., Baber, C., Cross, J., Knight, J., & Woolley, S.I. (2004). Defining and evaluating context for wearable computers. *International Journal of Human-Computer Studies, 60*, 798–819.

Brown, E. (Ed.). (2010). Education in the wild: Contextual and location-based mobile learning in action. *Report from the STELLAR Alpine Rendez-Vous Workshop Series*. Nottingham: Learning Sciences Research Institute, University of Nottingham.

Chan, T., Sharples, M., Vavoula, G., & Lonsdale, P. (2004). Educational metadata for mobile learning. In J. Roschelle, T. Chan, Kinshuk & S. J. H. Yand (Eds.), Proceedings from *The 2nd IEEE International Workshop on Wireless and Mobile Technologies in Education (WMTE)* (pp. 197–198). Los Alamitos, CA: Computer Society Press.

Cheverst, K., Davies, N., Mitchell, K., Friday, A., & Efstratiou, C. (2000). Developing context-aware electronic tourist guide: Some issues and experiences. Proceedings from *CHI 2000* (pp. 17–24). The Netherlands.

Cole, M. (1996). *Cultural psychology: A once and future discipline*. Cambridge, MA: Harvard University Press.

Dey, A., & Abowd, G. (2000). CyberMinder: A context-aware system for supporting reminders. In P. Thomas & H-W. Gellerson (Eds.), *Handheld and Ubiquitous Computing* (pp.172–186). Berlin: Springer-Verlag.

Dourish, P. (2004). What we talk about when we talk about context. *Personal and Ubiquitous Computing, 8*(1), 19–30.

Engeström, Y. (1996). *Perspectives on activity theory*. Cambridge: Cambridge University Press.

Goodyear, P. (2011). Emerging methodological challenges for educational research. In L. Markauskaite, P. Freebody & J. Irwin (Eds.), *Methodological choice and design: Scholarship, policy and practice in social and educational research* (pp. 253–266). New York, NY: Springer.

Kurti, A. (2008). Context modelling to support the design of mobile learning. Proceedings from *The 5th International Conference on Soft Computing as Transdisciplinary Science and Technology* (pp. 536–541). ACM.

Lonsdale, P., Baber, C., & Sharples, M. (2004). A context awareness architecture for facilitating mobile learning. In J. Attewell & C. Savill-Smith (Eds.), *Learning with mobile devices: Research and development* (pp. 79–85). London: Learning and Skills Development Agency.

Luckin, R. (2010). Learning contexts as ecologies of resources: A unifying approach to the interdisciplinary development of technology rich learning activities. *International Journal on Advances in Life Sciences, 2*(3&4), 154–164.

Nardi, B. (1996). Studying context: A comparison of activity theory, situated action models and distributed cognition. In B.A. Nardi (Ed.), *Context and consciousness: Activity theory and human-computer interaction* (pp. 69–102). Cambridge, MA: MIT Press.

Oppermann, R., & Specht, M. (2000). A context-sensitive nomadic exhibition guide. In P. Thomas & H-W. Gellerson (Eds.), *Handheld and ubiquitous computing* (pp. 127–142). Berlin: Springer-Verlag.

Perkins, D. N., & Salomon, G. (1988). Teaching for transfer. *Educational Leadership, 46*, 22–32.

Priestnall, G., Brown, E., Sharples, M., & Polmear, G. (2009). A student-led comparison of techniques for augmenting the field experience. In D. Metcalf, A. Hamilton & C. Graffeo (Eds.), Proceedings from *8th World Conference on Mobile and Contextual Learning (mLearn 2009)* (pp. 195–198). Orlando, FL. 28–30 October 2009.

Schilit, B., Adams, N., & Want, R. (1994). Context-aware computing applications. Proceedings from the *IEEE Workshop on Mobile Computing Systems and Applications (WMCSA'94)* (pp. 89–101). Santa Cruz, CA.

Spikol, D., Kurti, A., & Milrad, M. (2008). Collaboration in contact as a framework for designing innovative mobile learning activities. In H. Ryu & D. Parsons (Eds.), *Innovative mobile learning: Techniques and technologies* (pp. 172–196). Hershey, PA: IGI Global.

Vavoula, G., & Sharples, M. (2009). Meeting the challenges in evaluating mobile learning: A 3-level evaluation framework. *International Journal of Mobile and Blended Learning, 1*(2), 54–75.

Vavoula, G., Sharples, M., Rudman, P., Meek, J., & Lonsdale, P. (2009). MyArtSpace: Design and evaluation of support for learning with multimedia phones between classrooms and museums. *Computers and Education, 53*(2), 286–299.

Want, R., Hopper, A., Falcao, V., & Gibbons, J. (1992). The active badge location system. *ACM Transactions on Information Systems, 10*(1), 91–102.

Yang, S.J.H. (2006). Context aware ubiquitous learning environments for peer-to-peer collaborative learning. *Educational Technology & Society, 9*(1), 188–201.

# 10

# BEYOND INNOVATION IN MOBILE LEARNING

## Towards Sustainability in Schools

*Teresa Cerratto-Pargman and Marcelo Milrad*

## Introduction

Research efforts in the field of mobile learning have gained much attention in recent years. Mobile technologies and applications today play a central role in achieving a closer relationship between the information they offer, a physical location and the ways in which learning and communication can be mediated by the availability of the device (Sharples, Arnedillo-Sanchez, Milrad, & Vavoula, 2009). From the late 1990s, a substantial number of research projects on mobile learning have been conducted in both formal and informal learning settings to investigate the impact of the use of mobile technologies on learning activities and teaching practises.

According to Frohberg, Goth, and Schwabe (2009), Kukulska-Hulme, Sharples, Milrad, and Arnedillo-Sanchez (2009), and Wingkvist and Ericcson (2010), much of the research work conducted in the field of mobile learning has concentrated on design and development of technological solutions to support teaching and learning across contexts (e.g., formal and informal outdoors and indoors). Evidence of such a research orientation is reflected in European research projects, for example HandLeR (Sharples, Corlett, & Westmancott, 2002), CAERUS (Naismith, Sharples, & Ting, 2005), MOBIlearn (Lonsdale et al., 2004), MyArtSpace (Vavoula, Sharples, Rudman, Lonsdale, & Meek, 2007), and Mystery at the Museum (Cabrera et al., 2005). Other projects, particularly conducted in the UK and Sweden, have been salient for working in close collaboration with schools and museums. This is the case of research activities conducted in projects such as Savannah (Benford et al., 2004), The Treasure Hunt (Spikol & Milrad, 2008), Amulets (Kurti, Spikol, & Milrad, 2008), LETS GO (Vogel, Spikol, Kurti, & Milrad, 2010; Pea et al., 2012), MULLE (Eliasson, Cerratto-Pargman, Nouri, Spikol, &

Ramberg, 2011), Personal Inquiry (Mulholland et al., 2012), Mobile Learning Network (MoLeNET) (Attewell, Savill-Smith, Douch, & Parker, 2010), and English in Action (Walsh & Shaheen, 2013). A similar line of thinking can be observed in research activities aimed at exploring new design approaches and innovative uses of mobile technologies in a variety of collaborative and enquiry-based learning settings (Hwang, Tsai, & Yang, 2008; Hwang, Wu, & Ke, 2011; Looi et al., 2010; Nussbaum et al., 2009; Ogata et al., 2010; Roschelle, Rafanan, Estrella, Nussbaum, & Claro, 2010; Wong, Chin, Tan, & Liu, 2010).

The outcomes of these research efforts have contributed to a refined conceptualisation of learning with mobile technologies in schools, museums and on field trips, although most of the projects have been optimistic and expecting positive results just from the experience of taking learners outside the school and providing them with mobile devices. Research results obtained so far show that mobile learning initiatives are, as indicated by Wingkvist and Ericsson (2009), confronted with complex and dynamic settings; outcomes expected from research or from national or local implementation programs might not always live up to their promises and result in adoption of technology in sustainable ways. Indeed, few are the research efforts that have succeeded in integrating mobile devices, that are able to innovate pedagogical practises in sustainable ways and that have resulted in the implementation of useful learning tools that are in wide use (Traxler & Leach, 2006). Interestingly enough, research efforts in the mobile learning field have seldom reported on problems and limitations or different types of barriers and constraints. Although Yeh et al. (2006) reported on an initiative, the ButterflyNet, a mobile capture and access system for field biology research students based on the use of smartphones and cameras, the program did not work mainly due to the fact that the technology simply was not suited for the actual use. Likewise, Sharples, Lonsdale, Meek, Meek, and Vavoula (2007) pointed at problems and limitations during the study of the implementation of mobile phones supporting students on their field trips to museums. In the project MyArtSpace, museum curators who were initially responsible for handling and administrating the mobile phones expressed during the project that they were not interested in maintaining and charging phones and instructing visitors about their use.

Grounded in a review of research projects conducted in the US, Australia, Asia and Sweden, this chapter reflects on the lack of connection between mobile learning research and classroom practises as formulated earlier by Lagemann (2000), Johannessen and Pedró (2010), and Looi, Hyo-Jeong, Yancy, and Wenli (2011). In particular, we present an analysis that aims at disentangling the web of relationships amongst stakeholders and diverse factors playing a role in the sustainability of technological innovations in elementary schools in general and in Swedish schools in particular. The analysis is based on readings of academic literature focused on sustainability and scalability issues related to innovations in schools and presentations of past research experience introducing mobile devices in mathematics and science classrooms in Sweden.

The remainder of the chapter is organised as follows: First, we introduce the research field of mobile learning, focusing on perspectives and challenges that characterise this domain and point to the need to study sustainability issues associated with innovations in schools. Second, we articulate the problem of fostering sustainable learning innovations, taking research work reported on studies conducted in the US, Australia and Asia. Third, we turn the focus to three examples of research projects we have conducted in Sweden in order to provide a critical analysis of the barriers and constraints experienced by both researchers and teachers whilst integrating mobile devices in schools. Fourth, we discuss factors, stakeholders and lines of action identified when attempting to introduce mobile technologies and sustain innovative educational practises in Swedish schools.

## Researching Mobile Learning: Perspectives and Challenges

The foundation of mobile learning as a research field can be traced back to the 1990s. The rapid and general use of mobile devices in society has certainly triggered thoughts about the use of such devices in the field of education. Today after almost twenty years of development, researchers can observe a shift of focus in the orientation of the field. As stated by Nouri (2011), techno-centric perspectives on mobile learning were and still are dominating, although issues about social practises and learning cultures embedded in the classroom contexts have emerged in the last few years. Kukulska-Hulme, Sharples, Milrad, Arnedillo-Sanchez, and Vavoula (2011), for instance, have noted that early research projects explored the affordances of mobile devices and were thus interested in exploiting the new generation of pen tablet and personal digital assistant devices for supporting learning. Today, questions about what mobile technologies can bring into education are making room for enquiries about what educational institutions and established pedagogical practises can do with mobile devices. As a result of this change of perspective, research studies have started to explore social practises and learning cultures characterising educational contexts where mobile devices and applications are introduced (Pachler, Bachmair, Cook, & Kress, 2010). Emphasising learning activities and their contexts, Pachler et al. (2010), stated that "Mobile learning is the process of coming to know and being able to operate successfully in, and across, new and ever changing contexts and learning spaces" (p. 66). Focusing on concepts such as context and mobility, Kukulska-Hulme et al. (2011) suggested that "Research into mobile learning is the study of how the mobility of learners augmented by personal and public technology can contribute to the process of gaining new knowledge, skills and experience" (p. 159). Following this line of thinking, Sharples et al. (2009) suggested, amongst other things, to clarify what mobility embedded in technology means for learners and teachers, as well as what learning dispersed in time and space signifies for them. These research developments are in line with the need to investigate the study of mobile devices in use. By 'mobile devices in use', we do not refer to the sporadic use that a specific classroom can develop during a research intervention; we rather refer to the appropriation of tools that penetrate classrooms, shaping and transforming pedagogical practises and discourses. Specifically, we refer to socio-technical practises that continue to develop beyond the span of research studies.

Research on the social-technical realities of mobile technology use in everyday educational practises will confront researchers with the need to inevitably investigate the ephemeral life of mobile technologies in school classrooms. For instance, research studies carried out by Looi, Jonassen, and Ikeda (2005) and Looi et al. (2011) have contributed to understanding the problem of sustaining innovation in Singapore schools. In Europe, the reasons behind the few number of studies reporting on obstacles during the introduction of mobile devices in schools are certainly of a different nature, although they are related to an undeniable reality: mobile learning research and school practise are growing apart. Surprisingly, few are the studies interested in finding out how to maintain the use of innovative devices in schools and how technology can become part—or not—of the fabric of the school world. In the particular context of Swedish schools, such a research perspective will be more than welcome since hundreds of millions of Swedish crowns have been invested in the integration of technologies in schools (Tebelius, Aderklou, & Fritzdorf 2003). As suggested by Gravitz & Hernwall (2012), structural conditions, economics, policy documents, school facilities and other types of conditions that frame and influence the different learning processes are an area that needs to be further explored by research on technological innovations in Swedish schools. In the same line of thinking, Johannessen and Pedró (2010) outlined 10 salient aspects that point out, amongst other things, the imbalance between investments in infrastructure, content, support and teacher training and the required efforts to build a sustainable knowledge base regarding technology-based school innovations; tensions between technology and pedagogy; the importance to balance the expectations of the power of technology with the reality of what is feasible; the limitation of the current work of assessment that seems to be only focused on digital literacy; and the need for a social dialogue on educational innovations involving all stakeholders.

## Articulating the Problem of Fostering Sustainable Learning Innovations

As stated by Sabelli and Dede (2001), "Decades of funded study that have resulted in many exciting programs and advances have not resulted in pervasive, accepted, sustainable, large-scale improvements in actual classroom practise, in a critical mass of effective models for educational improvement, or in supportive interplay among researchers, schools, families, employers, and communities" (p. 13). Based on the statement above, the following question arises: Why has the adoption and appropriation of technology proven to be so cumbersome in schools? The question may be approached from different angles, as the reasons behind the sustainability of innovations and changes introduced in schools are certainly multiple. Indeed the complexity of educational systems is considerable, as it encompasses societal needs, policies, curriculum, pedagogy, practises, epistemic beliefs, competence, funding issues and other aspects (Looi et al., 2005). According to Johannessen and Pedró (2010), who applied a systemic perspective to fostering, supporting, monitoring, assessing and scaling-up technology-based school innovations, the complexity of the issues at stake requires a multilayered, multidisciplinary and multi-methodological approach.

For instance, Looi et al. (2005) presented two aspects that can be seen as the origins of the problem: either schools jump from one innovation to another (and one can ask if the jumping is then a strategy to avoid changes) or the implementation of educational programs that heavily rely on information and communication technologies (ICT) fails to consider the complexity of the educational system. Taking into account these aspects one can ask: How do we make sustainable learning innovations happen? And what is it that we would like to sustain?

Substantial research has been conducted in the area of sustainability of innovations in education. Our lines of thought in this direction have in particular been influenced by the work of Century and Levy (2004) and further developments presented in Looi et al. (2005). For Century and Levy (2004), who conducted a three-year study aimed at researching the sustainability of school reforms in nine urban schools districts in the US, sustainability refers to something more than merely making programs (i.e., changes) last or more than a secondary outcome of a well-implemented program. According to the authors, "A first step toward considering sustainability goes against our deeply rooted desire to think logically about effective strategies to improve education" (Century & Levy, 2004, p. 4). The idea of working with a rational model of social change as the key to the establishment, maturation and evolution of sustainable changes can, according to the authors, become inadequate, as it is troublesome to work with a rational model in an irrational system. This irrationality in the system has, according to Century and Levy (2004), mainly to do with two main sources of variability in the education system, namely the volatility of schools and school systems and the multiplicity of actors driving instructional and policy decisions, shaping organisational structures and influencing daily human interaction (i.e., classroom teachers, teachers leaders, school and district administration). These two main sources of variability highlight the problem of how to handle the effects of turbulence, inertia and teacher variability characterising the school system and how to promote sustainable innovations in schools. In order to specify the complexity of the educational system, the authors have identified 15 factors that characterised this situation (see Table 10.1). According to Century and Levy (2004), these factors support and/or inhibit the sustainability of programs or innovations in school districts. The factors are distinguished into tangible, intangible and contextual. Whilst the tangible and contextual factors were predictable according to the authors, the intangible factors were unanticipated, difficult to discern and in some cases unexpected.

**TABLE 10.1** Influences of sustainability: expected and unexpected supports and barriers (Century & Levy, 2004)

| Tangible Factors *(related to the concrete element of a program or innovation)* | Intangible Factors *(related to the program as a whole)* | Contextual Factors *(related to surrounding conditions)* |
| --- | --- | --- |
| Accountability | Adaptation | Culture |
| Implementation | Critical mass | Decision making and power |
| Instructional materials | Perception | Subject matter |
| Leadership | Philosophy | |
| Money | Quality | |
| Partnerships | | |
| Professional development | | |

It is the identification of such factors that brings the authors to define sustainability as: "The ability of a program to maintain its core beliefs and values and use them to guide program adaptations to changes and pressures over time" (Century & Levy, 2004 p. 4).

Within the tangible factors, we suggest to incorporate technology as a concrete element of a program or innovation in approaching technology-based schools innovations. The factor technology, which is tightly related to curriculum, is difficult to control, as it can be approached from different and even opposing perspectives. For instance, Haas (1996) synthesised two different myths associated with technology: one asserts technology as transparent and the other asserts technology as all-powerful.

Technology as something transparent, explains Haas (1996), conceives of technology as a kind of distortionless window; for instance, teaching and learning are not changed in any substantive way by the transparent medium through which they pass. Teachers and learners simply exchange their pens for writing software, transfer their books to hypertext and replace their face-to-face conversations with video or text-based communication. The only change that is accepted within this particular view of technology is that learning with technology is different because it increases efficiency. In this respect, teaching and learning with technology are certainly faster and fun, but they are not changed in how they get done. The belief that teaching and learning are not influenced by technology is thus interesting in the way that this presupposes that technology in reality does not matter.

Technology understood as all-powerful presupposes that technology may have effects on teaching and learning, but these effects are essentially one-way effects. By 'one-way effects', we mean that technology affects learning activities and teaching practises, but these activities and practises do not affect technology; technology is thus viewed as an independent agent of change. Haas (1996) synthesises this view, making explicit that "The belief that technology determines itself and its own uses and effects removes the space where both the development and critique of technology occur" (p. 35). These two myths, technology understood as transparent and technology understood as all-powerful, seem to have gained much attention and popularity in education despite a view that suggests that technologies' effects depend on how they are culturally represented and how people reason and talk about them.

For Looi et al. (2005), to make changes in a sustainable way implies that particular consideration has to be given to the factors at any level of the school system in the progression of each innovation, from establishment and maturation to evolution. Honey and McMillian-Culp (2000) made clear that to talk about sustainable changes entails talking about tensions between the desire to scale effective practise on the one hand, and issues of adaptation and customisation on the other. Cohen and Ball (2001) suggested analysing the problem of sustainability in terms of specifications versus development. Specifications make reference to the degree of detail with which an innovation is described for school take-up, such as specified curriculum and learning goals, whilst development points at the provision of resources required to make innovation happen. Both elements indeed have to be coordinated in piloting and promoting innovation in schools.

Implementing innovations in schools for sustainability is, according to Looi et al. (2005), best conducted in tight collaboration with the Ministry of Education and related policymakers who have knowledge of the ground. Succeeding in such endeavors would ensure cooperation between researchers and policymakers. In relation to fostering cooperation between researchers and policymakers, Looi et al. (2005) refer to three points that have earlier been put forward by Bosco and Bakia (2004). These three points are: providing better ways to make research accessible to practitioners and policymakers, developing structures that provide for communication between researchers, practitioners and policy-makers, and developing and implementing a national research agenda.

Currently in Sweden, there are significant attempts related to the introduction of 1:1 computing and mobile applications in a considerable number of public schools across the entire country (Hallerström & Tallvid, 2009). Previous results of research projects in the field of mobile learning have not led yet to major sustainable innovations, as many of these activities do not carry on after the project funding reaches an end. Moreover, most of these efforts have often been conducted outside of dialogue with policymakers and the Ministry of Education.

The next section presents a brief review of research projects touching upon issues of sustainability in relation to mobile learning and, in particular, describes challenges associated with the introduction of collaborative mobile learning in the particular context of Swedish schools. The aim of the section is not only to describe and discuss aspects related to design approaches and innovative learning activities of the research projects, but also to illustrate the problem of sustainability and scalability of educational technology innovations with examples from the Swedish educational context. We strongly believe that there is a need for developing models that may help us to identify factors and roles played by diverse actors in the complex process of introducing educational innovations in schools. A more detailed elaboration of these ideas will be described later in this chapter.

## Introducing Mobile Devices and Applications into the Classroom from a Sustainability Perspective

There are, so far, few studies that have had an explicit focus on sustainable mobile-based learning. According to Ng and Nicholas (2012), researchers have identified requirements for mobile learning, which include permanency, accessibility, immediacy, interactivity, situating of instructional activities and adaptability, but no specific requirement has been so far identified for its sustainability. As a consequence of a lack of studies on sustainability and scalability issues associated with mobile learning, today it is difficult to find a model of sustainability for mobile learning in schools in the literature. It is mostly the work conducted by Looi et al., (2010) and the Learning Sciences Lab in Singapore that has suggested a concrete framework and research agenda for bridging formal and informal learning that allows researchers to analyse how to work with mobile technology for sustainable and seamless learning in schools. The Learning Sciences Lab has, since 10 years ago, strived to design 'mobilised' curricula aimed at facilitating and scaffolding student-centred learning activities. The group, which has accomplished several research projects on enquiry-based mobile learning, has been unique in identifying, tackling, conceptualising and working towards sustainability and scalability issues (Looi et al., 2005; Looi et al., 2010; Looi et al., 2011).

For example, based on their research experiences, Looi et al., (2011) clearly suggested a systemic approach to innovative education reforms at the macro, meso and micro levels of education in Singapore. By macro levels, the authors refer to educational policy stated by the government, whilst by micro levels they refer to the interactions that occur in the classroom. By meso levels, the authors understand the socio-cultural factors and environment where learning and teaching take place. It is for Looi et al., (2011) the orchestration of the efforts from all actors across the macro, meso and micro educational levels that is key to the sustainability of an innovative educational intervention. According to what is reported by the authors, it is clear that the centralisation of the educational system in Asia, the combination of strong, explicit top-down directives and bottom-top desire for improving the educational system together with a close partnership between researchers and schools, makes the Singapore schools a fertile terrain to seed innovations.

The work on sustainable mobile learning in schools reported by Ng and Nicholas (2012) is also of interest, as it analyses and discusses the introduction of ubiquitous tools, such as a personal digital assistant (PDA), in a secondary school in Australia with the objective of providing just-in-time information for learning, thus encouraging cooperative learning between the students and also between the students and the teacher. 57 students and 25 teachers participated in the study, which was longitudinal and lasted three years, starting in 2007. The study has been the basis for the framework for sustainable learning in schools introduced in Ng and Nicholas (2012). The framework functions as an analytical tool that helps the researcher to focus on the interrelationships between the various stakeholders and their interactions with the devices within the mobile learning program. More particularly, the authors distinguish between interactions amongst the leadership team, the community, the technical support personnel and the users (namely teachers and students), and interactions between people and devices, as well as management's decision to provide the financial funding to support the interactions.

Amongst the findings obtained from the study reported by Ng and Nicholas (2012), the authors noted that: management and leadership were the most important part of sustaining the mobile learning program in the school and tensions between the principal and the program coordinator and between the principal and some of the teachers represented the least successful element of the program vis-à-vis its sustainability. In relation to leadership style, the authors pointed at the person-centred approach as crucial for technology projects to be successful, and they emphasised that it is important for all parts involved to work as partners towards common goals and expectations. Concerning students' and teachers' interaction with PDA devices, the authors made clear there were technical issues related to software limitations, wireless reliability, and internet accessibility that were especially expressed by the students. In that respect, the intention to provide more IT support in the following years to satisfy students' and teachers' demands was important to the longevity of the program.

At a pedagogical level, the authors pointed out, on the one hand, the need to consider the informal learning that the device facilitates and, on the other, how the informal learning connects with formal aspects of learning with mobile devices at school. They have highlighted that pedagogical sustainability is very dependent on the teachers and their knowledge about the capabilities and limitations of the device when used at school. It is crucial for the teacher to pilot and monitor the integration of the device into teaching activities in order to attain the learning objectives. The time factor, and more specifically the time invested by the teachers, was also found to be important for the sustainability of the program. In their study, the authors reported teachers were expected to find their own time and opportunities to work with colleagues to improve their skills and knowledge: "Just as students' pedagogy needs to be scaffolded, teachers' professional learning for mobile devices in their teaching needs to be scaffolded too" (Ng and Nicholas, 2012, p. 713). Finally, the authors emphasised the need to support the development of positive attitudes in students and teachers towards the program by, for instance, providing support for the maintenance of the innovative program, to assure effective communication between the stakeholders in order to have a chance to tackle potential conflicts and tensions in time, and to delegate responsibilities with trust amongst members of the management team and between management and the teachers, as well as between the teachers and their students.

## Attempts to Introduce Innovative Mobile Learning School Activities into the Subjects of Mathematics and Science

During the last six years, our groups at Stockholm University (IDEAL—Interaction Design and Learning) and at Linnaeus University (CeLeKT—Center for Learning and Knowledge Technologies) have been exploring new design approaches and innovative uses of social media and wireless and mobile technologies in a variety of collaborative and enquiry-based learning settings (Kurti et al., 2008; Milrad et al., 2011; Vogel et al., 2010; Nouri, Cerratto-Pargman, Elliasson, & Ramberg, 2011; Eliasson et al., 2011; 2012; Pea et al., 2012; Nouri, Zetali, & Cerratto-Pargman, 2013; Eliasson, 2013). These research projects are not simply characterised by the provision of novel uses of rich digital media combined with mobile and wireless computational systems and tools, but also by the exploration of new and varied learning activities that become available whilst applying innovative approaches for designing new technological solutions and utilising existing ones to support mobile learning. These research efforts have all been in close collaboration with schools, teachers and students, although not all of the innovative mobile learning activities presented in this section are today maintained in schools. The main objective of this section is to exemplify some of the problems contributing to the ephemeral life of innovative learning programs in schools that characterise mobile learning research in the Nordic countries, taking Sweden as an example.

### The Geometry Mobile (GEM) Project

Geometry Mobile (GEM) is an ongoing mobile learning project in the field of mathematics trying to find alternative ways to support the learning of geometry using mobile and positioning technologies (Sollervall et al., 2011). The project brings together a group of researchers from Linnaeus University (LNU) in the fields of media technology and mathematics education working very closely with teachers and schools. The activities in the project are related to enquiry-based geometric learning tasks involving transitions between different contexts, including outdoor and classroom tasks. The research focus is not only on the appropriation of technologies introduced to the students and teachers, but also on how the use of mobile technologies supports these transitions, and in particular how they support effective communication of mathematical strategies. The project has been motivated by the idea of designing learning activities able to stimulate students' engagement and active participation by means of spatial visualisation. Guided by design-based research and the notion of seamless learning (Chan et al., 2006), researchers have designed and implemented a series of learning activities in mathematics, where mobile and web technologies support transitions between outdoor and indoor learning contexts (Sollervall et al., 2011). The research team has developed a set of mobile applications that allows a student to measure distances between his or her own device and mobile devices held by other students, as well as to collect data and record audio annotations. The data collected by these mobile applications is stored in a central repository for using it later in the classroom. A web-based geovisualisation tool and an augmented reality application are used back in the classroom to visualise and reflect upon the activities conducted outdoors in the field.

Since 2009, the research group at LNU has conducted trials and empirical studies with five classrooms from four different elementary schools in the south of Sweden. Amongst the outcomes of the studies, it was observed that by participating in the activity, students are offered opportunities to experience geometrical constructions in full-sized space. Specifically, they are stimulated to make use of their orientation ability, which differs cognitively from the visualisation ability that is more commonly used to solve similar tasks in school. These kinds of learning activities are offering the participating students enacted experiences of school geometry that are not commonly offered in school contexts (Sollervall, Otero, Milrad, Vogel, & Johansson, 2012). However, these types of activities are highly demanding, as they are new for the teachers and the learners who need to adjust or even recreate adequate frameworks for communication and interaction with and through new technological devices. Furthermore, the fact that these activities are outdoor explorations that require the use of mobile technologies and organisation across time and locations poses pedagogical as well as technological challenges for the teachers and the school that call for careful considerations regarding the design of innovation in schools (Sollervall et al., 2012). Recently, we have been working with 16 teachers from three different local schools and AV-Media (the regional pedagogical centre) on how to transfer and integrate the results of the Geometry Mobile project into the content of the curriculum in mathematics for grades seven and eight. Since spring 2012, 16 teachers from these schools have been piloting different activities with almost 400 students. The National Agency of Education has supported these efforts as part of a program enabling in-service teachers in mathematics to become more competent with regard to the integration of ICT, including mobile and positioning technologies in everyday educational practises.

Regarding sustainability aspects of the pedagogical and innovative activities that the GEM project brings to the school, we observed the complexity inherent to the initiative, complexity that is in part due to the multiplicity of voices, interests and relationships involved in such a mobile learning program (i.e., the teachers, students, students' parents, researchers, designers, programmers, developers, school director and IT support personnel at the school, municipality representatives). This type of initiative is thus new for the school. Not only is it new because the school opens up its doors to a new technology, mobile devices, it is also new in the sense that the school opens up its doors to a new social universe of relationships, roles, responsibilities and competence. More precisely, the school opens up to a group of people, representing different interests, enacting different kinds of agency and bringing diverse competence to the school. The school position in such a social configuration is thus a delicate one, as often the schools, under the pressure of the municipality or the national curriculum, welcome a group of external actors who bring change to current established school practises. The risk is then that the school could identify itself as a patient whose symptom needs to be cured by a group of specialists who bring new tensions to the school, as they do not always coordinate their actions and are often in conflict with each other.

## *Math Education and Playful Learning (MULLE)*

MULLE was a mobile learning research project conducted in the field of mathematics. The goal of the project was to introduce mobile learning activities into primary schools, bringing children out of the classroom in order to establish a tangible way to learn mathematics in authentic contexts with concrete content and physical manipulatives. In particular, we were interested in providing children with the possibility to experience geometric concepts in-situ, in a physical environment. The mobile applications were designed to let children actively explore questions, measure distances and calculate areas and reflect on their answers (Gil, Andersson, & Milrad, 2010). More specifically, the research team designed and implemented geometry-learning activities where mobile devices present a GPS-based task structure and provide task-based clues, and these were used as contextual tools for measuring distance. These efforts have been guided by design practises from design-based research (Design-Based Research Collective, 2003), where we followed design methods from the co-design practise (Penuel, Roschelle, & Shechtman, 2007). The research study was conducted with small groups of fifth grade students of age 12. Four subactivities were designed and performed: two indoor introductory activities, an outdoor field activity and an indoor post-activity. The children worked with the area concept. The scenario was for the children to relocate an almost extinct species from the local zoo to a field close to the school. The task was to calculate onsite so that the new enclosures for the animals would have the right measurements.

The aim of the activities was for children to practise and experiment with central concepts related to the notion of area, on both procedural and conceptual levels. On the procedural level, the focus of the practise was on familiarising the students with different area calculation and construction methods, in terms of both formulas and approximation techniques. On the conceptual level, the aim was on providing tasks that encouraged the students to reflect upon how areas are constituted and how they can be decomposed, that different shapes can have the same area and, in general, that the relation between the lengths of the sides of a shape determine the area of that shape (Nouri, 2011). Measuring large enclosures required the students to use a particular mobile software application installed on their phones (Gil et al., 2010). The application measures the distance between two mobile devices using GPS. Each group had access to two devices. One of them was called the primary device and the other the secondary device. Apart from measuring, the primary device presented students with tasks based on where they were located and where they were in the task structure. The primary device was also used for submitting answers and providing feedback, whilst the only function of the secondary device was to display clues (Nouri, 2011).

The findings of the study indicated that researchers need to carefully examine what types of learning and collaborative opportunities mobile technology will be able to open up in the particular educational contexts selected so that collaborative mobile learning activities can be planned accordingly. Teachers, together with researchers, designers and developers, need to discuss technical configurations of devices and functionality that predetermines the dynamics of learners' collaboration. As stated by Nouri (2011), it becomes essential to ask ourselves how the configuration and the distribution of the mobile technology can scaffold learners in outdoor learning activities and what that entails for learners in terms of accessibility to essential learning processes.

The MULLE project tackled issues related to the nature of learning activities that are adequate to transform, the kinds of support necessary when learners interact with mathematical concepts in both outdoor and indoor contexts and design questions related to the adaptation of the mobile devices to the teachers' requirements. The results of the project were successful, as the study showed that mobile learning challenges traditional conceptualisations of learning as well as the assumption than the classroom is the optimal place for learning to take place. It was shown that mobile learning activities are an alternative way to teach about mathematical concepts in tangible and situated situations. In the relationship with questions about the sustainability of the project in the school, we noted a set of unrealistic conditions of this particular study, partly due to the disproportional number of students participating in the study (low number) in relation to the number of researchers assisting teachers and students during mobile school learning activities outdoors (high number). The study worked well from a research and methodological point of view, as tasks and activities were planned, discussed and designed between the researchers, developer and teachers. Even students have participated in workshops aimed at calibrating the form and content of the mobile learning intervention. However, the project did not awake any interest amongst the school leading team. The project worked as a teachers' project, but not as a school project. The teachers did not experience any type of hindrance in participating in the mobile learning project, but they did not get any support either.

From the experiences and knowledge gained in this project, we learnt that issues regarding sustainability of learning activities and software designed for the study were not fully explored in advance. Currently, two studies aimed at introducing mobile devices in the teaching of natural sciences and mathematics, conducted in three classes of 30 students (10 years old) each. On the one hand, the studies have been planned in collaboration with the teachers and the director of the school and, on the other, questions regarding the sustainability of mobile learning activities in schools have been identified and discussed from the very beginning.

## The Learning Ecology with Technologies from Science for Global Outcomes (LETS GO) Project

In the Learning Ecology with Technologies from Science for Global Outcomes (LETS GO) collaborative international project (2008–2012), researchers from Stanford and Linnaeus University, together with teachers and students from schools in Sweden and the US, have been developing, implementing, studying and scaling up novel ways for fostering secondary school student learning in teams for ecological and environmental sciences (Pea et al., 2012). During the last four years, the research group has been working with the design, development and implementation of web and mobile services that integrate geopositional sensing, multimedia communication and interactive visualisation techniques in specific ecology learning scenarios. The goal has been to create mobile science enquiry collaboratives with teachers, learners and developers, and learners and domain scientists on topics related to water and soil quality, ecosystems and biodiversity. So far, more than 500 students have been involved in different types of learning activities. These activities encompassed classroom lessons, field trips and lab work and included data collection in the field, taking images and notes, as well as data visualisation and discussions in the classroom (Vogel et al., in press). As part of the environmental science curriculum, students investigated topics related to soil quality (woodland ecology) and water quality in the surrounding lakes.

These activities usually comprised six to eight lessons over a period of five weeks, starting with the introduction of the enquiry process where basic concepts of the activity were introduced: students discussed the initial questions given to them about a specific topic (e.g., water quality). This activity was followed by the preparation for investigation and experiments to be conducted using different technologies (sensors, data loggers, mobile applications for data collection in the classroom). Additionally, learners conducted field experiments at a local environment and collected samples for lab analysis. The data gathered using the mobile data collection tool were geotagged content and sensor data (usually pH, dissolved oxygen, temperature, conductivity, moisture, etc., depending on the type of the activity). The learning activity usually ended with a discussion about their findings from the field and lab work, and an overall class discussion and reflection using the web visualisation tool, which tailored different geotagged sensor data and digital content collected using the mobile data collection tool. Furthermore, none of the participants in all these activities had prior knowledge regarding how to use the technologies we developed. The experiences and knowledge gained during these years enabled us to develop the LETS GO system to a sustainable and robust platform for mobile data collection, visualisation and collaboration.

Reflecting upon our latest development and deployment efforts (Vogel, Kurti, Milrad, Johansson, & Müller, 2014), the main findings of our research related to the issue of sustainability on mobile learning are presented below. During the lifetime of the LETS GO project, it has been noticed that rapid technological changes affect the flow of learning processes and educational organisations. To enable rapid changes to be smoothly reflected in everyday teaching and learning activities in this area, there must be well-defined processes to ensure the continual refinement of the applications developed. Facilitating communication between researchers and developers on the one hand and researchers and educators on the other is key to the success of these interventions and their sustainability. This approach would enable implemented technologies and applications to be closely integrated into everyday educational practises, thus maximising the benefits in terms of the long-term goals, costs and time, and to satisfy learners and educational institutions with their system. Furthermore, we have gained valuable insights related to integration, interoperability, extensibility and sustainability issues. A systematic view on those aspects and their implication for developing sustainable software solutions to support mobile learning could lead to a number of potential benefits:

- Standard-based systems
- Constant interaction with users/learners
- Incremental development
- Reduced time and costs
- Expandability
- Flexible change of technologies
- Increased usability
- Easy maintenance and sustainability

In terms of further implementation and integration with everyday teaching and learning practises, five secondary schools in the region have started to adopt and use the findings of the project. One of the main objectives of these efforts is to create and develop a community of teachers (approximately 50 teachers) in the field of natural science who can integrate and develop sustainable teaching practises in this field by adopting and refining novel mobile learning tools and methods.

## Discussion and Conclusions

The research projects described in the previous section described a wide range of learning activities supported by mobile devices that can be classified as promoting formal and social oriented learning. The activities described in the research projects presented exhibited a similar learning flow pattern characterised by teacher-facilitated classroom activities; out-of-class individual or small group activities; in-class data sharing or peer learning; and in-class consolidation activities. The research projects analysed attempted to strike a balance between learning outdoors, in the classroom, and in personalised and social settings. Furthermore, the research projects have developed and implemented a number of innovative learning activities that were well received by the schools at a classroom level, including both students and teachers. Our design approach was underpinned by current steering documents for Swedish compulsory school that prioritise the development of general abilities (problem solving, communication, reasoning, representation, choosing and evaluating methods) and naturally encompass both formal and informal contexts before specific content knowledge (arithmetic, algebra, functions, scientific experiments, natural science, etc.), which is more closely associated with the formal school context. By offering activities that are highly self-regulated and involve collaboration and communication with peers, we contribute to preparing the students for a future that requires them to take initiative, be creative and make informed decisions, and that puts high demand on their social skills. Moreover, results of the studies provided us with new insights and perspectives related to the design of mobile learning activities supported by a variety of pedagogical approaches and technologies. The learning trajectories described in the section "Attempts to Introduce Innovative Mobile Learning School Activities into the Subjects of Mathematics and Science" combined outdoor group-learning experiences with learning activities in the classroom to provide learners with meaningful activities in order to:

• learn and explore a topic in authentic settings;
• reason and argue in order to come to the solution of a problem;
• collaborate in order to construct common knowledge;
• visualise and reflect upon relevant matters and to support abstract thinking.

Jonassen, Hernandez-Serrano, and Choi (2000) claim that meaningful learning takes place when learners are engaged in the types of activities described above. The approach to technology-enhanced learning described in this chapter may contribute to a richer, more authentic grounded experience than conventional learning activities conducted in classroom settings using traditional material such as textbooks or demonstrations.

The research projects presented in the preceding sections can be considered as representative of how far technological innovations, and especially mobile learning activities, can come in the current dialogue between schools and research on mobile learning in Sweden. Although the relationship between classroom teachers (practitioners) and researchers is well established, it neither matures nor evolves, and most commonly it may also fade after a short period of time. According to Bosco and Bakia (2004), we can point at the absence of a third party in the development of sustainable learning ecologies, namely policymakers. In the rest of this chapter, we will address two of the questions presented in section three: How do we make sustainable learning innovations happen in the Swedish school context? And what is it that we would like to sustain?

Guided by the work presented in Looi et al. (2011) and Century and Levy (2004), we have identified six factors, understood as expected and unexpected supports and barriers for sustainable innovation, and a number of attributes of the Swedish educational system that may play a central role in the sustainability and scalability of educational technology innovations. On the one hand, there is a multiplicity of stakeholders involved in the Swedish educational system, as well as a strong tradition of institutionalised consultation between them. In Sweden, political decision-making is oriented towards reaching consensus between the different participants. On the other hand, the educational system can be described as highly decentralised (since the 1980s there has been a power shift from the central government to the municipalities), organised by principles of equity in education, and utilising a 'management by objectives' approach (schools can offer different study options, and teachers have a wide scope to interpret the steering documents and adopt flexible teaching practises to meet diverse students' needs).

## Tangible, Intangible and Contextual Factors Identified in the GEM, MULLE and LETS GO Projects

In the analysis of our work with the schools, we have identified five main factors out of the 15 earlier presented by Century and Levy (2004) in their work in the US, plus an additional one, namely technology. The factors that can be regarded as both barriers and supports for the sustainability and scalability of technological innovations in Sweden are *technology, implementation, partnerships, critical mass, perception* and *decision making and power*. These factors were identified by taking into account actual teaching practises observed during the running of the GEM, MULLE and LETS GO projects in several schools in Sweden on the one hand and taking into account today's organisation and main characteristics of the Swedish educational system on the other.

## Technology

Technology and education have always been strongly related. As Laurillard (2012) noted, "Tools and technologies, in their broadest sense, are important drivers of education, though their development is rarely *driven* by education" (p. 2). Technologies are often presented as achieved products able to be inserted in the teachers' practises. Technology is seldom viewed as a factor that needs to be unpacked, scrutinised and studied by the different actors involved in the integration of technologies in schools. Teachers and learners should adapt and adopt the new technologies that often make their entrance in schools with a label of supremacy and high status, and as a sign of progress and modernism. Technologies are rarely questioned in concrete ways in discussions that range from pedagogical content and value to issues related to technical support, viruses, dead batteries, lost power cables and various malfunctions.

The relationship with technology that teachers, as well as school leaders, municipalities and policymakers, seem to have is based on the myths already distinguished by Haas in 1996. It is necessary to unpack the concept of information technologies in order to fully explain its materiality. One important material aspect of today's uses of ICT is that its development is driven by industry for commercial and entertainment purposes. Education, which is not today driving technological innovation, is dealing with tools, applications and services that do not have educative purposes in the first place. Another important aspect is to make stakeholders aware of the relationships with and expectations of information technologies that each one of the actors maintains.

## Implementation

The implementation of technological innovations, such as the introduction of mobile devices and technologies in the teaching of mathematics and natural science, is in part tightly related to the specific culture of the municipality and school district the school belongs to. The schools chosen for the research studies belong to municipalities and school districts that have shown interest in being aligned with the changes that ICT has introduced to our society. These municipalities are also interested in offering modern programs and providing children with digital competencies. However, the interest of municipalities and teacher-leaders and teachers is not clearly supported by, for instance, the national curriculum for prep-rimary education and compulsory school published in 2011 (Skolverket, 2011). The document makes reference to the use of technology in quite general terms when stating, for instance, "The school principal is responsible for providing students with high quality learning resources and materials, such as the library, computers and other resources" (Skolverket p.18). This and other examples found in the document show that it is not specified what the teachers are expected to do in relation to the use of technology in schools. One can thus ask how teachers, teacher leaders, school principals, policymakers, municipalities and the government can clearly align their interests to use technology in schools as a catalyst for innovative learning activities.

## Partnership

Century and Levy (2004) found that partnerships with community institutions, "while contributing to the sustainability of programs in many ways can also carry a heavy cost or may even be a burden" (p. 7). We think that this factor applies to grounding the collaboration space that emerges between researchers and teachers in Sweden. Although the establishment of cooperation between teachers and researchers has been essential in our projects, it is not enough for maintaining innovative learning practises facilitated by mobile devices in schools. Teachers who enthusiastically open the doors to innovative technology and learning activities realise too soon that such innovations demand much from them in terms of time, effort, communication with other teachers and technical competence. But the solution to the problem does not only involve obtaining more time, putting in more effort or letting teachers participate in training programs. We think that solving the problem requires a partnership established with the teachers. It becomes clear that the teachers who have kindly cooperated in our studies have accepted to be part of a research team driving a specific learning innovation; teachers consequently do not see themselves as leaders of innovative projects in schools or they do not see themselves alone in trying to sustain innovative and challenging learning activities in schools. Questions about the specific role teachers should be invited to assume in partnership with researchers, as well as questions about what the school and the municipality can concretely provide to innovative projects, are important to discuss amongst researchers, schools leaders and policymakers.

## Critical Mass

The schools participating in our projects were all dependent on their local municipalities. Although one can think that the autonomy that municipalities possess in Sweden constitutes an advantage to support local democracy and promote increased flexibility and efficiency in finding solutions to meet local needs, this characteristic of the system becomes a disadvantage when it comes to the introduction of technological innovations. The number of teachers needed to participate in a reform effort to ensure that it will become standard for the school or district, is a central question. Our research efforts have not reached yet a critical mass of teachers, so questions such as how we should promote a culture of technological innovation and self-generation remain open.

## Perception

How others perceive the innovation is significant for supporting or inhibiting sustained innovations: "Perceptions could be a key driver of decision making for a program adaptation and implementation" (Century & Levy, 2004, p. 9). Florian (2000) argues that the role of perception is at the core of the definition of sustainability: "Sustainability is defined as the perception by those involved in the education system of continued implementation and practice of a change that occurred initially as a consequence of a reform program" (p. 4). In this particular direction there is much to do in Sweden, as the decentralisation of the educational system becomes a barrier for the systematic dissemination of successful results emerging from innovative learning practises supported by mobile technologies.

## Decision Making and Power

This factor is closely related to another one: culture. According to Century and Levy (2004), "culture" is defined as "the norms of communication, collegiality, organizational hierarchy and understandings of accepted practice" (p. 8). Decision making and power in Sweden are complex issues, as an essential value of the Swedish culture is making decisions based on general consensus. When changes are introduced in the educational system, this is generally preceded by wide consultations and submission for comments. The process can then become a long one, since involvement of *all stakeholders* and *transparency* in decision-making mechanisms are a must in Sweden.

The elaboration of the factors presented in this section aimed at gaining new insights about the lack of maturation and evolution of educational technology innovations introduced successfully at a classroom level. As already pointed out by Looi (2011), "Innovations should be weaved into the daily activities of all actors in the learning ecology" (Sollerval and Milrad, 2012: 9). In Sweden, we still have much to do to bring all actors in such a learning ecology to understand and to discuss the sustainability of educational innovation. From a research perspective, it will be essential to develop models that will allow us to conceptualise the complexity of learning ecologies in order to understand better how to make innovations sustainable. We strongly agree with Century and Levy (2004), who stated the following: "As individuals involved in educational improvement, we hope that our hard work will not fade, that our growth as learners and teachers will continue to develop, and that our students will benefit for many years" (p. 2).

In this sense, the framework for sustainable mobile learning in schools presented by Ng and Nicholas (2012) shed light on key aspects influencing the interaction between stakeholders and between users and devices. According to the authors, their model contains five components for sustainability in schools: economic, social, political, technological and pedagogical sustainability. These components are strongly interrelated and illustrate the complex relationships between the technical aspects and the people-related factors that include interpersonal relationships between leadership and management, teachers, students, technicians and the wider community consisting of parents, suppliers, policymakers, software developers and researchers. As the authors emphasise, the components of the framework need to be considered, putting the focus on people first, meaning that it is essential to pay attention to how the stakeholders interact with each other and with the technology.

We concur with the ideas proposed by Ng & Nicholas (2012), but it is not only discussing the type of technology, its cost and its infrastructure, but also what each of the stakeholders believe and expect from the technology with relation to the pedagogical and learning goals that need to be achieved. The combination of all these perspectives needs to be taken into consideration to make mobile learning innovations sustainable and endurable. In addition to the five components suggested in their framework, we would like to include two other dimensions: *design sustainability* and *knowledge management sustainability*. These dimensions are brought into consideration having in mind Goodyear's (2011) claims. The author points out that we are facing two perceptible changes in the field of educational research. The first is a shift in our sense of the spaces and contexts in which education takes place as different learning activities become more commonly distributed across a variety of contexts. The second change is a wider understanding about the conception of educational praxis, acknowledging the growing importance of design.

In this chapter we have presented and discussed our experiences and reflections with regard to which aspects need to be taken into consideration in order for mobile learning innovations to become more sustainable. This is quite a complex problem, which is far from being trivial as there are so many different stakeholders and variables involved. We agree with Pedro (2010), who points to a more systematic approach for understanding technology-based school innovations. He claims that:

> There is a need to know more about how governments promote, monitor, evaluate and scale up successful technology-based or supported innovations, paying particular attention to the role played by research, monitoring and evaluation, and the resulting knowledge base, both at national and international level. (p. 16)

We strongly encourage the international mobile learning research community to start developing collaborative efforts to promote new ways for thinking and taking concrete actions in these directions.

## References

Attewell, J., Savill-Smith, C., Douch, R., & Parker, G. (2010). *Modernising education and training: Mobilising technology for learning.* London: Learning and Skills Network.

Benford, S., Rowland, D., Flintham, M., Hull, R., Reid, J., Morrison, J., . . . Clayton, B. (2004). Designing a location-based game simulating lion behavior. Proceedings from *The Conference on Advances in Computer Entertainment* (ACE), Singapore. New York, NY: ACM Press. June 2004.

Bosco, J., & Bakia, M. (2004). National research agendas for ICT in education: A descriptive analysis. Presented at The CoSN International Symposium, Washington, DC. Retrieved from http://www.cosn.org/resources/international/2004_symposium_agenda_paper.pdf

Cabrera, J. S., Frutos, H. M, Stoica, A. G., Avouris, N., Dimitriadis, Y., Fiotakis, G., & Liveri, K. D. (2005). Mystery in the museum: Collaborative learning activities using handheld devices. Presented at *Mobile HCI 2005*, Salzburg, Austria.

Century, J. R., & Levy, A.J. (2004). Bringing theory of and research on sustainability to practice: Giving school improvement a "bottom line." Paper presented at *The SCALE Think Tank*. November 2003.

Cohen, D.K., & Ball, D.L. (2001). Making change: Instruction and its improvement. Kappan. Retrieved from http://www-personal.umich.edu/~dball/articles/CohenBallKappan.pdf

Chan, T.W., Roschelle, J., Hsi, S., Kinshuk, Sharples, M., Brown, T., Patton, C., Cherniavsky, J., Pea, R., Norris, C., Soloway, E., Balacheff, N., Scardamalia, M., Dillenbourg, P., Looi, C-K., Milrad, M.; & Hoppe, U. (2006). One-to-one technology-enhanced learning: An opportunity for global research collaboration. *Research and Practice in Technology Enhanced Learning Journal, 1*(1), 3–29.

Design-Based Research Collective. (2003). Design-based research: An emerging paradigm for educational inquiry. *Educational Researcher, 32*(1), 5–8.

Eliasson, J. (2013). *Tools for designing mobile interaction with the physical environment in outdoor lessons* (Doctoral dissertation). Stockholm University.

Eliasson, J., Cerratto Pargman, T., Nouri, J., & Ramberg, R. (2011). Mobile devices as support rather than distraction for mobile learners: Evaluating guidelines for design. *International Journal of Mobile and Blended Learning, 3*(2), 1–15.

Eliasson, J., Knutsson, O., Nouri, J., Karlsson, O., Ramberg, R., & Cerratto-Pargman, P. (2012). Evaluating interaction with mobile devices in mobile inquiry-based learning. Proceedings from *The 2012 IEEE Seventh International Conference on Wireless, Mobile and Ubiquitous Technology in Education* (WMUTE '12) (pp.92–96). Washington, DC: IEEE Computer Society.

Florian, J. (2000). Sustaining education reform: Influential factors. Aurora, CO: Mid-continent Research for Education and Learning.

Frohberg, D., Goth, C., & Schwabe, G. (2009). Mobile learning projects: A critical analysis of the state of the art. *Journal of Computer Assisted Learning, 25*(4), 307–331.

Gil, D., Andersson, A., & Milrad, M. (2010). Mobile virtual devices for collaborative m-learning. Proceedings from *The 18th International Conference on Computers in Education, ICCE 2010*. Putrajaya: Asia-Pacific Society of Computers in Education.

Goodyear, P. (2011). Emerging methodological challenges. In Markauskaite, Freebody & Irwin (Eds.), *Methodological Choice and Design* (Vol. 9, Part 4, pp. 253–266). Springer: Netherlands.

Gravitz, A., & Herwall, P. (2012). Ungas multimodala gestaltning i skolan. En arbetsrapport från forskningsprojektet UNGMODs våren 2011. Retrieved from http://mt.sh.se/ungmods/wp-content/uploads/2010/08/Arbetsrapport_2_maj-2011.pdf

Haas, C. (1996). Writing technology: Studies on the materiality of literacy. Mahwah, NJ: Lawrence Erlbaum.

Hallerström, H., & Tallvid, M. (2009). En egen dator i skolarbetet-redskap för lärande? *Utvärdering av projektet "En-till-en" i två grundskolor i Falkenbergs kommun.* Delrapport 2. Göteborg: Göteborgs universitet och Falkenbergs kommun, barn-och utbildnings förvaltningen.

Honey, M., McMillan Culp, K., & Carrigg, F. (2000). Perspectives on technology and educational research: Lessons from the past and present. *Journal of Educational Computing Research, 23*(1), 5–14.

Hwang, G.-J., Tsai, C.-C., & Yang, S. J.-H. (2008). Criteria, strategies and research issues of context-aware ubiquitous learning. *Educational Technology & Society, 11*(2), 81–91.

Hwang, G.-J., Wu, P.-H., & Ke, H.-R. (2011). An interactive concept map approach to supporting mobile learning activities for natural science courses. *Computers & Education, 57*(4), 2272–2280.

Johannessen, Ø., & Pedró, F. (2010). Lessons learnt and policy implications. *Inspired by technology, driven by pedagogy: A systematic approach to technology-based school innovations OECD Report.*

Jonassen, D. H., Hernandez-Serrano, J., & Choi, I. (2000). Integrating constructivism and learning technologies. In J. M. Spector & T. M. Anderson (Eds.), *Integrated and holistic perspectives on learning, instruction and technology: Understanding complexity* (pp. 103–128). Dordrecht: Kluwer Academic Publishers.

Kukulska-Hulme, A., Sharples, M., Milrad, M., & Arnedillo-Sanchez, I. (2009). Innovation in mobile learning. *Journal of Mobile and Blended Learning, 1*(1), 12–35.

Kukulska-Hulme, A., Sharples, M., Milrad, M., Arnedillo-Sánchez, I., & Vavoula, G. (2011). The Genesis and Development of Mobile Learning in Europe. In D. Parsons (Ed.), *Combining e-learning and m-learning: New applications of blended educational resources* (pp. 151–177). Hershey, PA: Information Science Reference (an imprint of IGI Global).

Kurti, A., Spikol, D., & Milrad, M. (2008). Bridging outdoors and indoors educational activities in schools with the support of mobile and positioning technologies. *International Journal of Mobile Learning and Organization, 2*(2), 166–186.

Lagemann, E. (2000). *An elusive science: The troubling history of education research.* Chicago, IL: The University of Chicago Press.

Laurillard, D. (2012). *Teaching as a design science: Building pedagogical patterns for learning and technology.* New York, NY: Routledge

Lonsdale, P., Baber, C., Sharples, M., Byrne, W., Arvanitis, T.N., & Beale, R. (2004). Context awareness for MOBIlearn: Creating an engaging learning experience in an art museum. In J. Attewell & C. Savill-Smith (Eds.), *Mobile learning anytime everywhere: A book of papers from MLEARN 2004* (pp. 115–118). London: Learning and Skills Development Agency.

Looi, C.-K., Hyo-Jeong, S., Yancy, T., & Wenli, C. (2011). The Singapore experience: Synergy of national policy, classroom practice and design research. *International Journal of Computer-Supported Collaborative Learning, 6*(1), 9–37.

Looi, C-K., Jonassen, D., & Ikeda, M. (2005). Towards sustainable and scalable educational innovations informed by the learning sciences: Sharing good practices of research, experimentation and innovation. Proceedings from the *13th International Conference on Computers in Education (ICCE 2005).* Singapore: IOS Press. 28 November—30 December.

Looi, C.-K., Seow, P., Zhang, B., So, H.-J., Chen, W., & Wong, L.-H. (2010). Leveraging mobile technology for sustainable seamless learning: A research agenda. *British Journal of Educational Technology, 41*(2), 154–169.

Milrad, M., Kohen-Vacs, D., Vogel, B., Ronen, M., & Kurti, A. (2011). An integrated approach for the enactment of collaborative pedagogical scripts using mobile technologies. *Proceedings of the International Conference on Computer Support for Collaborative Learning (CSCL)* (pp. 681–685). 4–8 July, Hong Kong: International Society of the Learning Sciences.

Mulholland, P., Anastopoulou, S., Collins, T., Feisst, M., Gaved, M., Kerawalla, L., ... Wright, M. (2012). nQuire: Technological support for personal inquiry learning. *IEEE Transactions on Learning Technologies, 5*(2), 157–169.

Naismith, L., Sharples, M., & Ting, J. (2005). Evaluation of CAERUS: A context aware mobile guide. In H. van der Merwe & T. Brown (Eds.), *Mobile technology: The future of learning in your hands, mLearn 2005 Book of Abstracts, 4th World Conference on mLearning* (pp. 25–28). Cape Town. October.

Ng, W., & Nicholas, H. (2013). A framework for sustainable mobile learning in schools. *British Journal of Educational Technology, 44*(5), 695–715. doi:10.1111/j.1467–8535.2012.01359.x

Nouri, J. (2011). *Towards orchestration of mobile learning: Scaffolding students' learning processes across contexts.* (Licenciate thesis). Stockholm University.

Nouri, J., Cerratto-Pargman, T., Eliasson, J., & Ramberg, R. (2011). Exploring the challenges of supporting collaborative mobile learning. *International Journal of Mobile and Blended Learning, 3*(4), 54–69.

Nouri, J., Zetali, K., & Cerrato-Pargman, T. (2013). *Mobile inquiry-based learning: A study of collaborative scaffolding and performance.* Las Vegas, NV: HCI International.

Nussbaum, N., Alvarez, C., McFarlane, A. E., Gomez, F., Claro, S., & Radovic, D. (2009). Technology as small group face to face collaborative scaffolding. *Computers & Education, 52,* 147–153.

Ogata, H., Li, M., Hou, B., Uosaki, N., El-Bishouty, M., & Yano, Y. (2010). Ubiquitous learning log: What if we can log our ubiquitous learning? Proceedings from the *International Conference on Computers in Education 2010* (pp. 360–367). Putrajaya.

Pachler, N., Bachmair, B., Cook, J., & Kress, G. (2010). *Mobile learning: Structure, agency, practices.* New York, NY: Springer.

Pea, R., Milrad, M., Maldonado, H., Vogel, B., Kurti, A., & Spikol, D. (2012). Learning and technological designs for mobile science inquiry collaboratories. In K. Littleton, E. Scanlon & M. Sharples (Eds.), *Orchestrating inquiry learning* (pp. 105–127). London: Routledge.

Pedró, F. (2010). The need for a systemic approach to technology-based school innovations. *Inspired by technology, driven by pedagogy: A systematic approach to technology-based school innovations OECD Report.*

Penuel, W.R., Roschelle, J., & Shechtman, N. (2007). Designing formative assessment software with teachers: An analysis of the co-design process. *Research and Practice in Technology Enhanced Learning, 2*(1), 51–74.

Roschelle, J., Rafanan, K., Estrella, G., Nussbaum, M., & Claro, S. (2010). From handheld collaborative tool to effective classroom module: Embedding CSCL in a broader design framework. *Computers & Education, 56*(3), 1018–1026.

Sabelli, N., & Dede, C. (2001). Integrating educational research and practice: Reconceptualizing goals and policies. Retrieved from http://ctl.sri.com/publications/downloads/policy.pdf

Sharples, M., Arnedillo-Sanchez, I., Milrad, M., & Vavoula, G. (2009). Mobile learning: Small devices, big issues. In N. Balacheff, S. Ludvigsen, T. de Jong, A. de, Lazonder, S. Barnes (Eds.), *Technology-Enhanced Learning: Principles and Products* (pp. 233–249). Berlin: Springer-Verlag.

Sharples, M., Corlett, D., & Westmancott, O., (2002). The design and implementation of a mobile learning resource. *Personal and Ubiquitous Computing, 6,* 220–234.

Sharples, M., Lonsdale, P., Meek, J., Meek, J., & Vavoula, G. (2007). An evaluation of MyArtSpace: A mobile learning service for school museum trips. In A. Norman & J. Pearce (Eds.), Proceedings from the *6th Annual Conference on Mobile Learning, mLearn 2007* (pp. 238–244). Melbourne.

Skolverket. (2011). Läroplaner, kursplaner och ämnesplaner. http://www.skolverket.se/om-skolverket/andra-sprak-och-lattlast/in-english; http://www.skolverket.se/om-skolverket/publikationer/visa-enskild-publikation?_xurl_=http%3A%2F%2Fwww5.skolverket.se%2Fwtpub%2Fws%2Fskolbok%2Fwpubext%2Ftrycksak%2FRecord%3Fk%3D2575

Spikol, D., Milrad, M., (2008). Promoting physical activities and playful learning using mobile games. *Journal on Research and Practice in Technology Enhanced Learning, 3*(3), 275–295.

Sollervall, H., Gil de la Iglesia, D., Milrad, M., Peng, A., Pettersson, O., Salavati, S., & Yau, J. (2011). Trade-offs between didactical and technological design requirements affecting the robustness of a mobile learning activity. Proceedings from *The 19th International Conference on Computers in Education.* Chiang Mai.

Sollervall, H., Otero, N., Milrad, M., Vogel, B., & Johansson, D. (2012). Outdoor activities for the learning of mathematics: Designing with mobile technologies for transitions across learning contexts. Proceedings from *The 7th IEEE International Conference on Wireless, Mobile and Ubiquitous Technologies in Education.* Takamatsu. Tebelius, U., Aderklou, C., &

Fritzdorf, L. (2003). ITiS som incitament till skolutveckling—den nationella utvärderingen av IT i skolan—surveystudien, *2000–2003*. Retrieved from http://www.itis.gov.se/content/1/c6/01/30/78/170947_3835_ITiS_slutrapport_dec2003.pdf

Traxler, J., & Leach, J. (2006). Innovative and sustainable mobile learning in Africa. Proceedings from the *Wireless, Mobile and Ubiquitous Technology in Education (WMUTE '06)* (pp. 98–102).

Vavoula, G.N., Sharples, M., Rudman, P., Lonsdale, P., & Meek, J. (2007). Learning bridges: A role for mobile learning in education. *Educational Technology Magazine, 47*(3), 33–36.

Vogel, B., Kurti, A., Milrad, M., Johansson, E., & Müller, M. (2014). Mobile Inquiry Learning in Sweden: Development Insights on Interoperability, Extensibility and Sustainability of the LETS GO Software System. *Educational Technology & Society, 17*(2), 43–57.

Vogel, B., Spikol, D., Kurti, A., & Milrad, M. (2010). Integrating mobile, web and sensory technologies to support inquiry-based science learning. Proceedings from the *6th IEEE International Conference on Wireless, Mobile and Ubiquitous Technologies in Education (WMUTE)* (pp. 65–72). Walsh, C., & Shaheen, R. (2013). English in action (EIA): Mobile phones as an agent of change for large-scale teacher professional development and English language learning in Bangladesh. Proceedings from the *American Educational Research Association Annual Conference 2013*. San Francisco, CA. 27 April–1 May.

Wingkvist, A., & Ericsson, M. (2010). A framework to guide and structure the development process of mobile learning initiatives. Proceedings from *The 9th World Conference on Mobile Learning* (pp. 184–191).

Wingkvist, A., & Ericsson, M. (2009). Sharing experience from three initiatives in mobile learning: Lessons learned. In S.C. Kong, H. Ogata, H. C. Arnseth, C. K. K. Chan, T. Hirashima, F. Klett, . . . S. J-H. Yang (Eds.), Proceedings from *The 7th International Conference on Computers in Education*. Hong Kong: Asia-Pacific Society for Computers in Education.

Wong, L.-H., Chin, C.-K., Tan, C.-L., & Liu, M. (2010). Students' personal and social meaning making in a Chinese idiom mobile learning environment. *Educational Technology & Society, 13*(4), 15–26.

Yeh, R., Liao, C., Klemmer, S. R., Guimbretière, F., Lee, B., Kakaradov, B., . . . Paepcke, A. (2006). ButterflyNet: A mobile capture and access system for field biology research. Proceedings from *CHI 2006*. Montréal. 22–28 April. Retrieved from http://hci.stanford.edu/publications/2006/butterflynet/ButterflyNetCHI2006.pdf

# 11

# CHALLENGES AND BARRIERS FOR MOBILE LEARNING IN SECURITY AND DEFENSE ORGANISATIONS

*Christian Glahn*

## Introduction

Mobile technologies have been amongst the key facilitators of recent political and economic change around the world. Technological innovations have impacted how people handle information and what they perceive as knowledge. In situations of emergency and crisis, mobile technologies have proved to be versatile and reliable tools for managing intra- and inter-organisational communication. Such advances have inevitably impacted upon the activities of security and defense organisations. This in turn warrants a closer inspection of the influence that mobile technologies have on professional education and training activities in the spheres of defense, security and international relations (IR).

Every defense and security professional requires adequate training, development and evaluation to ensure that they are capable of fulfilling key tasks. Technology has made a valuable contribution to satisfying these demands for many years. Training simulators using virtual reality and computer-based training, for example, form part of the educational activities of these organisations. Yet, a host of external factors—such as overseas operations or civilian emergency planning—often means that training and development requires more flexibility in terms of timing, accessibility and course structure. In professional contexts, offering face-to-face instruction alone cannot satisfy such requirements.

Just little over a decade ago the technologies of the World Wide Web introduced flexible ways for distributing and monitoring learning opportunities that assure the timely and cost-effective diffusion of relevant organisational information and knowledge. International standards and specifications that are part of the sharable content object reference model (SCORM) assure the interoperability of training material across systems, infrastructures and organisations (ADL Initiative, 2009).

The related technologies are typically summarised under terms such as e-learning or advanced distributed learning (ADL). As many organisations recently invested in ADL systems, frameworks and content, these novel mobile technologies are challenging for security and defense organisations not only because they offer new educational approaches, but also because unforeseen interoperability issues can emerge and because they interfere and conflict with organisational policies and regulations.

This chapter analyses challenges and barriers of introducing mobile learning in security and defense organisations. The chapter has three parts. The first part provides the analytical framework. The second part addresses the challenges for mobile learning in security and defense organisations as they were identified by previous research projects. Finally, the chapter focuses on organisational barriers for scaling up mobile learning solutions in security and defense organisations.

## Background

Like all educational technologies, mobile learning cannot be reduced entirely to the technology used by the learners. Indeed, technological aspects are not central in more recent definitions of mobile learning (Sharples, Arnedillo-Sánchez, Milrad, & Vavoula, 2009; Traxler, 2007). In order to operationalise this research, the following working definition of mobile learning is proposed:

> *Mobile learning refers to technology-supported learning processes and practises that take advantage of mobility of people and consider learning opportunities that are created by contexts as well as the relations and transitions between those contexts.*

This definition emphasises the educational design factors instead of technology factors. It also suggests that mobile learning cannot be reduced to translating conventional ADL solutions for the delivery on mobile devices. In order to identify the core characteristics that are specific to mobile learning, Börner, Glahn, Stoyanov, Kalz, and Specht (2010) conducted an expert study. The authors identified seven core challenges specific to mobile learning:

- *Organisational challenges* include strategies for adopting and applying mobile technologies in educational organisations;
- *Technological challenges* relate to the use and adoption of mobile technologies and infrastructures for learning;
- *Contextualisation* addresses the influence of contextual factors on learning;
- *Orchestrating mobile learning* focuses on educational strategies and instructional designs for mobile learning;
- *Access to learning* is related to new educational approaches for creating learning opportunities for mobile learners, as well as for the inclusion of remote or marginalised audiences;

*   *Personalisation and individualisation* within and across contexts emphasise the affordances of highly personalised technologies; and
*   *Collaboration* addresses the impact of mobility and contexts on group work and collaborative learning processes.

The working definition and the core challenges already emphasise context as the core concept of mobile learning. Dey (2001) defines context as:

> . . . any information that can be used to characterize the situation of an entity. An entity is a person, place, or object that is considered relevant to the interaction between a user and an application, including the user and applications themselves. (p. 5)

Zimmermann, Lorenz, and Oppermann (2007) identify five categories of contextual information: *individuality (identity)*, *activity, location, time*, and *relations*. Along these dimensions, it is possible to approximate and to match the contexts of two entities or to detect changes of the contextual focus. Typically sensors provide data that fall into one of these categories. These data are required for creating context-aware systems. Context-aware systems can automatically respond to contextual conditions and their changes.

*Context-aware* solutions integrate the analysis of contextual factors into the application logic in order to automatically adapt to a situation. Consequently, context-aware mobile learning solutions require active sensing mechanisms (sensors) for determining the contextual conditions of the learners. The most common examples of context-aware mobile learning are location-based or location-anchored instructional approaches. In these cases the location is used for selecting appropriate learning material for the learners. Sensors that are integrated into mobile devices, such as GPS receivers (Naismith, Sharples, & Ting, 2005), a camera for reading barcodes (De Jong, Specht, & Koper, 2008), or near field communication (NFC) readers (Hwang, Chu, Lin, & Tsai, 2011), identify the learner's location.

Context-aware solutions are best suited for scenarios in which learners need to become aware of environmental conditions, as they are relevant for their learning. This requires that these conditions remain stable for a group of learners. Location-based city or museum guides are good examples for such scenarios. However, not all learning opportunities can be related to external factors. Some mobile learning scenarios depend on contexts that are actively constructed by actors in the learning process. These learning scenarios cannot or do not need to be bound to strictly defined contextual conditions. Mobile learning solutions that address these scenarios consider contextual factors as part of the application or the instructional design, but these factors are only implicitly influencing the application logic. Such solutions are called *context-sensitive* and are not dependent on active contextual sensing. An example of a context-sensitive solution is casual mobile learning as described by Glahn (2012).

Glahn (2014) argues that mobile learning solutions can be divided into mobile learning management and mobile learning orchestration solutions. These two types of mobile learning systems focus on different aspects of mobile learning instructional designs. Mobile learning management systems typically provide access to and arrange tools that enable learners and facilitators to handle learning resources and objects. These types of systems primarily use context-sensitive approaches, as they do not include process management logic. Mobile learning orchestrating systems support the implementation of instructional designs. These systems are directly related to the procedural factors of learning activities: rules, tasks and contexts. Mobile learning orchestration systems with an explicit context model and rules for context matching are implemented as context-aware systems.

## Organisational Challenges for Adopting Mobile Learning

Integrating mobile learning into the organisational practise of education and training is a complex problem. Four challenges for adopting and implementing mobile learning have been identified by prior research:

1.  The technological challenge of adopting and integrating mobile technologies into the infrastructures of security and defense organisations.
2.  The organisational challenge of meeting the legal and regulative constraints under which security and defense organisations operate.
3.  The educational challenge of orchestrating novel scenarios of technology-enhanced learning.
4.  The content challenge of enabling trainers and educators to create educational learning material for the new medium.

The first challenge is strongly based on the characteristics of the professional work in security and defense organisations. The main scope of the related activities falls into the technological challenge of mobile learning. Mobile and wireless computing has its roots in performance support for mobile teams and improved communication between headquarters and other teams (Rodger, Pendharkar, & Khosrow-Pour, 2002). Squire, Haro, Mead, Schulz, and Adame (2011) analysed the benefits of rugged handheld devices over laptop equipment for supporting soldiers who were deployed in an operational environment. This work indicated a general acceptance of the technology amongst the target audience, but wireless data connectivity was identified as a main barrier for mobile performance support.

Another technical aspect of integrating mobile solutions into existing ICT infrastructures is the much smaller screen size of mobile devices compared to desktop systems. Two approaches to this challenge can be found in the literature. The first approach is to provide alternative interfaces for mobile devices. Alternate interfaces enable learners and teachers to access all functions of ADL systems from mobile devices (Beligan, Roceanu, & Barbieru, 2012; Hodges, 2013). These interfaces are designed for meeting the specific constraint of the small screen estate of mobile devices. Whilst the screen resolutions of contemporary smartphones would be sufficient to display most types of web content, it is the constraints of the human body that require special attention for enabling learners and trainers to interact with this content. The second approach is to provide supplementary learning opportunities based on the available learning material through mobile devices (Glahn, 2012). This approach considers mobile devices not as an alternative way for accessing the same functions as with desktop computers; instead, mobile devices offer new affordances that can be utilised for alternative learning experiences. Approaches to the technological challenge are typically related to context-sensitive solutions of mobile learning that consider contextual factors in their design.

The second challenge addresses the legal frameworks and operational regulations of security and defense organisations. This challenge focuses primarily on the organisational challenge for mobile learning. Given the complexity in which security and defense specialists operate, it is necessary to understand the legal frameworks and the security needs related to mobile learning. This is of particular relevance for innovating ADL solutions across organisations. In order to meet the legal and operational requirements of different organisations, common denominators are needed for the use of mobile technologies in related organisations. A first analysis indicates a great variation of regulations between organisations and nations that influences how research ethics can and have to be applied for studying using mobile learning (Hodges & Stead, 2012). The available findings indicate that context-aware mobile learning solutions are not only technically more complex, but are also influenced by a wider range of regulations than context-sensitive solutions.

The third challenge refers to the practical implications of applying mobile learning in educational practise. This challenge primarily addresses the orchestration challenge of mobile learning. The affordances of mobile technologies create new ways of supporting learning processes such as more authentic and situated learning. The literature discusses trainer monitoring and intervention (Ternier, Gonsalves, de Vries, & Specht, 2012), as well as rewarding mechanisms (Glahn, 2012) for approaching this challenge. This creates new opportunities for mobile scenario-based simulations for team training. Depending on the learners' performance, the trainer can decide to change parameters of the simulation script in order to escalate or ease the challenge for the learners. Mobile dashboards for the learners combine performance-based and effort-based metrics for self-assessment and formative evaluation. This enables the learners to monitor their learning progress. Furthermore, these metrics are synchronised with the ADL system, so trainers can analyse learner statistics and provide support if it is needed. The available approaches indicate that sensing and analysing sensor data are not exclusive to context-aware mobile learning, but also can have meaningful applications in context-sensitive solutions. However, the current approaches indicate that context-sensitive approaches rely on learner-centric data, whereas context-aware solutions can include a wider range of data.

The fourth challenge addresses the need for mobile learning content. Content authors need empowerment for supporting new delivery modes. This covers aspects of the technological and the organisational challenge of mobile learning. The learning material in security and defense organisations is often tailored to the special requirements and training procedures of the organisation. The trainers who use these resources are often those who create them. Therefore, it is necessary to provide easy-to-learn and easy-to-handle tools for creating appropriate material for mobile learning. In this regard, authors discussed automatic content conversion (Beligan, Roceanu, & Barbieru, 2012), reuse of learning resources from SCORM compliant content packages (Glahn, 2012), and process scripting (Ternier et al., 2012). Context-sensitive solutions can build on existing educational material that is reframed within the design of the mobile learning solution, whilst context-aware mobile learning requires revisiting educational concepts and creating new learning material.

## Barriers for Mobile Learning in Security and Defense Organisations

The available literature indicates high potential for adopting mobile technologies by security and defense organisations. However, apart from pilot projects there appears to be very little uptake of mobile learning on a larger scale. This raises the question of barriers to mobile learning in these organisations. In order to provide an answer to this question, a workshop with stakeholders from defense academies and military education was conducted in November 2012. About 40 international ADL experts and practitioners participated in this session and discussed the different dimensions for bringing mobile learning into practise. All participants had sufficient experiences with introducing ADL solutions into their organisations in the past. This ensured that this focus group had a good understanding of the conditions of implementing new technologies for innovating education and training within their organisations.

The session was organised as a prestructured open-space session in which the participants discussed mobile learning matters for 45 minutes. The open-space format is a bottom-up approach for group discussions on different topics. This means that the participants distribute themselves into different groups by choosing the topic of their interest. Given organisational constraints, the workshop facilitators implemented a variant of the open-space format by prestructuring the available topics and designating the chairpersons for discussion moderation. The entire session was implemented in a single large room in which four discussion tables were set up. This setup allowed the participants to easily move between the topics. In order to document the discussions, the chairpersons were asked to create concept- or mind-maps. For this purpose, they were provided with flipchart paper and colour pens. In contrast to the other participants, the chairpersons were not allowed to switch between topics. The following topics were open for discussion:

- Success factors for implementing mobile learning
- Barriers to mobile learning
- Mobile learning subjects
- Educational approaches to mobile learning

The following analysis focuses only on the barriers to mobile learning because it provided rich insights on the organisational requirements for mobile learning, whereas the other discussions mainly verified the expectations grounded on prior research results.

The participants acknowledge that support for mobile devices in education and training becomes increasingly necessary in security and defense organisations because an increasing number of young recruits will be well connected through mobile devices and expect the ubiquitous availability of mobile data services. Yet, mobile learning faces several organisational barriers. The participants indicated six distinctive areas that create barriers to introducing mobile technologies and mobile learning in these organisations:

1. Existing information security regulations and security requirements
2. Cryptographic requirements
3. Mobile data connectivity
4. Device features and interoperability
5. Device availability and financial constraints
6. Integration of mobile learning concepts into existing educational practises

The biggest barrier to mobile learning is related to the *existing information security regulations and security requirements* of security and defense organisations. Mobile technologies raise a number of challenges for such policies. These range from the carrier networks that are used for data transmission via a range of secure facilities, to the classification levels for information that can include education and training material. Only certified personnel under strict constraints can access classified resources. For ADL this can include the use of specially secured computer networks. Wireless data transmission is often not considered as sufficiently secure, specifically if alien data providers are responsible for the infrastructure.

The participants indicated large differences between their organisations at the level of specific regulations, but they generally confirmed that most ICT related security policies were not designed to be suitable for responding to the increasing availability of mobile handheld and personal devices. Whilst such regulations are typically unrelated to education and training, they have a direct impact on implementing mobile learning.

The second barrier has been identified as the *cryptographic requirements* for data transmissions and data storage. Since mobile learning requires data exchange between mobile devices and the organisation's infrastructure, it raises questions regarding protecting organisational information. Given the rapid growth of mobile data communication, many security risks of mobile technologies are either unknown or the understanding of security implications is in its infancy. One prominent example for this situation was the unrestricted access of installed apps to the contacts and calendar information on devices running Android, Blackberry OS and iOS. This function had been present in these systems at least since 2007, but it only received major attention in 2011 after it became public that many app developers 'harvested' addresses and calendar schedules for customer profiling, even if the respective app did not use this information. This incident indicated that this form of data exchange between applications on personal devices has not been considered as a security threat, although all affected platforms already provided strong cryptographic features for protecting application data against other forms of unprivileged access. The example illustrates that the cryptographic requirements are not only limited to data transmission, but also extend to storing and processing data on mobile devices.

The participants further referred to different and partially contradicting security protocols at the level of national organisations and international alliances that address *mobile data connectivity*. In order to take full advantage of mobile learning, it is necessary to analyse how these protocols can be aligned and standardised in order to enable the development of interoperable education and training services.

A related barrier for mobile learning is the wireless network infrastructure in military facilities. This infrastructure has to be independent from private sector partners if it provides access to information services. This barrier has two aspects: First, wireless network infrastructure is not available in all facilities—in some organisations, it is completely unavailable. Second, where the infrastructure is available, it is not clear if and how it can get used for education and training purposes. This poses a barrier for mobile learning because the related educational scenarios rely on wireless data transmission at some point.

The participants perceive the *device features and interoperability* as another barrier. Two aspects play a role in this respect. The first aspect involves the definition of mobile devices. The second aspect refers to the operating systems that are installed on mobile devices.

Approximately 10 years ago, the term mobile computing mainly referred to laptop computers and PDAs, whilst there are at least three relevant technologies of mobile ICT today: smartphones, tablet computers and laptops. In the literature, netbooks and PDAs are still present and communicated as independent device classes. Each of these device classes is clearly representing aspects of mobile ICT that are distinct from the other classes. Near future predictions on wearable computing indicate further diversification in this segment. Therefore, it is difficult to specify the key characteristics of mobile devices for educational purposes. This creates a barrier for mobile learning and ADL because it is unclear if mobile learning has to be optimised for a specific type of device, or if all device types need to be supported at the same time.

The second aspect of this barrier is related to the limited interoperability between mobile operating systems, which challenges the sustainability of investing in developing educational material for mobile learning. For the development of mobile ICT solutions, at least eight relevant platforms have to be considered, compared to only three platforms in desktop computing. These platforms are tightly coupled to the devices on which they are preinstalled. Unlike the situation in desktop computing, it is typically impossible to install a different mobile operating system on a mobile device. Even updating a mobile device to a new major release of its own operating system can be difficult (in the case of Android) or impossible (in the case of older Blackberry OS or Windows Mobile). The participants noted that the increasing success of HTML5 technologies holds the potential for overcoming this barrier. However, they also expect that their organisations will face a very diverse distribution of mobile operating systems.

Related to the wireless network infrastructure in security and defense organisations is the barrier of *device availability and financial constraints* of education and training departments. In the private sector particularly, smaller organisations follow a bring-your-own-device (BYOD) strategy to mobile ICT. Whilst this has the benefit of cost savings by relying on the infrastructure that is already in the hands and pockets of the staff, this path is difficult to follow for security and defense organisations due to the lack of controllability of information access. Yet, many organisations are unaware of the availability and distribution of privately owned mobile in their organisation. The alternative to BYOD is to provide a mobile device to all members in the organisation. However, this will necessitate major financial investments in devices, infrastructure and solution development. Such investments require an overarching organisational strategy because they are beyond the scope and financial capabilities of educational departments.

Finally, the participants identified the *integration of mobile learning concepts into existing educational practises* as a major barrier for mobile learning. Whilst mobile learning holds great potential to introduce new concepts to motivate learners, assessment and certification remains a major challenge. Casual learning and 'gamification' were discussed as ways of making learning more attractive, but the participants are not convinced that these new approaches are compliant with the legal requirements for certification and recertification. This requires a detailed analysis of mobile learning approaches with respect to their compliance with national and international regulations and policies.

## Conclusions

Mobile technologies have been identified as having great value for security and defense organisations. This includes the potential of mobile learning for innovating organisational education and training. The rapid adoption of mobile computing by individuals in industrialised countries creates an increasing demand for supporting mobile learning also for organisational learning. However, organisational adoption is far more complex than individual adoption. In this respect, security and defense organisations are unique. On the one hand, they heavily rely on continuous education and training to fulfill their duties. The great demand for training can only be satisfied by scalable, technology-supported educational solutions. On the other hand, security and defense organisations operate in dangerous and politically sensitive environments. This has created complex requirements and regulations for information security that affect all operational areas in these organisations, including education and training.

The analysis of the organisational challenges for adopting mobile learning indicates that present research responds to individual aspects of four core challenges: technological availability, organisational framing, educational approaches and authoring of learning resources. The findings suggest that the organisational factors have not received sufficient attention from research and development. This aspect is approached in the second part of the analysis that included the voices of educational stakeholders. Their input presents a complex network of security requirements, organisational policies and uncertainty of technological reliability. It appears that context-sensitive mobile learning approaches are easier to adopt by these organisations than context-aware solutions. The stakeholder responses also indicate that concepts of adopting mobile technologies for organisational mobile learning are less feasible for security and defense organisations.

## Acknowledgements

The research related to this chapter has been funded by the ADL Co-Lab and awarded by the Office of Naval Research Global (ONRG) under the grant no. N62909–12–1–7022. The views expressed herein are solely those of the author and do not represent or reflect the views of any academic, government or industry organisation mentioned herein.

The author thanks the members of the PfPC ADL WG for their contributions.

## References

ADL Initiative. (2009). Sharable content object reference model (SCORM) 2004 (4th ed.), version 1.1. Alexandria, VA: ADL Initiative.

Beligan, D., Roceanu, I., & Barbieru, D. (2012). Using mobile technology to enhance eLearning in CAROL I national defence university. In C. Glahn (Ed.), Proceedings from *The 1st Workshop on Mobile Learning in Security and Defense Organisations*. Helsinki. 15 October. Retrieved from http://ceur-ws.org/Vol-955/workshops/WS6Security.pdf

Börner, D., Glahn, C., Stoyanov, S., Kalz, M., & Specht, M. (2010). Expert concept mapping study on mobile learning. *Campus-Wide Information Systems*, 27(4), 240–253.

De Jong, T., Specht, M., & Koper, R. (2008). Contextualised media for learning. *Journal of Educational Technology & Society, 11*(2), 41–53.

Dey, A.K. (2001). Understanding and using context. *Personal Ubiquitous Computing, 5*(1), 4–7.

Glahn, C. (2014). Mobile learning operating systems. In M. Ally & A. Tsinakos (Eds.), *Increasing access through mobile learning* (pp. 141–157). Vancouver: Commonwealth of Learning and Athabasca University.

Glahn, C. (2012). Supporting learner mobility in SCORM compliant learning environments with ISN Mobler Cards. In C. Glahn (Ed.), Proceedings from *The 1st workshop on Mobile Learning in Security and Defense Organisations*. Helsinki. 15 October. Retrieved from http://ceur-ws.org/Vol-955/workshops/WS6Security.pdf

Hodges, J. (2013). Mobile learning environment (MoLE) project: A global technology initiative (Self-published report).

Hodges, J., & Stead, G. (2012). Research ethics in the MoLE m-learning program. In C. Glahn (Ed.), Proceedings from *The 1st workshop on Mobile Learning in Security and Defense Organisations*. Helsinki. 15 October. Retrieved from http://ceur-ws.org/Vol-955/workshops/WS6Security.pdf

Hwang, G.-J., Chu, H.-C., Lin, Y.-S., & Tsai, C.-C. (2011). A knowledge acquisition approach to developing Mindtools for organizing and sharing differentiating knowledge in a ubiquitous learning environment. *Computers & Education, 57*(1), 1368–1377.

Naismith, L., Sharples, M., & Ting, J. (2005). Evaluation of CAERUS: A context aware mobile guide. In H. Van Der Merwe & T. Brown (Eds.), *Mobile technology: The future of learning in your hands (mLearn 2005 book of abstracts, 4th world conference on mLearning)* (p. 50). Cape Town. 25–28 October. Retrieved from http://hal.archives-ouvertes.fr/docs/00/19/01/42/PDF/Naismith_2005.pdf

Rodger, J.A., Pendharkar, P.C., & Khosrow-Pour, M. (2002). Mobile computing at the department of defense. In A. Armoni (Ed.), *Effective healthcare information systems* (pp. 192–209). Hershey, PA: IGI Global. doi:10.4018/978–1–931777–01–8.ch012

Sharples, M., Arnedillo-Sánchez, I., Milrad, M., & Vavoula, G. (2009). Mobile learning: Small devices, big issues. In N. Balacheff, S. Ludvigsen, T. Jong, A. Lazonder & S. Barnes (Eds.), *Technology-enhanced learning* (pp. 233–249). Dordrecht: Springer Netherlands.

Squire, P., Haro, E., Mead, P., Schulz, J., & Adame, A. (2011). An extended user evaluation of the Apple, Inc. iPod Touch to aid the U.S. Marine Corps. Proceedings from *Human Factors and Ergonomics Society 55th Annual Meeting* (pp. 2088–2092). doi:10.1037/e578902012–443

Ternier, S., Gonsalves, A., de Vries, F., & Specht, M. (2012). Supporting crisis simulations with the ARLearn toolkit for mobile serious games. In C. Glahn (Ed.), Proceedings of *The 1st workshop on Mobile Learning in Security and Defense Organisations*. Helsinki. 15 October. Retrieved from http://ceur-ws.org/Vol-955/workshops/WS6Security.pdf

Traxler, J. (2007). Defining, discussing, and evaluating mobile learning: The moving finger writes and having writ.... *International Review of Research in Open and Distance Learning, 8*(2). Retrieved from http://www.irrodl.org/index.php/irrodl/article/view/346/882

Zimmermann, A., Lorenz, A., & Oppermann, R. (2007). An operational definition of context. In Kokinov (Ed.), Proceedings from the *Sixth International and Interdisciplinary Conference on Modeling and Using Context—The Context '07* (pp. 558–571). Berlin, Heidelberg: Springer. Denmark. 20–24 August.

# 12

## CONTEXT RECONSIDERED

*John Traxler*

### Introduction

In this chapter, we start by considering context-aware learning as a specific focus within mobile learning research, itself probably a cadre or vanguard within the wider community of researchers engaged in technology-enhanced learning and how its development has led to progressively richer conceptions of context. We then look at the impact of wider mobility and connectedness, specifically at how the conventional conceptualisation of context creates a dichotomy between *self*, the user or learner, and *other*, the environment and surroundings. The chapter extends and consolidates ideas from earlier tentative thoughts (Traxler, 2011).

### Context in Mobile Learning

The notion of *context* has been one of the defining contributions of mobile learning to the wider field of technology-enhanced learning, exploiting the personal and portable nature of the devices and their capacity to sense some aspects of their context, initially their location and trajectory. Context has been defined and classified in a variety of different ways. Working definitions include, "the formal or informal setting in which a situation occurs; it can include many aspects or dimensions, such as environment, social activity, goals or tasks of groups and individuals; time (year/month/day)" (Brown, 2010, p. 7). Another one is, "any information that can be used to characterise the situation of an entity, where an entity can be a person, place, or physical or computational object" (Dey & Abowd, 2000, p. 441). Thus, context-awareness or context-aware computing is "the use of context to provide task-relevant information and/or services to a user", according to

Dey and Abowd (1999, p. 1), "typically the location, identity and state of people, groups, and computational and physical objects". These definitions look at context from different perspectives. They make the distinction between, on the one hand, those contexts that relate to the user's environment including attributes such as their emotional state, focus of attention, social and informational state and, on the other hand, those contexts relating to the application's environment, surroundings, settings or states. Some attributes are common to both types of context including location, time of day, season, temperature, identities of people and objects around the user and changes to these identities.

At least two other classifications of contexts have been proposed. The first (Chen & Kotz, 2000, drawing in part on Schilit, Adams, & Want, 1994), defines four categories of contexts:

- Computing context including network connectivity, communication costs and bandwidth, and nearby resources such as printers, displays and workstations, though this becomes progressively less significant as the factors concerned become more stable, uniform, transparent and capable.
- Physical context including lighting, noise levels, traffic conditions and temperature, though these too may become less significant as devices become more independent of these aspects of physical context.
- User context including the user profile, location, people nearby and current social situation. Increasingly devices might give orientation and might sense or even recognise objects in their vicinity, so this aspect continues to become richer as the internet of things (Siorpaes et al., 2006) increasingly draws the physical world and its objects into the virtual world.
- Time context including time of day, week, month and season of year.

The second classification (Schmidt, Beigl, & Gellesen, 1998, p. 895) contains two categories with various sub categories:

- Human factors
  - User, their personal habits, mental state
  - Social environment, namely the proximity of other people, social relations, collaboration
  - Task, any goal directed activities or more general objectives
- Physical environment
  - Location
  - Infrastructure, the interactive and computing environment
  - Conditions such as the level of noise and brightness

There were also attempts to classify contexts specifically in relation to learning. For example, one source (Wang, 2004) breaks contexts of learning into six dimensions. These dimensions are identity, spatio-temporal, facility, activity, learner and community:

- Identity characterises the unique learner;
- Spatio-temporal is the time and location aspect of the learning process;
- Facility is the type of mobile device being used;
- Activity categorises the learning activity taking place, such as individual or collaborative;
- The learner dimension describes characteristics such as learning styles or preferences and knowledge level;
- The community aspect describes the social interactions between participants.

These distinctions are typical of attempts to define and delineate precise aspects of context. More recently, however, the distinction between the learner or user and their context or environment has been eroded by the notion of 'user-generated contexts' (Cook, 2010), a concept named to emphasise the role of learners themselves in shaping their own context: "The context within which communication takes place is augmented by users to suit the needs of the individual and/or the conversational community" (Cook, Pachler, & Bachmair, 2010, p. 4).

Alongside these developments, a more philosophical debate takes place in which our description so far is characterised as only one set of perspectives. There is, however, another set. As articulated by Dourish (2004, p. 20): context is "a technical notion, one that offers system developers new ways to conceptualise human action and the relationship between that action and computational systems to support it". This second set of perspectives draws "analytic attention to certain aspects of social settings" and argues that the earlier position was essentially positivist and that there is an alternative viewpoint, one of phenomenology. It leads to a different view of context. Rather than context as information, it is "a relational property that holds between objects or activities" and thus signifies relevance. Rather than delineated and defined in advance, context is defined dynamically; rather than being stable, context is local to each occasion of activity or action; rather than context and content being two separable entities, "Context arises from the activity. Context isn't just 'there', but is actively produced, maintained and enacted in the course of the activity at hand" (Dourish, 2004, p. 22).

Context can thus also be proximity and relevance as we have seen, and can also be difference and change; it can be seen as a description of that which differentiates, what is different in what is near or recent and what is further or earlier in relation to the subject. Originally these factors related to physical or geometric distance, but clearly there are other aspects, perhaps social proximity or pedagogic proximity, which might mean learning tasks or concepts near to one's own. An early definition of context gets near to these other ideas of proximity, defining it as "location and the identity of nearby people and objects" (Schilit & Theimer, 1994, p. 1). Others also argue for social dimensions, saying: "Context encompasses more than just the user's location, because other things of interest are also mobile and changing. Context includes lighting, noise level, network connectivity, communication costs, communication bandwidth and **even** [author's emphasis] the social situation, e.g., whether you are with your manager or with a co-worker" (Schmidt et al., 1998, p. 1).

The last word for the moment should be, "'Context' is a slippery notion. It is a concept that keeps to the periphery, and slips away when one attempts to define it" (Dourish, 2004, p. 29).

## How Things Have Changed

These developments in the ideas and practice of context-aware mobile learning came out of a particular historical and social milieu. They were embedded in the mobile computing community, and they became embedded deeply within the mobile learning research community. They were seen as a major development and contribution to the wider field of technology-enhanced learning. In the early days of mobile learning, perhaps the first six or seven years of this century, these developments helped place the mobile learning research community amongst the vanguard of technology-enhanced learning in an era when most people's and most learners' access to powerful and expensive educational technologies was through educational institutions. This was due to the relative cost, bulk and scarcity of different digital technologies at the time; consequently access was mainly through networked desktop computers running dedicated educational software integrated into wider institutional software systems, such as library software and student enrolment software.

This nature of access was and partly still is the corollary of an institutional culture in which research and development in technology-enhanced learning formed part of a 'research economy', where institutional research teams in many universities bid for project funding, conduct the research, often in-house, small-scale and by definition fixed-term, publish the results and move onto the next funding opportunity. There were of course exceptions to this pattern, and the EU funded several much larger projects of which MOBIlearn (Syvanen, Beale, Sharples, Ahonen, & Lonsdale, 2005; Da Bormida, Di Girolamo, Dahn, & Murelli, 2004; Taylor, 2004) in the current context is the most obvious in the early days. Nevertheless, there was an expectation that the institution would procure, provide, install and control any subsequent deployment of learning technology, and there was an expectation that the institution would promulgate technical and operational standards for learning technology in order to ensure equity, accessibility, uniformity and cost-effectiveness.

Now, for reasons of cost and sustainability, the focus has moved to 'learner devices', those owned by learners (Traxler, 2010a; CoSN, 2012), and with it the locus of agency and control has moved from the institution to the learner. This is challenging and complex and leaves much to be negotiated. It has become known as BYOD, or bring-your-own-device. If the professionals within institutions can accept the challenges, then scale and sustainability become distinct possibilities for mobile learning in general including context-aware mobile learning. Learner devices, actually just devices typical of the current retail domain, offer location-awareness and augmented reality along with much other sophisticated functionality. However attractive this may sound, the challenges include equity, standards, quality assurance, infrastructure, security and embedding and integrating with institutional 'blended learning'.

Much of the work so far could be seen in retrospect as an aspect of a Web 1.0 ideology, where the device user is merely the reader, consumer or recipient. There was, however, some work with a more Web 2.0 perspective, where users were writers, producers and contributors. This work was educational, recreational, reflective, expressive and creative.

One limitation of many early projects was that their temporal and sometimes spatial aspects were bounded or episodic; not only were the projects themselves fixed-term and often small-scale, but the experience of the individual learner or user was limited to a short time, and perhaps to a particular physical location such as a museum or heritage site and only for the duration of the visit. Outside these bounds of the episode, the experience was either exhausted or curtailed; the predominant aspects of context were usually just spatial and temporal. The increased technical capacity, functionality and connectivity, especially indoors and in metropolitan areas, however, offer a financially sustainable way to move beyond the merely local, impersonal and episodic experiences of much of this earlier informal context-aware mobile learning and offer a much richer experience as well. It is possible to imagine linked museums in the near future, for example the Ironbridge Gorge Museums in Shropshire, UK, or the South Kensington museums in London, or national organisations with heritage sites (such as English Heritage or the National Trust of England, Wales and Northern Ireland) where successive or repeat visits of groups or individuals using their own devices build a cumulatively richer, possibly incoherent and indiscriminate, but potentially more collaborative experience.

## The Mobility and Connection of Society

The last three or four years have seen a rapid change in the ownership of powerful digital technologies for learning. As indicated earlier, this was previously predominantly uniform networked desktop computers in educational institutions; now it is highly functional but diverse and rapidly changing personal mobile phones across the vast majority of technically sophisticated Western society, learners and others alike. This represents a change from uniform institutional hardware, not worth mentioning by virtue of its uniformity, to individual mobile phones, expressing individuality and thus taking a different emotional place in the learners' context.

Consequently, we now cross from the earlier technical or reformist account of context to a social account, and a shift of context-aware mobile learning from a component of mobile learning to the educational component of context-aware services and experiences as experienced outside education and its institutions: "[N]ew mobile communications systems are fundamentally rewriting the spatial and temporal constraints of all manner of human communications—whether for work, family, or recreation and entertainment" (Townsend, 2000, p. 5).

This is having dramatic, though maybe unnoticed, implications for the role, direction and significance of the mobile learning research community, as we shall see. It has implications for the relationships between learners and their educational institutions. It also has a profound, pervasive, but subtle impact on work, jobs, businesses and the economy; on perceptions of time, space and place; on the individual, their identity and the nature of communities; on knowledge, knowing, understanding and learning, and consequently on a changed meaning for context and its role in education. Our underlying contention is that earlier work on context-aware mobile learning was predicated on specific fixed ideas about self and other, as articulated within institutions, and that the impact of wide social mobility and connectedness in the way we describe has significantly transformed these ideas.

## Time and Space

We will start by looking briefly at time, space and place and their implications for context. We draw on what we have written elsewhere (Traxler, 2010b).

First, interacting with a desktop computer, especially before the mobile became ubiquitous, entering 'cyberspace' takes place in a bubble, in dedicated times and places where the user has their back to the world for a substantial and probably premeditated episode. Interacting with a mobile is different and woven into all the times and places of users' lives. Whereas the desktop computer would previously have imposed quite a rigid and separate set of contexts on a user or learner—they are either learning or they are doing something else equally specific—mobiles produce or enforce a more fragmentary and transient movement between multiple user-contexts. One consequence of this shift of cyberspace from desktop to mobile, perhaps entitled 'phonespace' (Townsend, 2000, p. 95), is that real and virtual spaces and the contexts that they represent become interwoven; the user works now in overlapping and fragmentary contexts, where other roles or contexts can easily intrude. Users are no longer dedicated learners, nor are there stable contexts.

Mobile technologies erode ideas of physical time as the common temporal context, and this temporal context, the way we understand the where and when of everyday life ". . . can instead be socially negotiated" (Sørensen, Mathiassen, & Kakihara, 2002, p. 3) alongside the "softening of schedules" (Ling, 2004, p. 73) afforded by mobile devices. Townsend (2000) uses similar phrasing: "The old schedule of minutes, hours, days, and weeks becomes shattered into a constant stream of negotiations, reconfigurations, and rescheduling" (p. 93). Nyíri (2007, p. 301) claims: "With the mobile phone, time has become personalized". Or perhaps, "...this means the replacement of one time by a series of overlapping times" (Cooper, 2002, p. 25) or overlapping temporal contexts. Nowadays:

> One can be interrupted or interrupt friends and colleagues at any time. Individuals live in the *phonespace*—they can never let it go, because it is their primary link to the temporally, spatially fragmented network of friends and colleagues they have constructed for themselves. It has become their new umbilical cord, pulling the information society's digital infrastructure into their very bodies. In fact, as technical evangelists at Nokia pondered, mobile communications could eventually evolve into an activity indistinguishable from telepathy. (Townsend, 2002, p. 70)

Mobile Times (n.d.), an Intel project, finds that time is becoming 'plastic', reporting:

> The experience of 'plastic time' frames modern life. It is an experience that is highly interruptible, shrinking and expanding around immediate concerns, and interleaving through multiple activities. . . . Conflicts arise not when people have more to do, but increasingly diverse things to switch between, creating the need to 'shift gears' frequently.

This sounds to a computer scientist like the overheads associated with the 'context-switching' of operating systems.

Agar (2003, p. 4) makes a direct comparison between the mobile phone and wristwatch in terms of intimacy and ownership. He also, however, makes a direct contrast in terms of personal freedom:

> . . . while it might have felt like liberation from tradition, the owner was caught anew in a more modern rationality, for, despite the fact that the pocket watch gave the owner personal access to exact time, accuracy depended on being part of a system. (p. 4)

In fact, it made the owner *part* of a system, part of a stable universal temporal context. Wristwatches are handcuffs, keeping the wearer in only one temporal context at a time. Time zones, another temporal artefact of the Industrial Revolution devised in the aftermath of the new national railway networks, had a similar effect, creating a large-scale unified and monolithic temporal context.

Now, of course, almost universal personal mobile connectedness (and the mobility of the car) erodes these too; international travellers are no longer locked into their local time zone, their own local temporal context. Mobile phones mean that they are also tethered to family temporal contexts back home and to the rhythms of their office and colleagues back at base or across a range of global offices rather than exclusively to their own physical context, location and contacts.

Staid (2008), in talking about 'the phone as mobile log', reminds us that mobiles are:

> . . . a kind of life diary that saves experiences, memories, thoughts, or moments in a visual and textual form. The SIM card in your phone could be seen to contain the story of your life (at least at the present time): not just text messages, photos and videos, but also chosen or given tokens such as icons, ring tones, music lists; and the diary, address book, alarm clock all save and display the experiences and activities of the user as they have been mediated and captured by the mobile. (p. 157)

This second-by-second account of our lives is another way in which mobiles transform our sense of time passing, populating our personal user-generated temporal context with an unprecedented level of detail and making it more finely-grained whilst at the same time plastic and fractured.

Furthermore, the increase of rolling news, off-air recording and domestic video-on-demand means that TV schedules no longer provide a synchronous and collective context that bound informal groups together in the way they used to a generation ago. Students rarely collectively discuss last night's TV programs when they arrive at university, each relating to that common temporal and social context. Ling (2008, p. 62) makes a similar point citing the lost rituals of watching national TV news in Norway, writing: "In this way the TV, and the particular news program, provided a kind of ontological security". At the same time, *news* is becoming more local, the news of your online community rather than global news (Bilton, 2010), altering the shape of the informational context of the user, reconfiguring the informational, historical and social contexts of users as the old landmarks are re-aligned, removed or replaced.

## Place, Space and Presence

Mobile devices are accelerating the erosion of physical place as the predominant aspect of the spatial context started by other networked digital technologies. It is being diluted by "absent presence" (Gergen, 2002), the phenomenon of physically co-located groups of people all connected online elsewhere and by the "simultaneity of place" (International Telecommunications Union, 2004, p. 20, paraphrasing Plant, 2000) created by mobile phones, that is the one physical space and multiple mobile virtual spaces of multiple conversational interactions. These are replacing a solid stable spatial context. Gergen does not, however, mention the corollary of absent presence, the experience when people emotionally and intellectually absent themselves from their shared physical location. The corollary is, of course, that others, people physically elsewhere, are now virtually present. At an Eduserv conference in London in 2010, delegates were asked not to watch the presentations on the live stream on their own laptops, presentations taking place literally a few feet in front of them. Is this some preference for the virtual, the next stage in absent presence?

A different account of identity (Truch & Hulme, 2004, p. 3) offers that, "social systems have become less location-based and more people-based". But on the other hand, "individuals now have the added complexity of having to operate in two distinct spaces: the locational space where they physically reside, and 'phone-space' (Townsend, 2000) where mobile communication takes place" (Truch & Hulme, 2004, p. 4). Our point is that self, roles and identity become more problematic, as well as the context in which these are situated, as we perform various context-specific roles.

Fortunati (2002) relates absent presence to a discussion of personal and public spaces, suggesting a preference for the known and private that forces us away from the physical:

> [Y]ou have the possibility of choosing between the public space of streets, stations, means of transport and the private space of interpersonal relationships, between chance socialness which may develop with those who happen to be passing by, and chosen socialness (e.g. with the friends you decide to call on your mobile phone). And it is obvious that the choice always falls on the second, if only because it represents the encroaching 'new'. (p. 515)

This means that, presumably in Fortunati's view, the familiarity of the personal and the intimate is less threatening. She continues by eliding absent presence with motion and then discussing the value and valorisation of space, reiterating the earlier point:

> This phenomenon is evident in means of transport. Compartment conversation, a typical communicative mode in which nothing very important is said, is increasingly often silenced by selected but artificial conversations (that is, by the mobile). The individual is in one place, as a physical presence, but virtually, as an immaterial presence, he or she is elsewhere. And elsewhere that takes on an ever-increasing fascination, because it gives the reality of space a new connotation.
>
> Physical space in fact is emptied of significance, becomes less dense as thickness, as the dimension of virtual space is grafted on to it. This phenomenon has, however, the implication that more and more distance is created with the unknown. Today it is difficult to surrender oneself to 'unknown lands' because one can face them armed with a mobile, thus defended by the socialness of one's point of departure . . . it is increasingly evident that between chosen and chance sociality the interest is much more on chosen,

even if this is virtual. In fact, the more one is forced into mobility, that is, into travelling great distances towards the unknown, the more one has to stress relations with what is familiar. (Fortunati, 2002, p. 515)

This has taken the speculative discussion of space, and the spatial context, to a discussion of agency and choices about which spaces to inhabit and which to avoid. It does, however, make the perhaps dubious equation between the safe and the familiar.

This analysis is not universally accepted. Some authors find evidence that mobiles attach people more strongly to existing social groups and contexts at the expense of joining or forming new ones; others find that they facilitate wide, shallow affiliations at the expense of fewer deeper ones (Geser, 2004, McEwen, 2010; Turkle, 2011). Whichever is actually the case, we are clearly seeing social proximity and social context changing from its established forms, being pulled and pushed and stretched differently.

Fortunati (2002), sees the underlying and unifying motivation for using mobile devices as somehow trying to wring more from both space and time:

> The attempt is to enlarge the surface of space and the duration of time by means of communicative technologies. Space has widened out horizontally, lengthened out vertically, and at the same time is perceived as a background; while time is experienced in all its extensions and expanded in thickness. Space and time have thus become the new frontiers of increased social productivity. (p. 514)

This portrays users' temporal and spatial contexts as some kind of resource or raw material (spatio-temporal capital, perhaps, or space-time as a commodity) resonating with the capitalist injunction that 'time is money' and with the earlier protestant valorisation of punctuality (Banks, 2006).

As time and space become more complex, they also become more confusing:

> What space and time has the mobile found itself interacting with? With a space that was already transformed before, developing its technological aspect, informative, multicultural, mobile and relational, in short, becoming a complex space, not immediately easy to understand. The increasing difficulty in people's immediate and effective relation with space, which has become increasingly difficult to understand, has been an important element at the base of the spread and success of the mobile phone. This instrument, in fact, has enabled people to somehow attenuate their anxiety and bewilderment in the face of this new quality and dimension of space. (Fortunati, 2002, p. 515)

This reiterates the notion that the familiar is reassuring and safe, and that it can now be easily accessed with a mobile connection. True or false, the discussion has implications for learning, almost by definition moving learners into the unfamiliar. Perhaps aspects of contextual support can provide reassurance.

Fortunati (2002) goes on to address the social context of mobiles:

> The mobile phone is a device that enables people, when they perceive the surrounding environment as extraneous to them, to contact somebody of their intimate circle, that is, to activate the reassuring procedure of recognition. In other words, people react to the lack of informative immediacy of the place, strengthening communicative immediacy with their social networks by means of the mobile. (p. 514)

Therefore, physical temporal and spatial contexts can become bewildering and unsettling, but social context offers reassurance.

## Different Spaces

Mobile devices are seen by many in the sociology of mobilities community as reconfiguring the relationships between spaces, between public spaces and private ones, between public and private contexts, and the ways in which these are penetrated by mobile virtual spaces. And in case we misunderstand these spaces, Childs (2013) argues that we do not inhabit the spaces we find, but rather we define spaces by inhabiting them. This reconfiguration is accompanied by what goes on within those spaces. Cooper (2002, p. 22) writes that the private "is no longer conceivable as what goes on, discreetly, in the life of the individual away from the public domain, or as subsequently represented in individual consciousness". Sheller and Urry (2003, p. 1) add that "massive changes are occurring in the nature of both public and private life and especially of the relations between them". Discussing media players, Bull (2005) writes:

> The use of these mobile sound technologies informs us about how users attempt to 'inhabit' the spaces within which they move. The use of these technologies appears to bind the disparate threads of much urban movement together, both 'filling' the spaces 'in-between' communication or meetings and structuring the spaces thus occupied. (p.344)

More so with the rise of noise-cancelling earphones, which further distance the local physical context.

This is part of a growing dislocation of time and place in which "everything arrives without any need to depart" (Virilio, 2000, p. 20): "Closer to what is far away than to what is just beside us, we are becoming progressively detached from ourselves" (p. 83). Owing to:

> . . . the tendency to previsit locations, through one medium or another; to actually arrive somewhere is no longer surprising in the way that it was . . . it

is becoming replaced by prevision. Thus according to this logic, the mobile would be one more technique by which the world became unsurprising. (Cooper, 2002, p. 26)

Another personal device, the in-car satellite navigation system, has a similar effect: that of previsiting places and locations. Other personal digital devices, such as the camcorder and the camera, allow us to recreate the past more and more vividly and to revisit places and locations, whilst augmented reality can supplement real places with imagined or imaginary ones. Moreover, "the instant availability of all types of information at any time or place means that there will be no need for physical motion" (Cooper, 2002, p. 25). Inertia or stagnation sets in, and the balance and proportions, the boundaries and the edges within the temporal context are transformed.

There are a growing number of augmented reality applications available as retail downloads for smartphones. These also add to the dilution of the immediate experience of the here-and-now. Examples include Layar, allowing developers to add layers onto the iPhone and Android phone's video, a 'mash-up' based on what the camera in the phone currently sees; Wikitude AR Travel Guide, which brings contextual Wikipedia information to what the camera currently sees; TAT Augmented ID, which uses the Flickr facial recognition technology to identify a person's face and overlay their image with their online profile and contact information; and TwittARound, which uses an iPhone's camera to overlay live video of the world around it with tweets. Ever increasing exposure to CGI and Photoshop, for example, must mean that our relations with what we used to think of as reality and context are becoming ever more complex and so does learning about this 'reality'.

Augmented reality applications (Papagiannakis, Singh, & Magnenat-Thalmann, 2008) and Google Maps with Street View both dilute the here-and-now; an ever-growing sense of surveillance and nervousness is implicit, too, as users become more known, visible and connected to their various contexts. Surveillance might be seen as a dilution of identity (certainly a diminution of privacy, an attribute of identity), at the same time as digital identities become more complex. Identity becomes more complex and fluid as we acquire and discard digital identities and join and leave digital communities within which these digital identities have meaning, making social contexts become more fluid.

## Interactive Travel through Contexts

Elsewhere in the literature of the sociology of mobilities, authors (Molz, 2010, p. 329) have commented on the "emergence of interactive travel, a mode of leisure travel that involves staying electronically connected while on the move", characterised by travellers using mobile technologies:

> …as a way of creating knowledge and negotiating on-the-road 'know-how'. Leisure travellers are increasingly integrating mobile technologies such as

laptop computers, wireless cards, MP3 players, GPS devices and mobile phones into their journeys in order to research and plan their trips, network with other travellers, share advice, and record, photograph and publish their experiences for the internet public. The result is a proliferation of online travel blogs, networked backpacker communities, mobile travel guides, hospitality networking sites, travel discussion boards, and the digital sharing of videos and photographs from travellers' journeys. (Molz, 2010, p. 88)

This is another way in which the real and virtual worlds, the real and virtual spatial contexts, are linked and interwoven; these travellers are "not only physically on the move, but are constantly moving amongst these overlapping virtual, imaginative, communicative and corporeal spaces of social interaction" (Molz, 2010, p. 330).

## Ragged and Uneven Contexts

Of course, mobility and connectedness do not sweep away the boundaries of time and spaces. Nor, as we have seen, are the spatial and temporal contexts more homogeneous or isotropic. They have moorings and tethering of their own. Spaces are now defined by the availability of varieties of network coverage, by mains power sockets and by ambient lighting levels without direct sunlight. Time is now measured by battery life; movement is restricted by cables, backing up and synching in much the same way that cars, the other symbol of modern Western mobility, are tethered to servicing schedules, flat tyres, traffic jams, car-parking spaces and filling stations: "Mobilities cannot be described without attention to the necessary spatial, infrastructural and institutional moorings that configure and enable mobilities. . . . There is no linear increase in fluidity without extensive systems of immobility. . ." (Hannam, Sheller, & Urry, 2006, p. 3).

## Individuals, Their Identities and Communities

Mobility and connection are also amongst the factors changing individuals and their identities, and the nature of communities. The rise of networked technologies has led to more complex ideas about identity, both formally, in relation to 'official' network technologies and the various sign-ons we acquire and collect, and informally, in relation to social networks, the various personalities we perform within them and the traces they leave. What constitutes the user, himself or herself, as opposed to his or her context changes and blurs? Some authors describe personal mobile devices as becoming prosthetic; Pertierra (2005) writes:

Unlike desktops and other immobile technologies, mobile phones more closely resemble tools or prosthetic devices as extensions of the body. They become extensions of the hand, allowing us to connect anytime, anywhere,

with anybody. Bodies themselves become writing devices as *phoneurs* negotiate new urban spaces. (p. 27)

Other authors describe them as becoming embodied (for example Rettie, 2005)
or claim, as Townsend (2002, p. 70):

> From pacifier, to nipple, to digital umbilical cord, the mobile phone rapidly
> progressed to assume a vital place in the virtual biology of urban informa-
> tion societies of the late twentieth century. At the final extreme, the mobile
> phone's connectivity might be completely subsumed into the body, and all
> other forms of communication become redundant, email, web, phone calls,
> all can be delivered over the universal handheld.

If context is a way of characterising the relationship between person and the
environment, then what we are seeing is this renegotiated in a variety of ways, in
this case of the body and its tools. A different aspect of the embodiment of mobile
phones was widely reported. "'I'd rather', deadpans Philippa Grogan, 16, 'give up,
like, a kidney than my phone. How did you manage before? Carrier pigeons?
Letters? Going round each other's houses on BIKES?'" (Henley, 2010). So we
see a much more fluid and fractured account of who we are, of our 'selves', and
likewise a more fluid and complex account of the physical environment and social
communities that constitute our context. These accounts will vary across every
conceivable variable.

## Knowledge, Knowing, Understanding and Learning

Mobile devices affect the processes by which ideas, images, information and
knowledge, and hence informal learning, are produced, stored, evaluated, valo-
rised, distributed, delivered and consumed. They are now part of a system that
allows everyone, including learners and potential learners, to generate and transmit content for learning—not just passively storing and consuming it, but making
mobile systems an integral part of the Web 2.0 ideology that takes users from
merely the web's readers to its writers. The impact of mobility and connectedness
on knowledge is to make it far more obviously relative, local, transient and partial.
Knowledge is local in being local to a community, local in being location-specific,
produced locally and consumed with defined communities, not necessarily geographically or spatially defined communities. The informational context is no
longer fixed, monolithic and external.

In formal learning, we already see changed ideas about space and knowledge
reflected in two emerging pedagogies: 'navigationism' (Brown, 2005) and 'connectionism' (Siemens, 2004). These grow out of networked and mobile learning
and shift the balance between ideas themselves and the relationships between
them, emphasising a kind of knowledge space, a topology of points rather than a

geography of bulky masses (of knowledge), thus transforming the intellectual or cognitive context within which learners move. Connectionism explicitly assumes "knowledge is distributed across a network of connections, and therefore . . . learning consists of the ability to construct and traverse those networks" (Downes, 2007). Therefore, we see changed perspectives on the relationships between knowledge and knower or learning and learner, with a far less straightforward relationship and boundary between each pair.

## The Future of Context

In the words of a newspaper article (Bilton, 2010):

> If you pull out your smartphone and click the button that says 'locate me' on your mapping application, you will see a small dot appear in the middle of the screen.
> That's you.
> If you start walking down the street in any direction, the whole screen will move right along with you, no matter where you go.
> This is a revolutionary change from the print-on-paper, where maps and locations are based around places and landmarks, not on you and your location.

The newspaper article's title makes the point more succinctly: "Where the individual is front and center". In any consideration of context, the learner or user is 'front and centre'.

Is this solipsism? Perhaps.

There is a counterpoint with a more scholarly or academic perspective, that of 'time geography' (Thrift, 1977). This also puts the learner or user front and centre, representing their movement through physical space as the trajectory of a point and enabling researchers to depict and analyse the use of places and spaces by different communities of users. This perspective could be extended for learners' multiple online identities and those proximate to them as some way into the multidimensional online places and spaces of cyberspace and phonespace, thus creating a new learning analytics.

The early half of our argument portrays the relationships between individual and environment as becoming increasingly richer and easier and as increasingly easy to exploit and deploy in support of existing enhanced or reformed pedagogies whilst recognising that we, not our surroundings, are now the focus and the source. The second part of our argument, however, is that the social changes we discussed earlier mean that this user at the front and centre is no longer distinct and separate, no longer 'a small dot', as described by time geography, but more smeared and blurred in time, space, knowledge, community and identity, the boundary between self and other becoming unsettled, dissolving and consequently ill at ease. Perhaps we must also question whether the technologies of context are contributing to an enriched and augmented reality or just distracting our attention from a reality that technology is not in fact augmenting but rather diluting, depleting and diminishing.

## References

Agar, J. (2003). *Constant touch: A global history of the mobile phone*. Cambridge: Icon.

Banks, K. (2006). L'Ordre du temps: L'invention de la ponctualité au XVIe siècle. *French Studies, LX*(1), 97–98.

Bilton, N. (2010, Sept. 14). Where the individual is front and center. *International Herald Tribune*, 19.

Brown, E. (2010). Introduction to location-based mobile learning. In E. Brown (Ed.), *Education in the wild: Contextual and location-based mobile learning in action* (pp. 7–9). Nottingham: Learning Sciences Research Institute, University of Nottingham.

Brown, T. H. (2005). Beyond constructivism: Exploring future learning paradigms. *Education Today, 2*(2), 1–11.

Bull, M. (2005). No dead air! The iPod and the culture of mobile listening. *Leisure Studies, 24*(4), 343–356.

Chen, G., & Kotz, D. (2000). A survey of context-aware mobile computing research. *Dartmouth Computer Science Technical Report TR2000–381*.

Childs, M. (2013). Defining space. *The Body Electric*. Retrieved from http://markchilds.org/2013/04/10/defining-space/

Cook, J. (2010). Mobile learner generated contexts: Research on the internalization of the world of cultural products. In B. Bachmair (Ed.), *Medienbildung in neuen Kulturräumen: Die deutschsprachige und britische Diskussion* (pp. 113–126). Wiesbaden: VS Verlag für Sozialwissenschaften.

Cook, J., Pachler, N., & Bachmair, B. (2010). Ubiquitous mobility with mobile phones: A cultural ecology for mobile learning. *E-learning and Digital Media, 8*(3), 181-195.

Cooper, G. (2002). The mutable world: Social theory. In B. Brown, N. Green & R. Harper (Eds.), *Wireless world: Social and interactional aspects of the mobile world* (pp. 19–31). London: Springer.

CoSN. (2012). *Making progress: Rethinking state and school district policies concerning mobile technologies and social media*. Washington, DC: Consortium for School Networking.

Da Bormida, G., Di Girolamo, M., Dahn, I., & Murelli, E. (2004). An open abstract framework for modeling interoperability of mobile learning services. In C. D. Kloos & A. Pardo (Eds.), *EduTech: Computer-aided design meets computer-aided learning* (pp. 113–120). Toulouse: Springer.

Dey, A.K., & Abowd, G.D. (2000). The context toolkit: Aiding the development of context-aware applications. In G. Abowd, G. Borriello, M. Gorlick, M. Karasick, & T. Starner (Eds.), *Workshop on software engineering for wearable and pervasive computing* (pp. 431–441).

Dey, A. K., & Abowd, G. D. (1999). Towards a better understanding of context and context-awareness. *GVU Technical Report GIT-GVU-99–22*. College of Computing, Georgia Institute of Technology.

Dourish, P. (2004). What we talk about when we talk about context. *Personal and Ubiquitous Computing, 8*(1), 19–30. Retrieved from http://www.dourish.com/publications.html

Downes, S. (2007). What connectivism is. Retrieved from http://halfanhour.blogspot.com/2007/02/what-connectivism-is.html

Fortunati, L. (2002).The mobile phone:Towards new categories and social relations. *Information, Communication & Society, 5*(4), 513–528.

Gergen, K. J. (2002).The challenge of absent presence. In J. E. Katz & M. A. Aakhus (Eds.), *Perpetual contact: Mobile communication, private talk, public performance* (pp. 227–241). Cambridge: Cambridge University Press.

Geser, H. (2004). Towards a sociological theory of the mobile phone. In A. Zerdick, K. Schrape, J.-C. Burgelmann, R. Silverstone, V. Feldmann, C. Wernick & C. Wolff (Eds.), *E-merging media: Communication and the media economy of the future* (pp. 235–260). Berlin: Springer.

Hannam, K., Sheller, M., & Urry, J. (2006). Editorial: Mobilities, immobilities and moorings. *Mobilities, 1*(1), 1–22.

Henley, J. (2010, July 16).Teenagers and technology: 'I'd rather give up my kidney than my phone'. *The Guardian.* Retrieved from http://www.guardian.co.uk/lifeandstyle/2010/jul/16/teenagers-mobiles-facebook-social-networking

International Telecommunications Union. (2004). Social and human considerations for a more mobile world. *Report from ITU/MIC Workshop on Shaping the Future Mobile Information Society.* Seoul. 26 February 2004.

Ling, R. (2008). *New tech, new ties: How mobile communication is reshaping social cohesion.* Cambridge, MA: MIT Press.

Ling, R. (2004). *The mobile connection: The cell phone's impact on society.* San Francisco, CA: Morgan Kaufmann Publishers.

McEwen, R. N. (2010). A world more intimate: Exploring the role of mobile phones in maintaining and extending social networks. Proceedings from the *Mobile Preconference, ICA Conference.* Singapore: SIRC.

Mobile Times. (n.d.). Intel Labs Research Project. Retrieved from http://web.archive.org/web/20100715175848/http://papr.intel-research.net/projects.htm

Molz, J.G. (2010) Connectivity, collaboration, search. In J. Urry, M. Büscher & K.Witchger (Eds.), *Mobile methods* (pp. 88–103). Routledge: London.

Nyíri, K. (2007). *Mobile studies: Paradigms and perspectives.*Vienna: Passagen Verlag, Hungarian Academy of Sciences.

Papagiannakis, G., Singh, G., & Magnenat-Thalmann, N. (2008). A survey of mobile and wireless technologies for augmented reality systems. *Journal of Computer Animation and Virtual Worlds, 19*(1), 3–22.

Pertierra, R. (2005). Mobile phones, identity and discursive intimacy. *An Interdisciplinary Journal on Humans in ICT Environments, 1*(1), 23–44.

Plant, S. (2001). *On the mobile:The effects of mobile telephones on individual and social life.* Motorola. Retrieved from http://www.it-c.dk/courses/MGB/F2002/on_the_mobile.pdf

Rettie, R. (2005). Presence and embodiment in mobile phone communication. *Psychology Journal, 3*(1), 16–34.

Schilit, B., Adams, N., & Want, R. (1994). Context-aware computing applications. Proceedings from the *First Workshop on Mobile Computing Systems and Applications, 1994* (pp. 85–90). IEEE.

Schilit, B., & Theimer, M. (1994). Disseminating active map information to mobile hosts. *IEEE Network, 8*(5), 22–32.

Schmidt, A., Beigl, M., & Gellesen, H.-W. (1998).There is more to context than location. Proceedings from the *International Workshop on Interactive Applications of Mobile Computing* (pp. 893–901).

Sheller, M., & Urry, J. (2003). Mobile transformations of 'public' and 'private' life. *Theory, Culture & Society, 20,* 107–125.

Siemens, G. (2004). Connectivism: A learning theory for the digital age. *International Journal of Instructional Technology and Distance Learning, 2*(1). Retrieved from http://www.elearnspace.org/Articles/connectivism.htm

Siorpaes, S., Broll, G., Paolucci, M., Rukzio, E., Hamard, J., Wagner, M., & Schmidt, A. (2006). Mobile interaction with the internet of things. Presented at the *4th International Conference on Pervasive Computing*. Dublin. Retrieved from http://www.medien.informatik.unimuenchen.de/fileadmin/mimuc/rukzio/Mobile_interaction_with_the_internet_of_things_final.pdf

Sørensen, C., Mathiassen, L., & Kakihara, M. (2002). Mobile services: Functional diversity and overload. Presented at *New Perspectives On 21st-Century Communications*. Budapest. 24–25 May.

Stald, G. (2008). Mobile identity: Youth, identity, and mobile communication media. In D. Buckingham (Ed.), *Youth, identity, and digital media* (pp.143–164). Cambridge, MA: The MIT Press.

Syvanen, A., Beale, R., Sharples, M., Ahonen, M., & Lonsdale, P. (2005). Supporting pervasive learning environments: Adaptability and context awareness in mobile learning. Proceedings from the *IEEE International Workshop on Wireless and Mobile Technologies in Education, 2005* (pp. 3–9). IEEE. November.

Taylor, J. (2004). A task-centred approach to evaluating a mobile learning environment for pedagogical soundness. In J. Attewell & C. Savill-Smith (Eds.), *Learning with mobile devices: Research and development* (pp. 167–171). London: Learning and Skills Development Agency.

Thrift, N. (1977). An introduction to time-geography. *Geo Abstracts*, Norwich: University of East Anglia.

Townsend, A. M. (2002). Mobile communications in the twenty-first century city. In B. Brown, N. Green & R. Harper (Eds.), *Wireless world: Social and interactional aspects of the mobile world* (pp. 62–77). London: Springer-Verlag.

Townsend, A. M. (2000). Life in the real-time city: Mobile telephones and urban metabolism. *Journal of Urban Technology, 7*(2), 85–104.

Traxler, J. (2011). Context in a wider context. In N. Pachler, B. Bachmair & J. Cook (Eds.), *Mobile learning in widening contexts: Concepts and cases*. Retrieved from http://www.medienpaed.com/en/Issues/#19

Traxler, J. (2010a). Students and mobile devices. *Research in Learning Technology, 18*(2), 149–160.

Traxler, J. (2010b). Sustaining mobile learning and its institutions. *International Journal of Mobile and Blended Learning, 2*(4), 129–138 Thrift, N. (1977). An introduction to time-geography. *Geo Abstracts*. University of East Anglia.

Truch, A., & Hulme, M. (2004). Exploring the implications for social identity of the new sociology of the mobile phone. Proceedings from the *Global and the Local in Mobile Communications: Places, Images, People and Connections Conference*. Budapest. January.

Turkle, S. (2011). *Alone Together: Why we expect more from technology and less from each other.* New York, NY: Basic Books.

Virilio, P. (2000). *Polar inertia.* London: Sage.

Wang, Y.-K. (2004). Context-awareness and adaptation in mobile learning. Proceedings from the *International Workshop on Mobile Technologies in Education (WMTE)* (pp. 154–158).

# CONCLUSION

## Contextual Challenges for the Next Generation

*John Traxler and Agnes Kukulska-Hulme*

This book very self-consciously addresses the next generation of mobile learning and identifies contextual learning as central to that next generation. This concluding chapter draws together the themes of the earlier individual contributions and explores the credibility of contextual learning as the next generation of mobile learning. Evolving factors and trends in the wider educational and social environment are relevant to this analysis. There are technical, demographic and business trends. There are trends around education, such as industrialisation, globalisation, competition and consumerisation, and within education itself, such as MOOCs (massive online open courses), the flipped classroom and BYOD (bring-your-own-device). There are also ongoing challenges such as scale, sustainability, ethics, theoretical base, evaluation and design. These trends and challenges shape the environment of contextual mobile learning and the environment of the next generation of mobile learning.

We must, however, first put these trends into an historical perspective. We have depicted the present as a tipping point, a watershed between an earlier decade, when mobile learning technology was expensive, fragile, difficult and scarce, and the current decade in which it has become cheap, robust, easy and universal. The transition is taking mobile learning from one of the leading innovative edges of e-learning research, development and deployment across formal education and within organisations, often underpinned by the foundations of educational and psychological theorising, to mobile learning as a ubiquitous, pervasive, diffuse and perhaps intrusive characteristic of a more mobile and connected world, underpinned by emergent sociological theorising. This transition must, however, be considered alongside a rather different tipping point or watershed: that of the global recession of around 2008–2009 (Eaton, Kortum, Neiman, & Romalis, 2011; Imbs, 2010), accompanied by a shift to the right in many Western liberal democracies (Apple, 2000, 2004). These political and economic forces may have militated against the kind of continued government support and government agencies that in the previous decade had supported innovative TEL research, including mobile learning research, in Western Europe, Asia Pacific and North America. At the same time, we have seen the rise of more market-driven globalised models of higher education, of which MOOCs, discussed later, are the TEL manifestation (Apple, Kenway, & Singh, 2005; Monahan, 2005; Spring, 2008). On a slightly smaller scale across the same period, we have seen the emergence of the apps economy (Genachowski, 2010, p. 3) in the global North, and in the global South we have seen the awakening of interest amongst international agencies such as UNESCO, World Bank, World Economic Foundation, USAID, ITU (International Telecommunication Union) and ILO (International Labour Organization) in mobiles as the vehicle for educational and humanitarian missions (Traxler, 2013). This is no doubt a rather ambitious interpretation of the global context of contextual mobile learning, but to a greater or lesser extent, these and other similar factors must inevitably skew the environment of a highly theorised research activity exploiting high-end technology such as contextual mobile learning.

A different account of e-learning, and the place of mobile learning within it, is that of the industrialisation of formal learning using computers, part of the massification of higher education driven initially by centre left governments in the 1990s (Traxler, 2010b), raising questions about whether mobile learning has been appropriated and exploited merely to make this process more modern, attractive and engaging in the interest of throughput, efficiency and unit costs. Contextual mobile learning research can be seen from this perspective, and the earlier chapters from our contributors could be revisited with this in mind.

This brief exploration of the environment of contextual mobile learning may seem distant and perhaps irrelevant to the daily concerns and activities of researchers, but the research community would be ill advised to forget the ultimate sources of funding for research, development and deployment, namely government and industry, or their ultimate accountability to their voters, customers and shareholders. The growth of the 'impact agenda' in various national research assessments exercises, notably the UK (Martin, 2011; Smith, Ward, & House, 2011; Bornmann, 2012), is in part a recognition of the accountability of researchers and is destined to develop in sophistication and to reach more and more of the Anglophone research communities. As above, the earlier chapters from our contributors could be revisited with this in mind.

This is not the place to critique the nexus between research funding and policy priorities. We should, however, remember that research is chiefly sponsored and supported on the basis of some public or corporate agenda. Economic realities and political priorities are part of these and account for research that promises to lead to sustainable business models, for societal impact and for various prominent themes such as cultural heritage and STEM teaching.

We should also bear in mind a different social perspective on research. The mobile learning research community is a research community, and as such can be characterised as working within a clearly defined paradigm, in the Kuhnian sense (Kuhn, 2012). This means that there are axioms that unite the community and underpin assimilation and acceptance by the community, that there is a research agenda that the community works to, that there are papers and books it routinely accepts and refers to and that there are pivotal incidents and personalities within the community. Whilst the mobile learning community might not explicitly articulate its axioms, they are clearly derived from the aspirations, methods, funding, rhetoric and history (and indeed, the personnel) of the e-learning community, but have given it a separate identity. It is not inconceivable that the mobile learning paradigm espoused by this community is under threat at its periphery; that what are perceived as unimportant errors or problems, for example difficulties with sustainability, scale or evidence, in fact represent the crumbling of one paradigm and the emergence of another, to which these earlier 'errors' or 'problems' are the foundational truths. The breadth but also the discontinuities and incommensurabilities amongst our current contributions may presage this.

So it is possible to portray learning with mobiles as about to undergo a paradigm shift, from a position where the research agenda was generated by a research community that grew up or grew out of desktop e-learning, using mobile technologies to enhance, extend and enrich the existing curricula, institutions and professions of education, to another paradigm that situates mobile learning into an account of a mobile and connected society, the part of the account built on the ways in which people and communities generate, transform, share and transmit ideas, opinions, identities, images and information, as they move and connect. If such a change is about to take place, then any theorising about contextual mobile learning takes place against a transformed background and on transformed foundations. The new foundational disciplines may include the sociology of mobilities (Hannam, Sheller, & Urry, 2006; Urry, 2007) and the methodological toolkit may come from the same source (Büscher & Urry, 2009). This in effect transforms what has been called 'mobile learning' from the mobile component of learning, actually e-learning, to the educational component of mobility and mobile societies, and our book's contributions could be reviewed through these two prisms or paradigms. We remember that a challenge for any account of mobile learning has always been future-proofing. The contributions have sufficient context, concepts and pedagogy to ensure that this has been addressed.

In our introductory chapter we briefly touched on the ordering of chapters in terms of increasingly broad and more theoretical perspectives; it is worth returning to this in order to ask about the historical development of theory and the likely trends and developments. Looking more closely at the development of mobile learning, we see that its theoretical perspectives deeply associated with its e-learning ancestry represent a shared theoretical gene pool. If we are now predicting a contextual mobile learning rooted in the popular consumption of mobile technologies, then perhaps we need a more social or sociological basis for theories of contextual mobile learning. Our latter chapters begin outlining how this might evolve.

## Technical, Demographic and Business Trends

The technical, demographic and business trends are likely to be generally smooth and rational; in the course of the gestation of this book, we have seen mobiles change from being scarce, fragile, expensive and difficult to being universal, robust, cheap and easy, shifting the research challenge from technology to pedagogy. In the same period, we have seen the technologies of mobile context change from research to retail and the coverage, functionality and ownership of high-end mobiles and networks continues to increase with no apparent saturation in sight. We have also seen the continued and growing influence of US technologies, pedagogies and business models, and this must have impacted on the balance and breadth of mobile learning activity, especially aspects of mobile learning with a theoretical research bias, for example contextual mobile learning where the mechanisms to generate profit by scaling up are potentially problematic unlike, say, messaging, apps or games.

The early days of mobile learning were sometimes characterised by hopes or expectations of a 'converged, generic device', somehow equivalent to the PC platform. The last decade has, if anything, seen increasing divergence, specialisation and polarisation in devices as the markets fragment and the manufacturers compete. In some senses this may have slowed the emergence of theories of mobile learning since the technology platform was never a stable, consistent and rational given but actually a diverse and unstable ecology of different platforms driven by commercial concerns in a consumer market place. The monolithic nature and lifetime of devices—throwaway rather than reparable and dedicated rather than flexible—obviously dictates different commercial strategies compared to those of laptops, which can often be upgraded, and those of desktops, which can often change or absorb different boards, racks, peripherals or connectors, and may have contributed to a certain conservatism. With different mobile devices often come different interfaces and operating systems. This has made cross-device development problematic, perhaps forcing developers in the direction of the lowest common denominator and away from exploiting unproven and highly device-specific features. The interplay of these various factors may have slowed down the commercialisation of informal contextual mobile learning.

Many research projects in mobile learning, including contextual mobile learning, have been predicated on the provision of institutional devices or project devices rather than learner devices. This is methodologically convenient—it removes a confounding variable—and logistically convenient. It does, however, produce findings that do not apply to the more sustainable situations where learners bring their own devices. This has consequences for the sustainability of contextual mobile learning based on BYOD strategies since designers need to make assumptions about platforms. Fortunately, the common features of web browsers, high-speed connectivity and location-awareness may mark the emergence of de facto common standards, as may image capture and audio capture standards. The ownership of location-aware, web-enabled smartphones may soon become an adequate user base for increased commercial development.

One specific technological and perhaps retail trend has been *wearables*, mainly wristwatches and goggles. Research interest has driven hesitant commercial product development, namely Google Glass (Johnson et al., 2013), Apple Watch (Walker, 2009) and Pebble (Esakia, Niu, & McCrickard, 2015). Some of the research projects have been location-aware and many can sense something of the user-context, for example heart rate (Lymberis, 2003) and by inference, mood (Picard & Healey, 1997). The immediate impact on mainstream contextual mobile learning is unclear as yet, but wearables certainly represent the trend in which technology becomes more prosthetic.

Accounts begin to talk of the transition of education systems from mass-production to mass-customisation (Freund, 2003) and of the long tail (Hartley, 2008; Waslander, 2007). This transition is manifest in increasing personalisation, contextualisation and now learner analytics. Recommender systems, systems that "support users by identifying interesting products and services in situations where the number and complexity of offers outstrips the user's capability to survey them and reach a decision" (Felfernig, Friedrich, & Schmidt-Thieme, 2007, p. 18), are now appearing in education and exploit mobile devices to provide data on the learner's context and to infer the optimal learning activity for the time, place and curriculum (Crane et al., 2012; Yau, 2011).

There is clearly much potential in formal learning for the convergence of learning analytics, contextual technologies and learner management systems. It is not difficult to imagine context and proximity becoming more comprehensive, embracing, connecting and inferring from social and academic context and proximity, as well as spatial and temporal context and proximity along with learning analytics, to give students personalised guidance and support through their courses and assessments. Convergence and synergy with the growing implementations of contextual information systems is also possible. These are being deployed in universities in the UK as the open-source, publicly-funded Mobile Oxford (Fernando, 2010) and the proprietary CampusM (Ombiel, 2015). They assume the ownership of location-aware, browser-enabled smartphones and give increasing sophisticated answers about geographically distributed events and resources using institutional and municipal data.

To return to our larger theme, that of technical, demographic and business trends, many national and international agencies collect data, for example ITU (2015), CTO (2013) and GSMA (2015), and provide analyses that explore social and technical issues. In very general terms these will inevitably describe cheaper, better devices connecting over wider, faster networks. We do know, however, that there is considerable granularity when we look at individual countries and specific economic classes. Furthermore, unlike technical, demographic and business trends, social trends and educational trends are more problematic and less easy to extrapolate. Fashion, politics and personalities all influence how these evolve.

## Trends around Education

These include competition, industrialisation, globalisation and privatisation of much of education. At the risk of over-generalising or over-simplifying, many observers would argue that the global higher education environment is increasingly the domain of large competitive institutions based in the global North (for example, Altbach, Reisberg, & Rumbley, 2009; Washburn, 2008; Hemsley-Brown & Oplatka, 2006). The target populations of contextual mobile learning research may be informal adult learning or school students or sometimes the global South, but the research itself is largely based in universities or research institutes, so the general climate of higher education influences research across the sectors globally. These may seem distant and abstract issues compared to the specificity and locatedness of contextual mobile learning, but its success and sustainability will depend on its capacity to align with these wider trends and forces.

There are, however, also questions about the extent to which the pedagogies embodied in the various kinds of contextual mobile learning are culturally specific. Higher education is increasingly globalised and homogeneous, driven partly by a global technical and professional curriculum and by the need to compete globally; this environment may foster circumstances in which contextual mobile learning could spread and develop. Informal, opportunistic and community education may be quite the reverse. The implicit values of individual and personalised enquiry, of authentic and situated learning and of active learner engagement may not align well with more conformist, collective, conservative or authoritarian cultures. The work of Hofstede (1997) and others that we discuss later identifies parameters that might predispose a culture towards or away from the types of learning that we describe here. This might seem an oblique connection, but these larger issues are the context in which contextual mobile learning thrives or withers.

## Trends within Education

The future of contextual mobile learning may depend on its perceived alignment with various other fashions, trends and developments elsewhere within education. At the moment these include MOOCs, the flipped classroom, OER (Open Educational Resources) and the changing nature of design. These are described in detail elsewhere, for example, the New Media Consortium's (2015) *Horizon Reports* and UK Open University's (2014) annual *Innovating Pedagogy* publications, in the scientific literature, the popular media and the professional press. They are of course not necessarily clearly and stably defined. MOOCs, OER and the flipped classroom do, however, share a concern for efficiency, the efficiency of the usage of resources and in the usage of time, a concern to leverage digital technology to save effort, redundancy and duplication.

The activity around MOOCs has been relatively sudden, intense and global. It is increasingly well documented and analysed (Ossiannilsson, 2014; Liyana-gunawardena, Adams, & Williams, 2013; Dillenbourg, Fox, Kirchner, Mitchell, & Wirsing, 2014; Conole, 2014). The principles of MOOCs were identified as distributed platforms, autonomy, diversity, openness, and connectivity (Downes, 2009, Downes, 2013), and the four key MOOC activities as: aggregation (filtering, selecting, and gathering personally meaningful information); remixing (interpreting the aggregated information and bringing to it personal perspectives and insights); repurposing (refashioning the information to suit personal purposes); and feeding forward (sharing the newly fashioned information with and learning from other participants) (Kop & Carroll, 2011). After the early experiments, including the MobiMOOC series on mobile learning (de Waard et al., 2011; de Waard et al., 2012), retrospectively labelled as a 'community MOOC', the phenomenon moved away from its early 'connectionist' principles. It became a much more pedagogically conservative albeit rich-media platform driven by plausible but unproven corporate or institutional business models, despite various attempts to prioritise educational factors (for example, Mackness, Waite, Roberts, & Lovegrove, 2013). Even FutureLearn (Ferguson & Sharples, 2014; Sharples et al., 2014, pp. 9–14), the UK national platform, whilst built on an explicitly rigorous pedagogy and designed to privilege mobile delivery, does not provide an experience of contextual mobile learning. There is perhaps an interesting connection to be made between connectionist pedagogy and contextual mobile technologies. Currently, however, contextual mobile learning does not seem well aligned to the MOOC phenomenon.

Learning analytics is a popular and growing area of educational enquiry that seeks to understand and exploit the big data increasingly available from institutional digital systems data harvested from learners' devices and learners' interactions. One definition is: "Learning analytics is the measurement, collection, analysis and reporting of data about learners and their contexts, for purposes of understanding and optimising learning and the environments in which it occurs." (Ferguson, 2012a, p. 305). It is now widely documented and reviewed (Ferguson, 2012b; Siemens & Baker, 2012; Siemens & Long, 2011). Key points are that contextual mobile learning systems will have contextual data, both rich qualitative data from learner interactions and quantitative data and metadata from technical systems; these are now starting to be explored (Aljohani & Davis, 2012a, 2012b) and there are links to the work on recommender systems mentioned earlier. Concerns about privacy and consent are increased with contextual mobile learning systems because of the richer data about the learners' context (Pardo & Siemens, 2014), and these become problematic as implementation moves from a regulated research environment to instances of informal and opportunistic mobile learning. These concerns are further emphasised when vulnerable learner groups such as immigrants are involved, yet for these learners, contextual mobile learning can be a lifeline when formal learning is not sufficiently relevant to their immediate needs, or it is too costly and inconvenient, as has been demonstrated in the MASELTOV project on social inclusion for immigrants (Gaved et al., 2014; Pearson et al., 2014). If contextual mobile learning becomes a commercial or retail phenomenon instead of a research phenomenon, the ethical framework changes from research ethics to public legislation or these two perspectives must find a way to coexist.

Perhaps the simplest definition of the flipped (or inverted) classroom is that "events that have traditionally taken place inside the classroom now take place outside the classroom and vice versa" (Lage, Platt, & Treglia, 2000, p. 32). Essentially a school phenomenon, it has nevertheless promoted discussion and reflection in the university sector. The flipped classroom is an attempt to systematically optimise face-to-face learning by moving as much learning out of the classroom, online or into the home. The flipped classroom can also be seen from a management perspective as the pretext or opportunity to reduce costs by reducing contact time. There are many reviews, histories and explanations (Bishop & Verleger, 2013, Hughes, 2012) and critiques (Tucker, 2012). In some respects, the flipped classroom is a response to make the most traditional teaching more effective and engaging (Berrett, 2012) and to provide an over-arching rhetoric and rationale for earlier piecemeal attempts such as personal response systems (PRS). There is little evidence to date of using contextual mobile learning in a consciously flipped classroom, though obviously mobile learning in a broader sense forms part of the flipped classroom repertoire (Herreid & Schiller, 2013). It may simply be that contextual mobile learning is largely a research topic and that teachers and lecturers do not normally have the expertise or experience to design, develop or procure a contextual mobile learning component for their flipped classroom; it may be that contextual mobile learning is quite structured and premeditated compared to the flexible and responsive nature of the flipped classroom.

Contextual mobile learning is historically and still largely an individual and hierarchic Web 1.0 broadcast pedagogy rather than a flat, social and participative Web 2.0 pedagogy where learners consume rather than create, though certainly some of our contributors show how consumers can become producers and learners are becoming teachers. This is a necessary development not only in terms of educational richness but also in terms of financial sustainability. As the costs of infrastructure, hardware and connectivity decrease and the notion of BYOD gains acceptance, the irreducible cost of contextual mobile learning seems to be the editorial and educational core of developing and managing the resources. This notion that learners can contribute contextually-specific ideas, opinions, images and information as well as consume them not only builds a progressively richer educational experience and resource but also suggests how the issues of editorial and educational cost might be reduced. The role of educators and designers might be to create the framework, the foundation and the stimulus for successive and cumulative contributions and interactions, opening the possibilities of contextually-specific expressive and creative experiences and contextually-specific memories and mementoes alongside (physical) rescue archaeology, the hurried attempt to find and preserve physical artefacts revealed in the course of construction work (Jones 1984). User generated content and the Web 2.0 ideology would a useful antidote to editorial and educational costs, and to perceptions of contextual mobile learning as a hard-wired top-down pedagogy.

BYOD policies are potentially problematic for contextual mobile learning in formal education. The term itself is rather vague and may mean anything from permission to compulsion; everything from laptops to mobile smartphones; some generic aspirations or some specifics about interface, connectivity and apps; something merely permissive, optional, enriching and thus perhaps irrelevant or something essential, assessed, enforced. There is furthermore currently little actual or documented experience of BYOD in the various sectors (CoSN, 2012; Handel, Ritter, & Marcovitz, 2014; Traxler, 2010a). The general implications in terms of hardware and infrastructure are, however, straightforward and can be itemised in terms of connectivity and electricity, in terms of routers and charging points. Contextual mobile learning may, however, be one area of the curriculum where connectivity, processing power or interface impose a higher threshold than the norm, but given the need for BYOD policies to be reasonably future-proof and to keep ahead of ever-increasing functionality and power, this is probably not a major consideration.

The more problematic aspects of BYOD policies for contextual mobile learning are specifying the devices that might be supported and specifying the nature of that support. Specifying the nature of the support is problematic because it is partly an academic issue and partly a technical issue, concerning who answers which kind of questions and responds with which kind of resources. Specifying the devices is problematic because of the sheer diversity and transience of devices, interfaces, operating systems and applications and the need or opportunity to provide support for licenses and institutional purchasing. Unfortunately mobile technologies are characterised by widely different technical and business models, one obvious example being the closed Apple technology and iTunes business model, another being the more open but anarchic Android model. App availability may be the overriding consideration, and currently this would take learners and their institutions towards Apple, that is iPhones and iPads, which are arguably leading the field in terms of pedagogy and technology but problematic as a business model in education. Moving contextual mobile learning must address these kinds of issues in order to achieve sustainable institutionalisation in formal education.

A rather different challenge is the changing and unresolved nature of design and consequently perhaps of teaching. We have observed or implied the increasing abundance of resources, both content and communities, for learners to access and in the movement from computers for learning to mobiles for learning, and we can see increasing contexts for learners to create or access. Learning with computers led to the design and construction of educational artefacts, from CAL packages to VLE/LMS systems and more besides, but artefacts that built on the assumption that they were monopolising the learner's digital resources and monopolising their attention and activity. Learning with mobiles, because mobiles are embedded in the world of learners' ongoing noneducational lives and because their role as the portal to the abundance of communities, contexts and content for learning, does not in practise have this monopoly. Design is more problematic, needing to shift the emphasis away from the design of educational artefacts and towards the design of educational experiences, specifically the design of experiences that recognise the demise of monopoly and the rise of abundance. This argument problematises the role of the teacher as well as challenges the work of the designer, since the teacher would have turned the artefact into an experience. Whilst this argument may offer a way forward for mobile learning designers in general, driving the development of new frameworks, methods and tools, it seems more problematic for the designers of contextual mobile learning—certainly it undermines any sense of immersion within the contextual mobile learning experience.

There is a shift in how the role and responsibilities of teachers are conceptualised, away from that of sole responsibility for creating content and stimulating discussion amongst a closed group of learners towards that of continually monitoring, evaluating and recommending resources, communities and materials from the wider world (Verhaart, 2012; Mihailidis & Cohen, 2013; Robson, 2013; Gadot & Levin, 2012). This has been called curating, transforming the role of teachers from the sole author and arbiter of content to the collector, organiser and guarantor of educational opportunities, including content and communities. These might include OER, YouTube, podcasts, blog posts and SIGs. It is not, however, immediately obvious how contextual mobile learning fits into this description.

The challenge now is to think about the design of contextual mobile learning experiences when the contextual mobile learning app no longer monopolises the learner's attention. These learners bring to contextual mobile learning the habits, expectations and experiences of digital inhabitants, not digital residents (White & Le Cornu, 2011), living in mobile cyberspace or phonespace as the default residence whilst multitasking or time-slicing between various modalities, communities, threads and apps confidently and frequently. Is there a model of context-aware mobile learning that integrates or incorporates the curation of resources, content and communities into a context-aware mobile learning experience?

## Trends within Mobile Learning

We have seen the early research-driven mobile learning research community working within universities being overtaken by a commercial *apps economy*, user-generated podcasts and web access based on rather different (implicit) theories of mobile learning. We have also seen, as we have observed elsewhere, a movement from mobile learning devised and deployed by experts and activists to learning with mobiles where the nature, level and granularity of the learning have become increasing ill-defined, where learners have access to almost unlimited websites, videos, podcasts and resources and where learning is being created by learners. This may mean much progress and discussion goes unreported.

In terms of mobile learning research and development activity, alongside the contextual mobile learning discussed here, we see a growing focus on mobile-assisted language learning (Miangah & Nezarat, 2012; Chinnery, 2006; Kukulska-Hulme & Shield, 2008; Kukulska-Hulme & Shield, 2007; Godwin-Jones, 2011), work-based learning (Pachler, Pimmer, & Seipold, 2011) and STEM (science, technology, engineering and mathematics, Crompton & Traxler, 2015a, 2015b) education. These are perhaps the emergent successes of the mobile learning research community. Within this research community, we are probably seeing a diversification, as illustrated by our contributors, away from theoretical foundations based in the behaviourism and social constructivism inherited from computer-based e-learning.

The current epoch poses several challenges to the theorising of contextual mobile learning. On the one hand, the universality of mobile technologies reduces the apparent need or demand for theory (since mobile learning is now obvious or might seem so to educational managers, educational policy makers and the general public, nearly all of whom now confidently use a mobile phone), but on the other hand, the universality of mobile technologies may mean a shift from essentially psychological accounts based around individual experiences to emerging sociological accounts based on social phenomena. If we look to likely sources of these, it might be the sociology of mobilities community mentioned earlier. This community is beginning to develop methodological innovation based on a mobile worldview or mobile axiology combined with smaller and more powerful empirical technologies that enable increasingly naturalistic experimental settings. The implications for contextual mobile learning in particular are as yet largely unclear.

## Challenges and Barriers

Several factors represent the constraints or challenges if contextual mobile learning is to make a sustained and substantial contribution to education. The evidence, however, upon which to base such a sustained or substantial contribution has always been problematic. Small-scale, fixed-term, culturally-specific projects were always challenging in terms of generalisation and transferability. The extra constraint that characterised many research projects in contextual mobile learning, that of working with the same handset platform across the learner cohort, exacerbated this challenge because it failed to address the irrefutable fact that financial sustainability depended on exploiting learners' own mixed and changeable devices. Now the popularity, indeed near-universality, of high-spec mobiles transforms the context of the evidence base and its purpose. It may be possible to make a pragmatic assumption about access to web-enabled, well-connected, location-aware smartphones as the basis for scale and sustainability. There might, however, be cultural or social limitations to scale. Having addressed the technical barriers, we may be left with an irreducible essence of contextual mobile learning that is local; once the technology has been scaled and the curriculum standardised or mapped and the assets tagged, we might still encounter the hurdle or barrier that context-aware mobile learning is by its nature local.

Perhaps the route to some kind of scalability is standards and technologies that build large-scale context-aware mobile learning out of the aggregation of local contexts. We must, however, also recognise the significance of culture. When we think about the sustainability of contextual mobile learning, we must think about its potential to transfer from one culture to another. Whilst much of the world's formal education systems are uniform and consistent, or at least trending and aspiring in that direction, the expectations and experiences of informal learning differ from culture to culture and are shaped by their host cultures. In order to understand the possibility and nature of transfer, we need to measure and compare the nature of culture. Drawing on the work of Hofstede (1997) is one way of tackling or conceptualising this (Traxler & Crompton, 2015). If we can identify cultural similarities between two cultures, then transferring a contextual mobile learning idea from one to the other may be more likely to be successful. Culture, however defined and measured, is not monolithic or homogeneous, and the success of an idea may depend on more similarities, such as similarities on the axis of risk-taking/risk-avoidance, short-term/long-term orientation, individualism/collectivism or some other measure. There are several other approaches to measuring or quantifying culture. Hofstede is far from unique (for example, Ingelehart & Welzel, 2005; Lewis, 1996) and certainly not universally accepted—these remarks are only intended to hint at the possibilities of this approach.

In both the formal sector and the informal sector, there is pressure to evaluate interventions and demonstrations. With public money at stake, this is understandable. The evaluations of mobile learning have, however, not always been trustworthy and convincing (Traxler & Kukulska-Hulme, 2006) and have consequently not always justified further investment or effort. To some extent, however, the quest for evidence is increasingly backwards looking and irrelevant, and associated with the recent past when society and personal mobile technology were separable. Looking forwards, a far better case for effort and investment in mobile learning, including contextual mobile learning, is that it represents authentic and credible learning in societies where the technologies of connection and mobility are pervasive and ubiquitous. It is, however, still the case that costs (and opportunity costs) have to be justified and budgets found; otherwise contextual mobile learning remains largely a research activity.

Another potential challenge is embedding or institutionalisation, meaning moving contextual mobile learning projects from the episodic, optional and un-assessed fringes of courses and programs of formal education to the core where they are ongoing, compulsory and assessed. This involves a transition from the culture of innovators and researchers to the culture of administration and teaching and into the realms of quality assurance and in some respects into the realms of the concerns alluded to earlier when we discussed the business and industrial aspects of education, reliability, cost-effectiveness, competitiveness and sustainability. The last issue takes us back to the faltering acceptance of BYOD strategies addressed elsewhere in this chapter. The culture issues are addressed elsewhere in the chapter too, though they should also be expressed and explored in terms of the 'diffusion of innovations' (Rogers, 2010; Frank, Zhao, & Borman, 2004). In either case the embedding of contextual mobile learning must be analysed in terms of the specifics of contextual mobile learning rather than any more general analysis in terms of mobile learning. Some of the factors around embedding involve building and transforming staff capacity; contextual mobile learning is very specific and different from, say, messaging or language learning. Another hurdle or challenge to the wider acceptance of contextual mobile learning might be concerns about equity. Some of these might already be embedded within any debate about BYOD strategies, but there should certainly be concerns for those physiologically and cognitively different learners and for the high price, for both handsets and connectivity, involved.

In general, there might also be ethical concerns about contextual mobile learning, and these will evolve as it moves from the domain of institutional research ethics to educational professional judgment in formal learning and public regulation and legislation in informal learning. There may be some tensions between the educational experience of context on the one hand, either Web 1.0, where learners consume, or Web 2.0, where learners also create or transform, and on the other hand, the social, recreational or retail experience of contextual mobile learning, and the issues of informed consent and data privacy may be problematic. Whilst the ethical question confronting any research is always, "Will it do harm?", this does, however, assume the benign professional neutrality of researchers; the next question should be, "Whose interests are served?" Researchers in contextual mobile learning must answer these two questions and not assume that either institutional ethics procedures or professional body regulations will absolve them. Contextual mobile learning is complex, abstract and fluid, and 'unexpected consequences' can be reliably expected.

In a wider context, educators probably have some moral obligation to think about the relevance of contextual mobile learning to poorer learners, poorer communities, poorer institutions and poorer countries. This may be a call for more contextual mobile learning research with low-end technologies such as SMS on entry-level phones. For instance, in metropolitan areas with high base-station density, the SatLav project in London provides contextual information (Sherwood, 2007)—it could perhaps be combined with the SMS-based decision-tree scenarios (Cornelius & Marston, 2009) used in real-time simulations.

In looking at ethics and equity, especially in looking at the possibilities of extending contextual mobile learning to the global South, we must remember that the interfaces, design and delivery of mobile technologies are deeply, indeed structurally, biased in favour of US technologies and corporations, and in favour of US Anglophone language, culture, metaphors and gestures. Localisation and contextualisation are in practise, not processes that start from some abstract, universal and neutral concept or artefact, but more often mean a translation from or replacement of US English originals.

## Conclusion

In attempting to summarise this chapter and draw together a variety of very disparate factors and forces, we must recognise the rapidity of change and the complexity of the environment. At the time of writing, it does, however, seem that contextual mobile learning is a vibrant and progressive research topic with the capacity to contribute much to a wider understanding and delivery of learning in digital and mobile societies. The challenges and uncertainties are large, but these represent opportunities to push the thinking and development further and in new directions, increasing impact and relevance with unique insights.

## References

Aljohani, N.R., & Davis, H.C. (2012a). Learning analytics in mobile and ubiquitous learning environments. Retrieved from http://eprints.soton.ac.uk/342971/1/mlearn2012_Full_Paper-_Aljohani_and_Davis.pdf

Aljohani, N.R., & Davis, H.C. (2012b). Significance of learning analytics in enhancing the mobile and pervasive learning environments. Proceedings from the *6th International Conference on Next Generation Mobile Applications, Services and Technologies (NGMAST)* (pp. 70–74). IEEE. September.

Altbach, P.G., Reisberg, L., & Rumbley, L.E. (2009). *Trends in global higher education: Tracking an academic revolution.* Moscow: UNESCO.

Apple, M.W. (2004). Creating difference: Neo-liberalism, neo-conservatism and the politics of educational reform. *Educational Policy, 18*(1), 12–44.

Apple, M.W. (2000). Between neoliberalism and neoconservatism: Education and conservatism in a global context (pp. 57–77). In N. C. Burbules & C. A. Torres (Eds.), *Globalization and education: Critical perspectives* (pp. 57–77). New York, NY: Routledge.

Apple, M.W., Kenway, J., & Singh, M. (Eds.). (2005). *Globalizing education: Policies, pedagogies, & politics (Vol. 280).* New York, NY: Peter Lang.

Berrett, D. (2012). How 'flipping' the classroom can improve the traditional lecture. *The Chronicle of Higher Education, 12*, 1–14.

Bishop, J.L., & Verleger, M.A. (2013). The flipped classroom: A survey of the research. Proceedings from the *ASEE National Conference.* Atlanta, GA. June. Retrieved from http://www.studiesuccesho.nl/wp-content/uploads/2014/04/flipped-classroom-artikel.pdf

Bornmann, L. (2012). Measuring the societal impact of research. *EMBO Reports, 13*(8), 673–676.

Büscher, M., & Urry, J. (2009). Mobile methods and the empirical. *European Journal of Social Theory*, *12*(1), 99–116.

Chinnery, G.M. (2006). Going to the mall: Mobile assisted language learning. *Language Learning & Technology*, *10*(1), 9–16. Retrieved from http://www.llt.msu.edu/vol10num1/pdf/emerging.pdf

Conole, G. (2014). A new classification schema for MOOCs. *INNOQUAL-International Journal for Innovation and Quality in Learning*, *2*(3), 65–77.

Cornelius, S., & Marston, P. (2009). Towards an understanding of the virtual context in mobile learning. *Research in Learning Technology*, *17*(3), 161–172.

CoSN. (2012). *Making progress: Rethinking state and school district policies concerning mobile technologies and social media.* Washington, DC: Consortium for School Networking (CoSN). Retrieved from https://www.nsba.org/sites/default/files/reports/MakingProgress.pdf

Crane, L., Awe, A., Benachour, P., & Coulton, P. (2012). Context aware electronic updates for virtual learning environments. Proceedings from the *12th International Conference on Advanced Learning Technologies (ICALT)* (pp. 173–175). IEEE.

Crompton, H., & Traxler, J. (Eds.). (2015a). *Mobile learning and mathematics.* New York, NY: Routledge.

Crompton, H. & Traxler, J. (2015b). *Mobile learning and STEM: Case studies in practice.* New York, NY: Routledge.

CTO. (2013). Retrieved from http://www.cto.int/country-ict-data/

de Waard, I., Koutropoulos, A., Hogue, R.J., Abajian, S.C., Keskin, N.Ö., Rodriguez, C.O., & Gallagher, M.S. (2012). Merging MOOC and mLearning for increased learner interactions. *International Journal of Mobile and Blended Learning*, *4*(4), 34–46.

de Waard, I., Koutropoulos, A., Keskin, N., Abajian, S.C., Hogue, R., Rodriguez, O., & Gallagher, M.S. (2011). Exploring the MOOC format as a pedagogical approach for mLearning. Proceedings from *mLearn 2011, 10th World Conference on Mobile and Contextual Learning.* Beijing. Retrieved from http://mlearn.bnu.edu.cn/source/ten_outstanding_papers/Exploring%20the%20MOOC%20format%20as%20a%20pedagogical%20approach%20for%20mLearning.pdf

Dillenbourg, P., Fox, A., Kirchner, C., Mitchell, J., & Wirsing, M. (2014). Massive open online courses: Current state and perspectives. *Dagstuhl Manifestos*. Retrieved from http://ethicalforum2013.fuus.be/sites/default/files/dillenbourg_MOOC.pdf

Downes, S. (2013). The quality of massive open online courses. Retrieved from http://mooc.efquel.org/week-2-the-quality-of-massive-open-online-courses-by-stephen-downes/

Downes, S. (2009). Connectivism dynamics in communities. Retrieved from http://halfanhour.blogspot.com/2009/02/connectivist-dynamics-in-communities.html

Eaton, J., Kortum, S., Neiman, B., & Romalis, J. (2011). *Trade and the global recession.* New York, NY: National Bureau of Economic Research.

Esakia, A., Niu, S., & McCrickard, D.S. (2015). Augmenting undergraduate computer science education with programmable smartwatches. Proceedings from *The 46th ACM Technical Symposium on Computer Science Education* (pp. 66–71). ACM. February.

Felfernig, A., Friedrich, G., & Schmidt-Thieme, L. (2007). Recommender systems. *IEEE Intelligent Systems*, *22*(3), 18–21.

Ferguson, R. (2012a). Learning analytics: Drivers, developments and challenges. *International Journal of Technology Enhanced Learning*, *4*(5/6), 304–317.

Ferguson, R. (2012b). The state of learning analytics in 2012: A review and future challenges. *Technical Report KMI-2012, 1, 2012.* Milton Keynes: Knowledge Media Institute.

Ferguson, R., & Sharples, M. (2014). Innovative pedagogy at massive scale: Teaching and learning in MOOCs. In C. Rensing, S. de Freitas, T. Ley, P. J. Muñoz-Merino (Eds.),

*Open learning and teaching in educational communities* (pp. 98–111). Cham, Switzerland: Springer International Publishing.

Fernando, T. (2010). Erewhon project final report. Oxford: Oxford University. Retrieved from http://www.webarchive.org.uk/wayback/archive/20140615053731/http:// www.jisc.ac.uk/media/documents/programmes/institutionalinnovation/jisc%20ere whon%20-%20final%20report.pdf

Frank, K.A., Zhao, Y., & Borman, K. (2004). Social capital and the diffusion of innovations within organizations: The case of computer technology in schools. *Sociology of Education*, 77(2), 148–171. Retrieved from https://dschool.stanford.edu/sandbox/groups/k12/wiki/222bb/attachments/8c9c7/frank.pdf?sessionID=51531c9908403b46ec2ac 20403f74a9e40f8a86d

Freund, R. (2003). Mass customization and personalization in education and training. *ElearnChina2003*. Retrieved from http://robertfreund.de/blog/wp-content/uploads/2008/12/robert-freund-2003-elearnchina-paper-update-2004–03.pdf

Gadot, R. & Levin, I. (2012). Digital curation as learning activity. Proceedings from *EDU-LEARN12* (pp. 6038–6045).

Gaved, M., Luley, P., Efremidis, S., Georgiou, I., Kukulska-Hulme, A., Jones, A., & Scanlon, E. (2014). Challenges in context-aware mobile language learning: the MASELTOV approach. Proceedings from the *13th World Conference on Mobile and Contextual Learning 2014* (pp. 3–5). Istanbul. November. Retrieved from http://oro.open.ac.uk/40758/

Genachowski, C.J. (2010). Mobile broadband: A 21st century plan for US competitiveness, innovation and job creation. Presented at New America Foundation, Washington, DC.

Godwin-Jones, R. (2011). Emerging technologies: Mobile apps for language learning. *Language Learning & Technology*, 15(2), 2–11. Retrieved from http://www.llt.msu.edu/issues/june2011/emerging.pdf

GSMA. (2015). Retrieved from http://www.gsma.com/newsroom/gsmai/

Handal, B., Ritter, R., & Marcovitz, D. (2014). Implementing large scale mobile learning school programs: To BYOD or not to BYOD. Proceedings from the *World Conference on Educational Multimedia, Hypermedia and Telecommunications* (Vol. 2014, No. 1, pp. 796–801). June.

Hannam, K., Sheller, M., & Urry, J. (2006). Editorial: Mobilities, immobilities and moorings. *Mobilities*, 1(1), 1–22.

Hartley, D. (2008). Education, markets and the pedagogy of personalisation. *British Journal of Educational Studies*, 56(4), 365–381.

Herreid, C.F., & Schiller, N.A. (2013). Case studies and the flipped classroom. *Journal of College Science Teaching*, 42(5), 62–66.

Hofstede, G.H. (1997) Cultures and organizations: Software of the mind. New York, NY: McGraw-Hill.

Hughes, H. (2012). Introduction to flipping the college classroom. Proceedings from the *World Conference on Educational Multimedia, Hypermedia and Telecommunications* (Vol. 2012, No. 1, pp. 2434–2438). June.

Imbs, J. (2010). The first global recession in decades. *IMF Economic Review*, 58(2), 327–354.

Ingelehart, R. & Welzel, C. (2005). *Modernization, cultural change, and democracy: The human development sequence*. Cambridge: Cambridge University Press.

ITU. (2015). Retrieved from http://www.itu.int/en/ITU-D/Statistics/Pages/stat/default. aspx

Johnson, L., Adams, S., Cummins, M., Estrada, V., Freeman, A., & Ludgate, H. (2013). The NMC horizon report: 2013 higher education edition. Retrieved from http://www.editlib.org/p/46484/

Jones, B. (1984). *Past imperfect: The story of rescue archaeology*. London: Heinemann.

Kop, R., & Carroll, F. (2011). Cloud computing and creativity: Learning on a massive open online course. *EURODL*. Retrieved from http://www.eurodl.org/?p=special&sp=articles&inum=2&article=457

Kuhn, T.S. (2012). *The structure of scientific revolutions*. Chicago, IL: University of Chicago Press.

Kukulska-Hulme, A., & Shield, L. (2008). An overview of mobile assisted language learning: From content delivery to supported collaboration and interaction. *ReCALL, 20*(03), 271–289.

Kukulska-Hulme, A., & Shield, L. (2007). An overview of mobile assisted language learning: Can mobile devices support collaborative practice in speaking and listening? Presented at *EuroCALL 2007*.

Lage, M. J., Platt, G. J., & Treglia, M. (2000). Inverting the classroom: A gateway to creating an inclusive learning environment. *The Journal of Economic Education, 31*(1), 30–43.

Lewis, R. D. (1996). *When cultures collide*. Boston, MA: Nicholas Brealey Publishing.

Liyanagunawardena, T.R., Adams, A.A., & Williams, S.A. (2013). MOOCs: A systematic study of the published literature 2008–2012. *The International Review of Research in Open and Distributed Learning, 14*(3), 202–227. Retrieved from http://www.irrodl.org/index.php/irrodl/article/view/1455/2531

Lymberis, A. (2003). Smart wearables for remote health monitoring, from prevention to rehabilitation: Current R&D, future challenges. Proceedings from the *4th International IEEE EMBS Special Topic Conference on Information Technology Applications in Biomedicine* (pp. 272–275). IEEE. April.

Mackness, J., Waite, M., Roberts, G., & Lovegrove, E. (2013). Learning in a small, task-oriented, connectivist MOOC: Pedagogical issues and implications for higher education. *The International Review of Research in Open and Distributed Learning, 14*(4). Retrieved from http://www.irrodl.org/index.php/irrodl/article/view/1548/2636?utm_source=ednak.com&utm_medium=link&utm_campaign=edtech-trending

Martin, B.R. (2011). The research excellence framework and the 'impact agenda': Are we creating a Frankenstein monster? *Research Evaluation, 20*(3), 247–254.

Miangah, T.M., & Nezarat, A. (2012). Mobile-assisted language learning. *International Journal of Distributed and Parallel Systems, 3*, 309–319. Retrieved from http://mosavit.ir/images/Articles/18_Mobile_Assisted_Language_Learning.pdf

Mihailidis, P., & Cohen, J.N. (2013). Exploring curation as a core competency in digital and media literacy education. *Journal of Interactive Media in Education*. Retrieved from http://jime.open.ac.uk/article/view/2013-02/472

Monahan, T. (2005). *Globalization, technological change, and public education*. Abingdon: Routledge.

New Media Consortium. (2015). *Horizon Reports*. Retrieved from http://www.nmc.org/nmc-horizon/

Ombiel. (2015). Retrieved from http://www.ombiel.com

Ossiannilsson, E. (2014). Lessons learned from the European eMOOCs 2014 stakeholders summit. Proceedings from the *International EIF/LINQ Conference 2014* (pp. 109–116). Retrieved from https://oerknowledgecloud.org/sites/oerknowledgecloud.org/files/LINQ_2014_Proceedings_final.pdf#page=109

Pachler, N., Pimmer, C., & Seipold, J. (Eds.). (2011). *Work-based mobile learning: Concepts and cases*. London: Peter Lang.

Pardo, A., & Siemens, G. (2014). Ethical and privacy principles for learning analytics. *British Journal of Educational Technology, 45*(3), 438–450.

Pearson, C., Gaved, M., Brasher, A., Jones, A., Kukulska-Hulme, A., Scanlon, E., . . . Busta, M. (2014). *Mobile situated language learning: Deliverable 7.5.2.* Graz: MASELTOV Project Consortium. Retrieved from http://oro.open.ac.uk/42108/

Picard, R.W., & Healey, J. (1997). Affective wearables. *Personal Technologies, 1*(4), 231–240.

Robson, R. (2013). The changing nature of e-learning content. In R. Huang, Kinshuk & J. M. Spector (Eds.), *Reshaping learning: Frontiers of learning technology in a global context* (pp. 177–196). Berlin: Springer.

Rogers, E.M. (2010). *Diffusion of innovations.* New York, NY: Simon and Schuster.

Sharples, M., Adams, A., Ferguson, R., Gaved, M., McAndrew, P., Rienties, B., . . . Whitelock, D. (2014). *Innovating pedagogy 2014.* The Open University. Retrieved from http://www.open.ac.uk/blogs/innovating/

Sherwood, J. (2007, Nov. 29). Spend-a-penny SMS service starts flowing. *The Register.* Retrieved from http://www.theregister.co.uk/2007/11/29/westminster_satlav_texting_service/

Siemens, G., & d Baker, R.S. (2012). Learning analytics and educational data mining: Towards communication and collaboration. Proceedings from the *2nd International Conference on Learning Analytics and Knowledge* (pp. 252–254). ACM. April. Retrieved from http://users.wpi.edu/~rsbaker/LAKs%20reformatting%20v2.pdf

Siemens, G., & Long, P. (2011). Penetrating the fog: Analytics in learning and education. *EDUCAUSE Review, 46*(5). Retrieved from http://www.educause.edu/ero/article/penetrating-fog-analytics-learning-and-education

Smith, S., Ward, V., & House, A. (2011). 'Impact' in the proposals for the UK's research excellence framework: Shifting the boundaries of academic autonomy. *Research Policy, 40*(10), 1369–1379.

Spring, J. (2008). Research on globalization and education. *Review of Educational Research, 78*(2), 330–363.

Traxler, J. (2013). mLearning solutions for international development: Rethinking the thinking. *Digital Culture and Education, 5*(2), 74–85.

Traxler, J. (2010a). Students and mobile devices. *Association for Learning Technology Research Journal, 18*(2), 149–160.

Traxler, J. (2010b). e-Learning: The next wave. Proceedings from *ALT-C, Association for Learning Technology.* Oxford. Retrieved from http://repository.alt.ac.uk/798/2/Abstracts_Handbook_web.pdf

Traxler, J., & Crompton, H. (2015). The cultural implications of learning with mobile devices. *Distance Education in China.* Retrieved from http://en.ouchn.edu.cn/index.php/research/journal-of-distance-education-in-china

Traxler, J., & Kukulska-Hulme, A. (2006). The evaluation of next generation learning technologies: The case of mobile learning. Proceedings from *ALT-C 2006.* Oxford: ALT.

Tucker, B. (2012). The flipped classroom. *Education Next, 12*(1), 82–83. Retrieved from http://wardwcom.webstarts.com/uploads/the_flipped_classroom_article.pdf

UK Open University. (2014). *Innovating Pedagogy 2014.* Retrieved from http://www.open.ac.uk/blogs/innovating/

Urry, J. (2007). *Mobilities.* Cambridge: Polity.

Verhaart, M. (2012). Curating digital content in teaching and learning using wiki technology. Proceedings from the *12th International Conference on Advanced Learning Technologies (ICALT)* (pp. 191–193). IEEE. July.

Walker, G. (2009). Display week 2012 review: Touch technology. *Information Display, 7*(10), 10.

Washburn, J. (2008). *University, Inc.: The corporate corruption of higher education.* New York, NY: Basic Books.

Waslander, S. (2007). Mass customization in schools: Strategies Dutch secondary schools pursue to cope with the diversity-efficiency dilemma. *Journal of Education Policy, 22*(4), 363–382.

White, D.S., & Le Cornu, A. (2011). Visitors and residents: A new typology for online engagement. *First Monday, 16*(9). Retrieved from http://firstmonday.org/ojs/index. php/fm/article/view/3171/3049

Yau, J.Y.K. (2011). *A mobile context-aware learning schedule framework with Java learning objects* (Doctoral dissertation). University of Warwick. Retrieved from http://wrap.warwick. ac.uk/36869/

# INDEX